RADICAL
ROAD MAPS

James H. Hansen

RADICAL
ROAD MAPS

Untangling the
Web of Connections
Among Far-Left Groups
in America

WND BOOKS

AN IMPRINT OF CUMBERLAND HOUSE PUBLISHING, INC.

NASHVILLE, TENNESSEE

RADICAL ROAD MAPS
A WND BOOK
PUBLISHED BY CUMBERLAND HOUSE PUBLISHING, INC.
431 Harding Industrial Drive
Nashville, Tennessee 37211

Cover design by Linda Daly

Library of Congress Cataloging-in-Publication Data

Hansen, James H.
    Radical road maps : untangling the web of connections among far-left groups in
America / James Hansen.
        p. cm.
    Includes bibliographical references.
    ISBN-13: 978-1-58182-530-5 (hardcover : alk. paper)
    ISBN-10: 1-58182-530-7 (hardcover : alk. paper)
    1. Radicalism—United States. 2. Left-wing extremists—United States. I. Title.
HN90.R3H37 2006
320.530973—dc22   2005032881

Printed in the United States of America

1 2 3 4 5 6 7 8 9 10—10 09 08 07 06

CONTENTS

INTRODUCTION

THIS BOOK EXAMINES THE significant groups of the Far Left in America today and discusses how they connect and interact, how they operate, what they profess, and why this matters. My goal is to reveal the many connections between these Far-Left groups and to explore the range of their actions. In doing so, I have applied analytical techniques and provided diagrams that clarify the webs connecting these groups and expose their radical cores.

The main subject of this study is a group of twenty-nine Far-Left organizations. Also examined are key groups within the entertainment industry; the feminist, black, and gay movements; the educational and legal industries; the media; and the Congress. There are no sacred cows here, as I point out specific actions of specific individuals.

Who are these people? None of those who head the Far-Left groups have been elected by the general public, yet they have as much impact and leverage as our elected officials in Washington. These individuals will be prominent in the 2006 and 2008 elections and in key political events for the foreseeable future. Like it or not, we are engaged in a cultural civil war, and because there is a great deal at stake—the hearts and minds of mainstream America—we should have a grasp of the nature and organization of the Far Left in our midst.

Perhaps this book will speak to you. Perhaps you are concerned about the cultural and moral decay in our society. Perhaps you are a student outraged by what you see on campus every day. Perhaps you are a law-enforcement officer or a prosecutor weary of watching your efforts thwarted by the social-justice or victimization lobbies. Perhaps you are a religious person tired of being vilified for your beliefs. Perhaps you are an ordinary citizen puzzled by the shrillness and poisonous invective coming from some Far-Left groups.

Radical Road Maps may help to pave the way for a conservative counteroffensive against the ongoing anti-American con job of the Far

Left. This con job is based on the lie that is trying to convince us that the United States is a militarist, imperialist, racist country that does not deserve to be defended. This book contains many facts that expose the nature of Far-Left groups behind this distortion. It exposes the lunacy of their arguments and claims, revealing the radical origins and connections that Far-Left groups do not want the general public to know. And this book just may encourage some readers to take back the terms of debate.

Why is this book relevant now? Our country is deeply divided, polarized by sharply differing and contending ideas of who and what is responsible for the condition of our political system and society. Issues such as the Iraq War, national disaster-relief efforts after Hurricanes Katrina and Rita, rising gasoline prices, divisive religious issues, and the travails of political figures have taken a toll. As our country's leadership struggles in the midst of these events, many leftists—still traumatized after the 2004 election—are anxious to exploit these difficulties for their own political ends. Given the many challenges this country faces, it is important now more than ever before to identify those forces behind this avalanche of discord and negativity.

To summarize the structure of this book, I propose to focus on:

THE ISSUE: The presence of Far-Left groups as a permanent component of the American political scene. Which leads to . . .

THE NEED: To understand these organizations and their mind-sets, techniques, and overall effectiveness. Which calls for . . .

THE APPROACH: Establishing and assessing the linkages between these Far-Left groups and their leaders. Which yields . . .

THE OUTCOME: An enhanced understanding of the Far Left in America today.

YOUR ROAD MAP

Chapter 1 is a statement of why this matters in the current U.S. political climate.

Chapter 2 examines the tools and tactics that America's adversaries used during the cold war, some of which have been utilized by Far-Left groups in recent times.

Chapter 3 adds historical context by highlighting selected groups of Americans who, for one reason or another, collaborated or supported the Nazis in the 1930s, the Soviets since the 1920s, and the Vietnamese Communists in the 1960s and 1970s.

Chapter 4 offers an overview of some analytical techniques that will be utilized in these pages to clarify the linkages or expose the radical cores and origins of the Radical Left in America today. It also offers examples of how these techniques can be used to address today's issues and dilemmas.

Chapter 5 examines the oldest and most established Far-Left groups still active today and also explores some interesting family connections. It might be surprising to learn just how long some of these groups have been around.

Chapter 6 discusses those groups that emerged during the cold war, including a nostalgic trip to a radicalized college campus.

Chapter 7 covers the period since 2000 and looks at those groups that now stand at the forefront of the organized Far Left. Many of them will be prominent throughout the immediate future.

Chapter 8 looks at some of the larger enterprises that are in step with the Far-Left organizations described in chapters 5–7. These larger enterprises include the entertainment industry; elements of the feminist, black, and gay movements; the educational and legal establishments; the mass media; and Congress.

Chapter 9 explores how individuals in the Far-Left groups express themselves.

Chapter 10 offers a few snapshots from the career of John Kerry, a dedicated, committed liberal with radical ties.

Chapter 11 explores what the Far-Left groups are likely to do in the future and what concerned citizens might be able to do in response.

I entitled the appendix "Outrageous Quotations," a small selection of some of the most bombastic, stupefying, and breathtaking quotes uttered by prominent persons of the Far Left. To balance these distortions, I included some perceptive quotes to offer encouragement for the struggle ahead.

INTRODUCTION

TRUTH IN ADVERTISING: WHAT YOU WILL FIND

This book is more about groups than individuals, because it is more revealing to examine groups and their connections. It is one thing to catalog a series of idiotic celebrity rants, and such books are readily available already. It is another thing to systematically explore the various Far-Left organizations, their connections, their similarities, and their differences.

There is an emphasis on recent history, with a host of documented facts about people and events. This is because a grasp of recent U.S. political history enables one to find continuity, shared experiences, and linkages among the various groups and individuals who comprise the Far Left.

Particular attention is also focused on the mass media as well as the various techniques of propaganda, opinion shaping, perception management, and linguistic distortion. Now more than ever we have come to recognize the many ways in which news and political reporting can be distorted so as to affect public opinion for a desired outcome. The presidential campaign of 2004 was replete with many examples, as Dan Rather and CBS News demonstrated in spectacular fashion.

Most chapters have diagrams of various types. I have used these diagrams to illustrate the points within the text or to shed additional light on the subject.

You will also see that the chapters are laden with endnotes. I have used a variety of book sources as well as Internet sources. Given my reliance on a large number of Web sites, I probably could not have written anything like this book ten years ago, before the emergence of so many politically charged Web pages.

MY POINT OF VIEW

Most of my life experiences have resulted in a world view that has become increasingly conservative over time. These experiences included a stint in the U.S. Air Force in the mid-1960s with duty in Southeast Asia, followed by an eye-opening (even astonishing) three years on a radicalized campus in the late 1960s and early 1970s. Having spent thirty years as a civilian in Uncle Sam's intelligence services (the CIA and the Defense Intelligence Agency [DIA]), I am reluctant to comment on much of that, although I remember best those episodes of working against some of the most infamous police states that existed during the cold war and thereafter. My career clearly showed me those tactics and techniques that our country's hardened enemies have used against us, but it also gave me hope that we are fighting back. My teaching experiences at several institutions have convinced me that succeeding generations must be informed about earlier struggles so that they can face the future without losing sight of what we strive for in this country, and this is why we must be concerned about what goes into their minds from the first grade throughout graduate school.

Parts of this book have been reviewed by the CIA to assist in eliminating any possibly classified information. That review does not constitute endorsement of the accuracy of factual material nor of the views expressed in this book, which are the author's alone.

ACKNOWLEDGMENTS

I am profoundly grateful for those at Cumberland House Publishing who saw the merit of this approach and accepted this project for publication. These include Chris and Stacie Bauerle, Ed Curtis, and especially Ron Pitkin. As acquisitions editor, Chris recognized the linkages approach in February 2005 and was most encouraging. In mid- and late 2005, Stacie proved to be an invaluable facilitator in her role as assistant publisher. As the project neared printing, Ed Curtis was most helpful in the editing role. Ron Pitkin, the president of Cumberland House, accepted this manuscript for publication and recognized where it fit into the big picture. One telephone discussion with Ron in late 2005 convinced me that his vision and leadership would result in a successful launch of *Radical Road Maps*. Thanks to you all.

I am most grateful to my wife, Linda, for all her help in so many ways. Over nearly forty years, we have accumulated some extraordinary life experiences that have been all the more enjoyable and memorable because we have done them together.

I should offer some thanks to those of the loony Far Left who never hesitated to offer their opinions, platitudes, invective, and bloviation. Without such individuals this project would not have been possible.

Finally, I must recognize and applaud all those who stand against tyranny of any type. These include U.S. military troops at home and abroad as well as civilian intelligence, security, and law-enforcement officials who work to keep us safe 365 days a year.

This also includes those who fought and won the cold war, the U.S. and Allied officials who worked to bring down the Berlin Wall, not to mention the Hungarians of the 1956 armed uprising, the Poles of the 1980s Solidarity movement, and other dissidents in the East. Moreover, it includes those brave Iraqis and Afghans who are now building their political institutions and societies free of dictatorship and oppression, as well as those in still-imprisoned countries who hope and dream.

LIST OF ABBREVIATIONS

AAADC	Arab-American Anti-Discrimination Committee
AAUP	American Association of University Professors
ABM	anti-ballistic missile
ACDA	Arms Control and Disarmament Agency
ACLU	American Civil Liberties Union
ACT	America Coming Together
ACW	advanced conventional weapons
ADA	Americans for Democratic Action
AFC	America First Committee
AFSC	American Friends Service Committee
AFSCME	American Federation of State, County, and Municipal Employees
AFT	American Federation of Teachers
ALF	Animal Liberation Front
ANC	African National Congress
ANSWER	Act Now to Stop War and End Racism
ATLA	Association of Trial Lawyers of America
AV	America Votes
BBC	British Broadcasting Corporation
BW	biological warfare
CAF	Campaign for America's Future
CAIR	Council on American-Islamic Relations
CAP	Center for American Progress
CBC	Canadian Broadcasting Corporation
CBC	Congressional Black Caucus

CC&D	camouflage, concealment, and deception
CBRN	chemical, biological, radiological, nuclear
CBS	Columbia Broadcasting System
CC	Central Committee (of CPSU)
CCNY	City College of New York
CCR	Center for Constitutional Rights
CEP	Council on Economic Priorities
CIA	Central Intelligence Agency
CIP	Center for International Policy
CLRA	Civil Liberties Restoration Act
CLW	Civil Liberties Watch
CNN	Cable News Network
CNSS	Center for National Security Studies
CP	CodePink
CPSU	Communist Party of the Soviet Union
CPUSA	Communist Party USA
CW	chemical warfare
D&D	denial and deception
DCI	Director of Central Intelligence
DGI	General Directorate of Intelligence (Cuba)
DNC	Democratic National Committee
DNI	director of national intelligence
DSA	Democratic Socialists of America
DSEA	Domestic Security Enhancement Act
ELF	Earth Liberation Front
EU	European Union
FAIR	Fairness and Accuracy in Reporting
FBI	Federal Bureau of Investigation
FFP	Fund for Peace
FISA	Foreign Intelligence Surveillance Act
FISC	Foreign Intelligence Surveillance Court
FOIA	Freedom of Information Act
FOR	Fellowship of Reconciliation

LIST OF ABBREVIATIONS

GE	Global Exchange
GLCM	ground-launched cruise missile
GPS	Global Positioning System
HUD	Department of Housing and Urban Development
IAC	International Action Center
IADL	International Association of Democratic Lawyers
IAEA	International Atomic Energy Agency
ID	International Department (of CPSU Central Committee)
IFCO	Interreligious Foundation for Community Organization
IID	International Information Department (of CPSU Central Committee)
IIG	Iraqi interim government
IIS	Iraqi Intelligence Service
IMF	International Monetary Fund
INS	Immigration and Naturalization Service
IOW	Iraq Occupation Watch
IOWC	International Occupation Watch Center
IPA	Institute for Public Accuracy
IPS	Institute for Policy Studies
IRS	Internal Revenue Service
ISO	International Socialist Organization
IWCT	International War Crimes Tribunal
IWW	Industrial Workers of the World
KGB	Committee for State Security (Soviet Union)
LAGPAC	Lesbian and Gay Political Action Committee
LCCR	Leadership Conference on Civil Rights
LCV	League of Conservation Voters
LGBT	lesbian, gay, bisexual, and transgender
MCPL	Members of Congress for Peace Through Law
MEK	Mujahideen al-Khalq
MFS	Mobilization for Survival
MMA	Media Matters for America
MPLA	Popular Liberation Movement of Angola

MRBM	medium-range ballistic missile
MRE	meal ready to eat
NAACP	National Association for the Advancement of Colored People
NACCA	National Association of Claimant's Compensation Attorneys
NACLA	North American Congress on Latin America
NAFTA	North American Free Trade Association
NARAL	National Abortion and Reproductive Rights League
NATO	North Atlantic Treaty Organization
NBC	National Broadcasting Corporation
NCC	National Council of Churches of Christ in the USA
NCLB	National Civil Liberties Bureau
NEA	National Education Association
NECLC	National Emergency Civil Liberties Committee
NGLTF	National Gay and Lesbian Task Force
NION	Not in Our Name
NLF	National Liberation Front (Vietcong)
NLG	National Lawyers Guild
NOW	National Organization of Women
NPR	National Public Radio
NPT	Nuclear Non-Proliferation Treaty
NRDC	Natural Resources Defense Council
NSC	National Security Council
OSI	Open Society Institute
PA	Peace Action
PCPJ	People's Coalition for Peace and Justice
PD	Propaganda Department (of CPSU Central Committee)
PDN	Progressive Donor Network
PFAW	People for the American Way
PFP	Pastors for Peace
PLO	Palestine Liberation Organization
PWA	Public Works Administration

R&D	research and development
R&R	Refuse and Resist!
RAN	Rain Forest Action Network
RCP USA	Revolutionary Communist Party USA
RIM	Revolutionary Internationalism Movement
RU	Revolutionary Union
RYM II	Revolutionary Youth Movement II
SANE	Committee for a SANE Nuclear Policy
SAT	Scholastic Aptitude Test
SCDP	Soviet Committee for the Defense of Peace
SDI	Strategic Defense Initiative
SDS	Students for a Democratic Society
SEIU	Service Employees International Union
SLA	Symbionese Liberation Army
SNCC	Student Nonviolent Coordinating Center
SRBM	short-range ballistic missile
SVR	Foreign Intelligence Service (Russia)
SWP	Socialist Workers Party
TNF	theater nuclear forces
UFPJ	United for Peace and Justice
UNESCO	United Nations Educational, Scientific and Cultural Organization
UNHCR	United Nations High Commissioner for Refugees
USA PATRIOT Act	Uniting and Strengthening America by Providing Appropriate Tools Required to Intercept and Obstruct Terrorism Act
USPC	U.S. Peace Council
VMC	Vietnam Moratorium Committee
VVAW	Vietnam Veterans Against the War
WFDY	World Federation of Democratic Youth
WFTU	World Federation of Trade Unions
WIDF	Women's International Democratic Federation
WILPF	Women's International League for Peace and Freedom

LIST OF ABBREVIATIONS

WMD	weapons of mass destruction
WPC	World Peace Council
WRL	War Resisters League
WSI	Winter Soldier Investigation
WSP	Women's Strike for Peace
WTO	World Trade Organization
WUO	Weather Underground Organization
WWP	Workers World Party

RADICAL
ROAD MAPS

WHAT'S AT STAKE NOW

NO MATTER WHAT YOUR political persuasion, we clearly live in interesting, emotional, and highly charged times! Our political process is moving faster, further, and in more directions than ever before. An exciting time—but the United States seems to be at war with itself. If the German philosopher George Hegel were alive today, he might cast the issues into his framework of "thesis-antithesis-synthesis."

THESIS: The United States is attempting to secure itself through a position of strength and is trying to spread freedom throughout the world.

On February 2, 2005, President George W. Bush stood before a joint session of Congress to spell out his vision of extending freedom beyond American borders and ensuring a stronger America based on the freedom that other nations pursue and attain. It was a State of the Union address of memorable proportions.[1]

The war in Iraq was a prime topic. The president stated: "The new political situation in Iraq opens a new phase of our working in that country. We will increasingly focus our efforts on helping prepare more capable Iraqi security forces—forces with skilled officers, and an effective command structure. We are standing for the freedom of our

Iraqi friends, and freedom in Iraq will make America safer for genera-tions to come."

The campaign against international terrorism was also high on his agenda that night. He noted: "In the next four years, my administration will continue to build the coalitions that will defeat the dangers of our time. In the long term, the peace we seek will only be achieved by elimi-nating the conditions that feed radicalism and ideologies of murder. . . . The only force powerful enough to stop the rise of tyranny and terror, and replace hatred with hope, is the force of human freedom." He noted the necessity of "pursuing our enemies" as vital to the war on terror and further noted, "We must continue to support our military and give them the tools for victory."

At the same time, he noted that the U.S. aim is to "preserve and build a community of free and independent nations, with governments that answer to their citizens and reflect their own cultures. And because democracies respect their own people and their neighbors, the advance of freedom will lead to peace." In this phrase, President Bush tied to-gether the advance of freedom on a global scale with enhanced security for Americans and American interests. In short, this marked a fusion of Wilsonian idealism with Reaganesque muscularity.

There was recognition in this speech that the spread of freedom would not be primarily a matter of arms. The United States has many nonmilitary tools of "soft power" as well as a first-class military estab-lishment. Our vast array of tools includes diplomacy (making our case quietly), public diplomacy (making our case publicly), economic power, and covert action (political influence operations), not to men-tion a host of cultural influences as well (Hollywood, MTV, and English as the dominant language of the World Wide Web).

Even before President Bush delivered his State of the Union speech that night, Secretary of State Condoleezza Rice had put several foreign governments on notice that their human rights records were lacking. The governments of Myanmar (Burma), Zimbabwe, Belarus, North Korea, Cuba, and Iran were singled out by name. Some of these coun-tries had not appeared on this list with such a high profile, although North Korea, Cuba, and Iran had long been cited for giving varying de-grees of support to terrorism.

Within only two weeks of that address, events abroad coalesced as if to underscore what a dangerous world President Bush had inherited in 2001.

President Bush singled out Iran by name in his speech: "Today Iran remains the world's primary state sponsor of terror, pursuing nuclear weapons while depriving its people of the freedom they seek and deserve. To the Iranian people, I say tonight: As you stand for your own liberty, America stands with you." Shortly thereafter, the Iranian regime hardened its already-defiant stance on its nuclear goals. At that juncture it appeared that the combined efforts of the "EU Three" (the United Kingdom, France, and Germany—with whom Iran had been negotiating) had no discernible impact on Tehran's nuclear goals.

He also singled out Syria, which was cited for allowing its territory and even parts of Lebanon "to be used by terrorists who seek to destroy every chance of peace in the region." Within two weeks, Syria stood accused of involvement in the massive bomb explosion in downtown Beirut that killed former Lebanese prime minister Rafik Hariri, and the United States withdrew its ambassador home "for consultations," a sign that relations between the two countries were spiraling downward.

At this same time, North Korea announced that it had indeed attained a nuclear capability. The regime of Kim Jong-il had long been suspected of developing nuclear weapons and had already tested long-range missile delivery systems. This marked the first public announcement from the secretive, reclusive regime in Pyongyang. All that would remain would be some kind of nuclear test in the future, an event that would surely evoke an array of nervous reactions throughout Asia and beyond.

Indeed, the events of early 2005 only began to illustrate the many hurdles lying in the path of U.S. aspirations to spread peace and freedom on a global scale. These were times that would certainly challenge to the utmost those keystone officials of the second Bush administration: Secretary of State Rice, Secretary of Defense Donald Rumsfeld, national security adviser Stephen Hadley, Attorney General Alberto Gonzales, Secretary of Homeland Security Michael Chertoff, Director of Central Intelligence (DCI) Porter Goss, and National Intelligence Director John Negroponte.

ANTITHESIS: Determined and influential forces are mightily opposing these initiatives.

Before, during, and after the contentious election of 2004, there was a swirl of raucous, strident, and militant voices that spoke out forcefully against the Bush administration and its objectives and policies. Many of those in this crowd expressed a venomous hatred for Bush in shrill tones. Some called this the "SSS" affliction (Sputtering and Spewing Syndrome), and a few of those so afflicted were booking one-way tickets to Canada by early 2005.

This level of hatred has been seen on only several occasions throughout American history. The names given to some of our most notable presidents remind you that American politics is a rough (sometimes bare-knuckle) enterprise. Thomas Jefferson of 1800 was an "atheist," an "infidel," a "Jacobin," and by 1804 had attained the vaunted status of "anti-Christ." In 1868 Ulysses S. Grant was known as the "drunkard," the "butcher," and by 1872 had graduated to "Useless Grant," the "swindler" and "ignoramus."

George Bush could take some solace from the fact that Abraham Lincoln and Franklin D. Roosevelt were also targets of ridicule. In 1860 Lincoln was called the "big baboon." By 1864 he was the "Illinois Ape, the "tyrant," and the "prince of jesters." Many had spoken out against Franklin D. Roosevelt. In 1932 FDR was called a "demagogue," "Bolshevist," "Little Lord Fauntleroy," and an "amiable boy scout" as well as a "traitor to his class." By 1940 he was known to some as "King Franklin," "Dr. Jekyll of Hyde Park," a "dictator," a "warmonger," and an "appeaser" (quite the opposite of a warmonger, but why bother with trivialities?).

The names called George Bush are one thing, but it is more significant that determined forces have been marshaling, organizing, raising money, and calibrating their efforts to oppose nearly every initiative the United States puts forward. The overall level of organization and cohesion of these groups is not well known, nor is the extent of their connections to one another. Their levels and sources of funding are certainly not known to a great extent. For anyone who bothers to look, the level of their vitriol is most evident, but their organizational nuances are not. This book will try to fill in those blank spots in our common understanding of these organizations, focusing on what they believe in, how they work together, and what it means to us.

The actions of these Far-Left groups have brought about a reaction from many elements of mainstream America. As such, the country is divided to the point of polarization. Just as there was a proverbial wall that existed during the days of Vietnam, separating those who served there and those who did not, there is such a wall today as well. If anything, the wall is just as high and just as thick as it was some forty years ago. If it has been the deliberate intention of these groups to cause alienation and polarization in American society, they have succeeded remarkably.

SYNTHESIS: The outcome of this great political collision will hinge greatly on the common person's understanding of these oppositional forces and the degree of support that they garner.

Average citizens should try to find out a few things about those groups that have taken such an adversarial approach to U.S. policies. The key questions include these:

- What do these groups really believe? This includes their perceptions of reality, their understanding of their own capabilities, and whether they truly believe what they are telling themselves and their audiences.
- Do these groups mean well? Do they have the best interests of democracy in mind?
- Who is behind the Far-Left groups today?
- How well are they succeeding in forming and sustaining their groupings? This includes their abilities to fund, organize, and control their movements.
- How are Far-Left viewpoints getting injected into the mainstream of liberal thought, and how much are these Far-Left viewpoints becoming dominant themes of liberal thought?
- Can the non-Far-Left elements of the liberal movement reassert control?

This book will examine these questions in subsequent chapters, but for now it is useful to sketch out the essence of what many of these groups truly believe if we are to take their own slogans and terminology at face value.

- The United States has used the war against Iraq as a first step toward world domination and empire.
- The United States is a hegemonic, imperialistic nation eager to impose its version of democracy on all other nations.
- President Bush is a moron, a bully, a liar, a murderer, and a warmonger.
- The terror inflicted upon the United States on September 11, 2001, was well deserved, justifiably brought on by our own aggressive policies.
- The terrorist threat is greatly overstated.
- The campaigns against al-Qaeda and Iraq are some of the greatest crimes in modern history.
- Nothing can possibly justify the Bush administration's criminal wars on foreign soil or its widespread violation of human rights.
- Most Americans are truly ashamed of their government's arrogance.
- The United States is using homeland security as a tool to stifle dissent as well as harass those who oppose its policies.
- The United States is well on the way to jailing people for their political opinions or otherwise taking extreme measures that violate the Bill of Rights.

IMPLICATIONS

WHAT'S AT STAKE: POLITICAL OUTCOMES

The opposition forces rely greatly on their abilities to mobilize large numbers of people to support their causes. It does not matter whether such people show up on the streets in demonstrations or appear in the print or broadcast media. These forces know that there is strength in numbers.

The force of numbers has been decisive on several occasions in modern history. On one occasion President Lyndon B. Johnson finally gave in to the forces that were rising against his policies in Vietnam in March 1968, when he announced on national television, "I will not seek, nor shall I accept, the nomination of my party for President of the United States." Much more recently, voters in Spain turned out the government of U.S. ally Jose Maria Aznar in March 2004, just two days after a series of deadly terrorist bombings of the Madrid commuter rail network. The new Spanish government under Jose Luis Rodriguez Zapatero set about immediately to withdraw its troops from Iraq.

WHAT'S AT STAKE: WHETHER HUGE NUMBERS OF PEOPLE SUCCUMB TO PERCEPTION MANAGEMENT AND OPINION MANIPULATION

In order to mobilize a large number of people, clever organizers often rely on the manipulation of perceptions through advanced media techniques. These techniques might be called opinion making, opinion shaping, and opinion policing. *Opinion making* refers to generating formative themes that many can rally behind. "No war for oil" remains a favorite even now. *Opinion shaping* refers to channeling or bending existing issues in a way that is favorable to a group's point of view. One example would be trying to prove that systematic torture of Iraqi and other foreign detainees is standard U.S. policy. *Opinion policing* refers to defining what topics are within the bounds of acceptable discourse and what are out of bounds. The topic of hate speech—and decisions on what topics are tolerable for debate on college campuses—comes to mind here.

The aim of clever organizers is to influence people's opinions and their resulting behavior rather than merely communicate facts. Many of the individuals cited here have sought to change how people understand an issue or a situation for the purpose of changing their actions in ways that favor their groups. Many of them are skilled artists of the spoken and written word—adept at influencing opinions through persuasion or else through deception and confusion. In recent years there has been a substantial increase in deceptive and confusing tactics that have targeted U.S. society and its perceptions of U.S. policies.

The most clever organizers and opinion makers are well versed in all propaganda techniques. These include appeals to fear, appeals to authority, the "bandwagon effect," demonization, glittering generalities, oversimplification, stereotyping, scapegoating, and sloganeering. Given the many ways in which opinions can be shaped and altered, average people have to have some way to assess and ultimately accept or reject these various claims and statements. Rest assured that no hard-Left radical demonstration organizer wants average people to have the "tools of awareness and filtering" to see through the organizer's array of "tools of persuasion." Likewise, the radical professor who uses his classroom to propagandize students does not want them to use their own tools of awareness and filtering.

WHAT'S AT STAKE: AN ENDURING IMAGE OF AMERICA ABROAD

The sloganeering and hyperbole of Far-Left groups have been given wings abroad, especially in Europe and the Middle East. Many political activist groups in Europe have readily adopted the jargon and the tactics practiced by American Far-Left groups. Many disillusioned youths who inhabit the "Arab street" parrot those slogans in front of cameramen from Aljazeera. Given that many Far-Left groups in the United States wish to project their message worldwide—using every tool of the twenty-first-century communications revolution—it is inevitable that this message is replayed and amplified on a global scale. The allies of the Far-Left groups who inhabit the newspapers and major U.S. television networks greatly assist in this process, as they can trim out various embarrassing details about the affiliation of such groups while transmitting the most captivating sound bites instantaneously.

WHAT'S AT STAKE: ALIENATION OF THE VOTING PUBLIC

Even though the election of 2004 resulted in a large voter turnout, there is no doubt that a huge number of Americans have become thoroughly alienated from politics. The appropriate term, to borrow from the German, is *politikverdrossenheit*, meaning "fed up with politics." There are many reasons for this alienation, but the techniques and tactics employed by radical elements likely account for a significant measure of it.

WHAT'S AT STAKE: OUR OWN STANDARDS OF CIVILITY

In recent years everyone has witnessed a stupefying number of attack ads, use of the Big Lie, caricature and stereotyping, demonizing the opposition, extreme metaphor, mudslinging, the politics of personal destruction, ritual defamation, and smears. The years 2003 and 2004 witnessed a veritable flood of books from Far-Left authors (published gladly by liberal publishing houses) that amounted to unlimited character assassination. All of this has eroded our own standards of civility. Only forty years ago, those on opposite sides of the aisle in the Senate and House of Representatives saw one another as opponents, not as enemies, as is often the case today. Policy makers of opposing parties could mingle at Capitol Hill watering holes at day's end. Likewise, most average citizens on both sides of the Democratic-Republican divide were far more civil to one another when they had to mix.

SCOPE NOTE

This book is not intended to be a complete account of all the groups that have opposed current U.S. policies. Instead it concentrates on those organizations that have demonstrated continuity from their early founding period and remain active up to the present. There is special emphasis on those that emerged over the past ten years and continue to play a major role today.

This book is not intended to document the various stages of development and decline of the New Left. That history is best left to others, and any effort to get into all the twists, turns, splits, mergers, and other permutations that the New Left has experienced would either require a new book on that topic or would significantly derail the discussion from what is intended here.

Any author who tries to show the linkages that exist between groups is tempted to assume that these various associations act with a greater level of coherence and cohesion than may exist in real life. It is well to remember that these groups—while coordinating their activities—may not always work as a smoothly functioning united front. Just to take the examples of the European Union (EU), or NATO, or the UN for that matter, different members can bring differing perceptions and expectations to the table—factors that can get in the way of a higher degree of group cohesion. Any author examining this topic must use some degree of caution and not allow conspiracy theories to get out of hand. Likewise, it is necessary to determine whether these groups pose a dagger to the heart, an irritating pinprick, or something else. Not all of them pose the same degree of threat to our republic.

Finally, it is wise not to overestimate the ultimate leverage and influence such groups may have on actual events. Many of these Far-Left groups denigrated Iraqi efforts to hold its first election on January 30, 2005, or else tried to explain it away as insignificant. Yet their combined efforts could not prevent or dismiss the groundswell of democratic movement occurring in the Middle East in early 2005 alone: the "purple finger" Iraqi election; an election within the Palestinian Authority in the post-Arafat era; the emergence of "people power" in Lebanon and a popular upwelling of rage against the continued Syrian occupation; and Egyptian president Mubarak's announced plans to hold some form of multiparty election in September 2005. It is a fair question whether the hard-line stridency and logical contortions of these radical organizations will doom them to utter irrelevance.

KEY FINDINGS

1: THESE ORGANIZATIONS EMPLOY RECURRING PATTERNS OF
   OPERATIONS AND TACTICS.

To cite the example of the "anti-intelligence lobby" of 1974, there were interlocking directorates and advisory boards among the chief groups. The leading figures moved relatively freely between the Institute for Policy Studies (IPS), Center for National Security Studies (CNSS), National Emergency Civil Liberties Committee (NECLC), Center for Constitutional Rights (CCR), and the American Civil Liberties Union (ACLU). These groups had the ultimate goal of dismantling U.S. intelligence and security agencies, or at the very least rendering them toothless. According to S. Steven Powell, "They sat on one another's advisory boards, participated in one another's conferences, and wrote for one another's journals. The different arguments being made by apparently separate groups which reinforced one another were at the core basically of a single argument being repeated over and over again."[2]

To cite the best example today, there is a close interactive relationship between today's organizations, now consisting of United for Peace and Justice (UFPJ), Global Exchange, CodePink, and the Iraq Occupation Watch (IOW). There is the same interlocking leadership among these groups, and they all tend to reinforce one another in a variety of demonstrations, forums, conferences, and publications. At the same time, the groups formed in the 1960s and 1970s have not gone away, as the anti-intelligence lobby groups of the 1970s are continuing and operating in concert just as they always have.

2: THEY ARE PURSUING NEW WAYS TO UNDERMINE THE ABILITY OF THE
   UNITED STATES TO DEFEND ITSELF AT HOME AND ABROAD.

During the 1960s and 1970s, these groups campaigned hard against the U.S. intelligence agencies as well as any new improvements in the U.S. military arsenal. Had they gotten their way on all these issues, the United States would have been defenseless, isolated, and saddled with some kind of socialist government. Some prominent individuals in these groups opposed any measures taken against foreign terrorists over concerns about the terrorists' privacy or civil rights.

By the same token these groups are working hard now against any efforts to police or defend our borders—even in the face of an overwhelming surge of illegal aliens. They are also working hard against the USA PATRIOT Act, passed by a substantial vote of Congress in October 2001, as well as any further enhancements in our homeland security posture. By the same token some of these groups today are obstructing efforts to identify and strike back against foreign terrorist groups.

3: "UNITED FRONT" ALLIANCES HAVE EMERGED BETWEEN RADICAL
   ISLAMIC ELEMENTS AND THOSE WITH A TRADITIONAL PRO-
   COMMUNIST BACKGROUND, AS WELL AS A NUMBER OF APOLOGISTS,
   ALLIES, AND PROTECTORS OF BOTH OF THESE GROUPS.

The confluence of interests began in the 1970s. Both the USSR and some radical Islamic groups were opposed to "U.S. imperialism" and found a common enemy: the United States. There is no question today about the support to a host of terrorist groups offered then by the USSR, Cuba, East Germany, and other Communist countries.

An examination of today's umbrella groups shows that such alliances have continued. The "united front" is as active as always. To cite the example of UFPJ, its member groups include the Arab-American Anti-Discrimination Committee (AAADC), Communist groups such as the Communist Party USA (CPUSA) and the International Socialist Organization (ISO), and radical lawyers' groups such as the CCR, NLG, as well as traditional radical groups such as the American Friends Service Committee (AFSC) and IPS. Many of these groups have taken up the charges of "torture" against detainees from terrorist groups or they have worked hard to change the laws governing our policies vis-à-vis terrorist groups.

Other linkages emerge as the evidence is examined. There are now working partnerships between Far-Left groups and the Council on American-Islamic Relations (CAIR) and the Arab-American Institute. There is ample evidence of some Americans offering assistance to Saddam's regime ("solidarity" trips) as well as the recent deliveries of material aid to the insurgent stronghold of Fallujah, Iraq, in the postwar period.

4: THE LAWS THAT SUCH ORGANIZATIONS SPONSOR REALLY MATTER BECAUSE THE UNITED STATES IS GOVERNED BY THE RULE OF LAW.

Much as we would like to, we cannot ignore the efforts of the ACLU, CCR, NLG, and their allied organizations to change existing laws. Their campaigns have been fought on the floors of Congress and in the back corridors and lobbies as well—usually out of sight of the U.S. public. There has been a concerted effort to influence members of Congress and their staffs as well. Lobbyists for such groups also work their wiles on members of the Executive Branch as well as the Judicial Branch. The laws that come out of all these efforts govern what we can or cannot do vis-à-vis foreign terrorists, illegal aliens, and others who seek to harm U.S. interests.

5: THE INFLUENCE OF SOME OF THESE ORGANIZATIONS HAS BEEN UNDERCUT—FOR NOW—BY THE "MIDDLE EAST SPRING."

Starting with the elections in the Palestinian movement and in Iraq in early 2005, and proceeding through the "Cedar Revolution" in Lebanon and the announced plans of Egyptian president Hosni Mubarak to hold elections in September 2005, a number of dramatic events have combined to suggest that perhaps President Bush was correct in staying the course with the Iraqi election and in promoting freedom in other Middle Eastern nations. It is interesting to note that on the second anniversary of the start of the Iraq War, on March 19, 2005, the number of demonstrators was reported to be in the "hundreds" in large U.S. cities—not thousands or tens of thousands. At the same time a widespread opposition movement centered on these groups could reemerge quickly should the United States undertake another military venture against another foreign dictatorship posing a threat with weapons of mass destruction (WMD).

6: THE NOTORIOUS RADICAL GROUPS GIVE AID AND COMFORT TO U.S. ENEMIES WHILE AT THE SAME TIME LIBERAL GROUPS GIVE AID AND COMFORT TO THESE RADICAL GROUPS.

For more than four decades, officials of the IPS have collaborated with opinion makers and policy makers (U.S. and foreign) against U.S. interests. The radical IPS people have been assisted by a number of liberals in the media and in the U.S. Congress. The spin-off groups of IPS, such as the CNSS, enjoyed great support from a host of influential liberals. Many have ignored the various interactions that such radical groups had with foreign officials and ignored the material aid and moral support that they gave to countries such as the USSR, North Vietnam, and Cuba.

Today, radical groups such as the troika of the Workers World Party, International Action Center, and Act Now to Stop War and End Racism (WWP-IAC-ANSWER) have sponsored and organized the largest demonstrations against the U.S. war in Iraq. The radical troika is helped by a host of liberal groups that participate in these demonstrations, that ignore any warnings of the troika's true character, or that otherwise give radicals a stage or a media outlet. To this day, liberals in the print and broadcast media have obscured the nature of radical groups while liberal members of the U.S. Congress have gone out of their way to accommodate and support various radical groups.

7: THE MONEY FLOW REALLY MATTERS BUT IS LITTLE UNDERSTOOD.

Research into these organizations reveals that staggering sums of money are flowing in the system. Yet we know relatively little and can view

33

these money flows only as snapshots for a given period of time. By one policy decision and a few strokes of a pen, someone such as George Soros can redirect the flow from one group to another. Moreover, there is very little known about his vast holdings, such as his accounts in Curacao, which can go to radical causes. Other than Soros, the names of other influential money movers are barely known, which is unfortunate because they also direct and redirect the flow of untold millions of dollars toward radical causes.

8: THERE IS A GREATER NEED TO CHECK ONE'S SOURCES OF INFORMATION THAN EVER BEFORE.

It has long been the case that the most radical groups have resorted to lying, distortion, hyperbole, half truths, and exaggeration. But in recent years groups that have become prominent have done the same thing, especially when regarding the elections of 2000 and 2004. Groups that took every opportunity to twist and distort issues and reporting about events spent great sums of money to do so—especially in 2004. Large-membership groups such as MoveOn.org have raised issues that serve to undercut the legitimacy of the 2004 presidential election and have thrown together a number of "scare tactics" statements with regard to any proposed reforms in the Social Security system.

9: THERE IS PROBABLY MORE INTERACTION BETWEEN THE RADICAL AND LIBERAL U.S. GROUPS AND FOREIGN OFFICIALS THAN IS COMMONLY KNOWN OR REPORTED.

There is never a shortage of conferences, seminars, workshops, demonstrations, or other kinds of gatherings where there are unlimited opportunities to criticize the United States and its policies. There are some within the U.S. organizations who have acted as de facto agents of influence in the past—even though the U.S. government had not labeled them as such—and these persons remain active today. By the same token there are foreign officials who would have sought to influence U.S. politics through interaction with our opinion makers and public officials. In view of the communications revolution and unlimited opportunities to connect with foreign officials, it is highly likely that there is sustained, ongoing interaction between the groups discussed in this book and some foreign officials who wish us ill.

10: THE BEST WAY TO COUNTERACT THE INFLUENCE OF RADICAL AND HARD-LINE LIBERAL GROUPS IS TO USE THE TOOLS OF EXPOSURE AND AWARENESS.

We need to throw light on the various statements made by the officials of these groups. It pays to take them at their word and to assume that they mean exactly what they say. The more light is shed on these sentiments, the better understanding we will all have of their true intentions. A general level of awareness is useful for everyone who is concerned about the direction that these groups are trying to steer the United States and the way they are going about it.

At the same time it does not hurt to return to our own democratic principles to ask these questions:

- Who elected George Soros to public office?
- Who elected Eli Pariser to public office?
- Who elected Ramsey Clark to public office?
- Who elected Leslie Cagan to public office?
- Who elected Ed Asner to public office?
- Who elected Michael Moore to public office?

LESSONS FROM THE COLD WAR

A S A FORMER PARTICIPANT in the cold war during 1965–68 (military service) and 1971–2003 (civilian service in intelligence), I do not miss it. More than many other people, I am delighted that we have stepped back from those times of U.S.-Soviet confrontation, tensions, and anxieties about far-flung crises that might rapidly escalate to a nuclear exchange.

At the same time, there are lessons from that period that are very applicable today. These lessons involve techniques and tactics for the manipulation of opinion, what some call "perception management." Those techniques and tactics are part of the "war of manipulation." That aspect of the cold war was far more subtle and nuanced than the military-versus-military aspect. The manipulative aspect was truly the "game of the foxes."

The old institutions of Soviet power included the Communist Party of the Soviet Union (CPSU) and its leadership organizations, the Politburo and Central Committee. The former Committee for State Security (KGB)—the "action arm" of the party that carried out its directives—was supplanted by the Foreign Intelligence Service (SVR). The party institutions have been gone since 1991, but their legacies live on in the form of the techniques and tactics that they developed and perfected.

Some of the radical groups discussed here practice those same techniques and tactics or variations of them adapted to the present day.

This chapter will review some of the most significant aspects of the war of manipulation. These include the broad concepts of active measures and denial and deception (D&D). Other concepts relevant to today are: agents of influence, disinformation, the big lie, the principle of leading masses from hard-core elements, the "long march through the institutions," and the resort to intimidation and physical violence.

ACTIVE MEASURES

The Soviets used the term "active measures" (*aktivnyye meropriyatiya*) primarily to refer to covert influence operations intended to provoke a policy effect. They long considered active measures as an unconventional adjunct to traditional diplomacy. Specifically, active measures were designed "to influence the policies of foreign governments," to "disrupt relations between other nations," to "undermine confidence in foreign leaders and institutions," and to "discredit opponents." One interagency intelligence study of 1982 notes that active measures consisted of a "wide range of activities, both overt and covert," that included (among others) manipulation or control of the media, written or oral disinformation, use of foreign Communist parties and front organizations, and manipulation of mass organizations.[1]

Active measures emanate from a rich tradition in Soviet history, going back to right after the Russian Revolution and the 1920s. One of the best known was a massive deception operation known as the Trust, which was planned and executed by Felix Dzerzhinsky, the head of the Cheka secret police. This operation lasted from 1921 until 1927 and convinced many Western European intelligence services to support and fund a notional anti-Bolshevik "resistance" movement inside the USSR.

During the cold war days, the Soviets saw active measures as a way to weaken opponents of the USSR and to create a favorable environment for advancing Moscow's view and international objectives worldwide. The United States was often the main target for these active measures, and that situation had not changed even in the era of East-West détente. Those U.S. experts in this area recognized that the Soviets had institutional memories as well as recurring patterns of operations.

PRINCIPAL TECHNIQUES OF SOVIET ACTIVE MEASURES

Covert Media Manipulation
- Placement and reply of articles
- Purchase of media outlets
- "TV offensive"

Agents of Influence
- Recruited and controlled agents
- "Special contacts" (nonrecruited)
- "Trusted contacts" (nonrecruited)

Disinformation
- Written
- Oral

Use of Foreign Communist Movements
- Nonruling Communist parties
- Other leftist parties

Use of Front Organizations
- Traditional fronts
- Soviet mass organizations
- Friendship societies
- Professional groups

People-to-People Contact Operations
- Individuals
- Groups
- Delegations

Forgeries
- Public forgeries
- "Silent forgeries" (victim unaware)

Defamation Operations
- False rumors
- Blackmail

Street Activities
- Demonstrations
- Strikes
- Intimidation operations

Active measures usually involved a complex blend of overt and covert activities, and occasionally Moscow would coordinate several different types of tactics, in what was called a "combination" (*kombinatsiya*). They would use a combination in what they believed were critical campaigns, such as their effort to prevent the deployment of NATO's long-range missiles in Europe or to derail the Strategic Defense Initiative (SDI) announced by President Ronald Reagan in 1983.

In trying to sway or bend opinion, the Soviets would often use naturally occurring sentiments and then distort them in a pro-Soviet or anti-Western direction. They would often allude to peace, freedom of the press, freedom of speech, and human rights.[2] And they would seek to play on mankind's genuine concerns over peace, security, and social justice. Often Moscow would take advantage of the U.S. propensity for "mirror imaging," wishful thinking, preconceived notions, and misunderstanding of the Soviet system.[3]

The two most prominent players in Soviet active measures were the International Department (ID) of the Central Committee of the CPSU and Service A of the First Chief Directorate (foreign intelligence) of the KGB.[4] The ID had an overarching role in Soviet indirect warfare and would set the tone and coordinate affairs from Moscow. The ID would sponsor trips for leaders of foreign Communist parties to the USSR, and the ID would also place some of its representatives in selected embassies abroad. The KGB's Service A would plan and coordinate active measures and oversee their implementation in the field. Both the ID and Service A were relatively small organizations in terms of staffing, with about two hundred to three hundred persons apiece, although both played a major role in the cold war. The International Information Department (IID) and the Propaganda Department (PD) of the Central Committee played supporting roles as well.

Moscow took active measures seriously. It was estimated that the USSR spent some three billion to four billion dollars each year in its active measures campaigns.[5] Just as significantly, the ID and KGB realized that Washington DC was an ideal arena for their active measures. No place else in the world is there a free press with greater access to high government officials. Accordingly, the Soviets spared little effort to play to the Washington press corps in efforts to swing U.S. opinion.

During the early 1980s Moscow was involved in a number of influence operations intended to thwart the implementation of NATO's decision to enhance its theater nuclear forces (TNF). The United States and NATO had intended to deploy Pershing II ballistic missiles and the ground-launched cruise missile (GLCM) as counters to the much-feared Soviet SS-20 missile that had previously been deployed in the western USSR and targeted on Europe.

The plan to modernize NATO's missile force led to the largest and best-coordinated protests in decades. The nuclear freeze movement demanded that the West unilaterally halt nuclear weapons development, testing, and deployment. The freeze movement in the United States was organized by Terry Provance and Randall Forsberg, who used popular entertainers such as Bruce Springsteen to draw audiences to nuclear freeze rallies.[6] Moreover, a host of books, authored by pro-freeze intellectuals, lambasted President Reagan and his "confrontational" approach that could lead to a nuclear war. Before the advent of George W. Bush's presidency, Reagan was a favorite target for the Left to bash as a "simple-minded warmonger."

The active measures planners in the ID and KGB used journalists, political figures, and academicians to try to influence the decision-making process in several West European countries. They brought out a number of front groups and offshoots of these front groups to sponsor or exploit various conferences, symposiums, and demonstrations opposed to NATO's new missiles. Ultimately this campaign was not successful, as the new missiles (108 Pershing IIs and 464 cruise missiles) were deployed in the United Kingdom, Germany, and Italy.[7]

At the same time, the Soviets used active measures to promote the leftist insurgency in El Salvador. In late 1981 President Reagan had authorized the CIA to furnish arms and training to the "contra" rebels fighting the Sandinista regime in Nicaragua and then-DCI William Casey had persuaded the president to funnel support to anti-Marxist elements in the Salvadoran government. Moscow's plan also was motivated by a variety of objectives: to establish another Communist (or at least a pro-Soviet leftist) government on the U.S. doorstep, to divert attention from Soviet action in Afghanistan, and to damage the U.S. image abroad by distorting U.S. policy on El Salvador and linking the United States with objectionable aspects of the Salvadoran government through a coordinated disinformation and propaganda campaign. This "combination" included such classic techniques as forgeries, front groups, covert press placements, disinformation, and the manipulation of mass organizations. Some Salvadoran leftists created a number of "solidarity committees" abroad—evidently with Soviet and Cuban encouragement and backing—to serve as propaganda tools, conduits for material aid, and organizers of meetings and demonstrations.[8]

Soviet active measures tended to retain certain long-range strategic objectives:

- "To influence both world and American public opinion against U.S. military, economic, and political programs" perceived to be threatening to Soviet objectives.
- To demonstrate that the United States was an aggressive, "colonialist," and "imperialist" power.
- "To isolate the United States from its allies and friends and discredit those that cooperate with it."
- To demonstrate that the policies and goals of the United States were "incompatible with the ambitions of the underdeveloped world."
- "To discredit and weaken U.S. intelligence efforts—particularly those of the CIA—and expose U.S. intelligence personnel."
- "To create a favorable environment for the execution of Soviet foreign policy."
- "To undermine the political resolve of the United States and other Western states to protect their interests against Soviet encroachments."[9]

It is now interesting to see some of these themes recycled as recently as 2006. True, the Central Committee and its ID have departed the scene, but new radical U.S. groups have emerged since the hammer-and-sickle flag was lowered over the Kremlin, and some new groups have adopted the various objectives that the Soviet groups developed earlier.

Some of the Far Left's propaganda techniques are even identical to those used by the ID and KGB forty to fifty years ago. These include the systematic denigration of the United States, its culture, political system, and belief structures; imputing false motives to U.S. policy; and debasing the meaning of words—especially when applied to the United States or its policies.

DENIAL AND DECEPTION

Denial and deception (D&D) refers to a range of measures that one takes to conceal his hand and to mislead his opponent. In the military context, D&D had earlier been called CC&D (camouflage, concealment, and deception). The essence of D&D is to strike at the mind of the enemy commander by leading him astray.

The first D of denial simply means measures to present the other side from gaining information. This could include masking or hiding one's capabilities. The second D of deception is the more active side, referring to a concerted program to mislead or confuse the adversary.

The U.S. experience with Iraq confirms that the Iraqis were masters at D&D. They repeatedly hid their weapons of mass destruction (WMD) and often resorted to playing an elaborate shell game with weapons inspectors. Moreover, they transmitted false and misleading messages about their capabilities and intentions, either through controlled sources (plaiting false information on agents of foreign intelligence services) or else broadcasting this information to the world in public forums.

TWO EXAMPLES OF D&D TODAY

One good example of D&D occurred in a 1988 book by Bill Moyers entitled *The Secret Government: The Constitution in Crisis*, a work that emerged in the wake of the Iran-Contra scandal.[10] In this case, Moyers practiced both denial and deception in one short book.

Moyers brought in denial when he refused to mention the powerful role played by President Lyndon B. Johnson in ordering the involvement of the CIA in Operation CHAOS in 1967, a role that ran against the agency's charter for overseas operations. As a former aide to LBJ, Moyers would have no interest in revealing this significant fact. Further denial was evident as Moyers masked or obscured the ideological bent of some who had contributed significantly to this book (and to the television program that this work was taken from). These persons included the notorious radical Morton Halperin, black activist and IPS senior fellow Roger Wilkins, liberal columnist Richard Strout, and rogue former CIA employee-turned-radical Ralph McGehee.

Moyers brought in deception when he implied that there was a "constitutional crisis" in the first place. Reagan's aides had made serious miscalculations and missteps, and they and Reagan paid a high political price, pure and simple. But it was no constitutional crisis. Moyers further added deception when he referred to the Center of Defense Information under retired Adm. Gene LaRocque as a "public interest group," with no further discussion of its actual radical orientation. Finally, deception came in the form of linguistic exaggeration and hyperbole, as Moyers compared William Casey's "Enterprise" working out of the National Security Council with the murderous Cheka secret police established by Dzerzhinsky in the USSR after the Bolshevik Revolution.

An excellent example of D&D emerged in early 2003. Denial occurred during a large antiwar demonstration on January 18, 2003, in Washington DC. In covering this event, the combined resources of the major news networks never once indicated the involvement of organizers from the Workers World Party (WWP). Neither C-SPAN nor Lisa Sylvester of ABC nor Dan Lothian of NBC nor Joie Chen of CBS found it possible to mention the pedigree of the principal figures who had organized and led this demonstration. Instead, the networks touted the "diversity" of the people and groups that comprised the demonstration, portraying them all as a cross section of America.[11]

Deception occurred a few weeks later. On this occasion, Amy Goldman, the radical host of a radio program called *Democracy Now!* just happened to have several guests "drop by" her New York City studio. These guests were Ramsey Clark, Danny Glover, Susan Sarandon, and Harry Belafonte.[12] These, of course, are four of the most vociferous and hard-core individuals adamantly opposed to any Bush administration effort and to George Bush himself. What resulted was a stereo broadcast of a hate-America, hate-Bush message, quite typical on *Democracy Now!*

AGENTS OF INFLUENCE

This term refers to people whom the Soviets used to advance their plans and goals, influential individuals usually close to the levers of policy and power in their own countries. Agents of influence were

DENIAL AND DECEPTION

Denial in General

- An effort to hide or block information, which can be used by an opponent to learn the truth
- Methods to conceal secrets, especially from foreign intelligence collection
- Examples of methods:
    - Signals security
    - Countermeasures to satellite/aerial reconnaissance
    - Camouflage
    - Underground or covert facilities

Deception in General

- An effort to convey false information, causing an opponent to believe something that is not true
- The manipulation of information and perceptions designed to change an opponent's course of action
- Examples of methods:
    - Disinformation
    - Cover stories
    - Staged activities
    - False installations

D&D in 1988 Book by Bill Moyers

DENIAL:
- Critical role of LBJ in ordering CIA to act in Operation CHAOS
- Radical/liberal orientation of Halperin, Wilkins, Strout, and McGehee

DECEPTION:
- There really is a constitutional crisis
- Portrayal of CDI as "public interest group"
- Linguistic hyperbole and exaggeration ("Enterprise" = Cheka)

D&D in Case of 2003 Demonstrations

DENIAL:
- No mention by networks of WWP affiliations of organizers

DECEPTION:
- Messages of guests who "drop in" to *Democracy Now!* radio program (Clark, Glover, Sarandon, Belafonte)

sometimes recruited by Soviet intelligence and sometimes not, although they were under some form of control. They were sometimes paid for their services and sometimes not. And they were sometimes fully aware of their Soviet sponsors and sometimes not, and not all agents of influence knew that they were being used in this way.[13]

There were several different categories of people whom the Soviets tried to use for influence operations. Agents of influence were under the control of either the KGB or the ID. Using Soviet intelligence terminology, a "special contact" was someone who was under less control, and someone in a "trusted relationship" was under even less control.

The Soviets relied on developing strong personal relationships with political, economic, academic, and media figures abroad who could be used to further Moscow's agenda. The Soviets usually entrusted this task to the KGB, which tried to secure the active collaboration of these persons on matters of mutual interest while the individuals retained their integrity on other issues. In return for collaboration, the KGB would offer intangible rewards tailored to meet the specific requirements or vulnerabilities of the persons involved. Such rewards included publicity for the collaborators' accomplishments and promises of special communications channels to the Kremlin.

PIERRE-CHARLES PATHE

One example is the remarkable case of French journalist Pierre-Charles Pathe. In 1980 Pathe was convicted for acting as a Soviet agent of influence since 1959. "During his career as a Soviet agent, Pathe was handled by KGB officers who worked under the cover of either the Soviet delegation to UNESCO or the Soviet Embassy in Paris." Early contacts between Pathe and his handlers were overt, taking place at receptions or restaurants. After 1962 all these meetings were clandestine. "His articles, sometimes written under the pseudonym Charles Morand, were published in a variety of French newspapers and journals, including *France-Observateur, Liberation,* and *Realities.* All of the articles subtly pushed the Soviet line on a wide range of international issues. The Soviets reviewed Pathe's articles and provided information that formed the basis of others. Pathe also published a private newsletter, *Syntheses,* with funds provided by the Soviets."

Pathe did not receive a regular agent salary from the Soviets, but he was paid for individual analysis of French and international political developments he provided to them. "His established reputation among journalists and political figures, many of whom took his information and views at face value, made Pathe a valuable asset. He was well integrated into the political establishment."[14]

ARNE HERLOV PETERSEN

Another example concerns the case of Arne Herlov Petersen of Denmark. In early 1981 the Danish government expelled a Soviet diplomat for activities inconsistent with his diplomatic status. It also reported that a Danish citizen, Arne Herlov Petersen, had been arrested and charged for his activities as the Soviet official's agent. This interesting case showed the different ways in which an agent of influence can be used.

For several years Petersen was in clandestine contact with a succession of KGB officers. Under their direction, he functioned as a propagandist, an activist, and a clandestine conduit of funds to support Soviet-induced "peace movement" activities. Petersen was also "a source of information on 'progressive' Danish journalists and other Danes of interest to the KGB, as well as purveyor of forgeries." Below is a sample of some of his activities:

- "In 1979 Petersen published a pamphlet entitled *Cold Warriors*. The pamphlet, based on a KGB-supplied draft, contained brief but scathing attacks" on major Western political figures: Prime Minister Margaret Thatcher, Senator Henry "Scoop" Jackson (D-WA), Senator Barry Goldwater (R-AZ), and major European political figures. The pamphlet was published in Dutch and English.
- "In 1980 Petersen published *True Blues: The Thatcher that Couldn't Mend Her Own Roof.*" This pamphlet attacked the foreign and domestic politics of the British government, and the text was supplied by one of Petersen's KGB contacts.
- "The May 30–31, 1981, issue of the newspaper *Information* carried an appeal bearing the signatures of 150 Danish artists endorsing Soviet proposals for a nuclear-free zone in northern

Europe. The Soviet Embassy is known to have promised Petersen that it would finance at least part of the expenses for such newspaper appeals. Those who signed the appeals, a number of which were published, were apparently unaware of who paid for their publication."

- Petersen, who was actively involved in the Denmark–North Korea Friendship Society, was used by the Soviets to pass a forged report dealing with alleged negotiations between the United States and China that were intended to discourage negotiations between the two Koreas. The Soviets apparently believed that if the North Koreans believed the Chinese were negotiating with the United States over Korean issues, "Pyongyang would feel threatened and seek closer ties with Moscow. Petersen was chosen to pass the report to the North Koreans, without revealing the Soviet role, because of his role in the friendship society."[15]

WILFRED BURCHETT

The third example of a prominent agent of influence concerns Australian journalist Wilfred Burchett. In late 1974 Burchett lost a libel suit challenging allegations that he had been engaged in espionage activities for the USSR. During his long and controversial career as a foreign correspondent, Burchett was known as a "confidant of former Vietnamese premier Ho Chi Minh as well as former Chinese premier Chou en-Lai." Burchett also "wrote for a wide variety of newspapers and news agencies throughout the Western and Communist world."[16] He conducted a guided tour of North Vietnam for reporter Harrison Salisbury in 1966 to support Salisbury's book *Behind the Lines—Hanoi*. Burchett was a prominent participant in the International War Crimes Tribunal that took place in Sweden and Denmark in 1967 and made his influence known in other ways while covering the Vietnam War.

ORLANDO LETELIER

The fourth example of an agent of influence connected to the Far Left was the case of Orlando Letelier. During the rule of socialist Salvador Allende, Letelier had been named Chile's ambassador to the United

States; he later served as Chilean foreign minister, head of the national police, and defense minister. After the 1973 coup that toppled Allende, Letelier worked tirelessly to restore socialism to Chile. To this end, he organized exiled Chilean Marxists and cultivated ties not only with terrorist groups and Communist governments but also with liberal American congressmen.

Saul Landau introduced Letelier to the Institute for Policy Studies, and by 1975 Letelier had come to Washington to take a position there. In September 1976 he was assassinated in Washington DC. The FBI recovered his briefcase from his bombed-out car and found evidence that Letelier was acting as an agent of influence for the Cuban intelligence agency, the General Directorate of Intelligence (DGI), and the Chilean Socialist Party apparatus exiled in East Germany.

"Letelier was receiving financial support from Cuba for his political activities in the United States, and he had extensive contacts" with the Communist world. Listed in his address book were "eleven Cuban officials, thirteen East German addresses" (including Politburo and Central Committee members), and many other contacts in the East. Among his American friends and associates, those in the media composed the largest group. He was in contact with "twenty-seven journalists, reporters, and editors"—seven of whom worked for the *Washington Post*.

According to S. Steven Powell, this case showed conclusively how the IPS used fashionable issues to manipulate liberals into supporting a radical agenda. The case further showed the "proclivity of the IPS to join hands with parties behind the Iron Curtain, parties that, when not denying individual human rights in general, wonder at the incorrigible naivete of American liberals."[17]

DISINFORMATION

Disinformation, or *dezinformatsiya* in Russian, is "false, misleading, or incomplete information that is passed, fed, or confirmed to a targeted individual, group, or country." Disinformation is carefully crafted with regard to the nature of the message, the intended recipient, and the expected result. Propaganda may be used as a support element of disinformation, but propaganda "lacks the precision and bite of disinformation." As practiced by the Soviets, disinformation became more widely used in the 1960s, and the Soviet KGB and their allied intelligence services grew better at it as time went by.

During the mid-1960s Soviet disinformation had three principal aims:

- "Destroy the confidence of the Congress and the American public in U.S. personnel and agencies engaged in anti-Communist and cold war activity.
- "Undermine American prestige and democratic institutions and denigrate American leadership with NATO governments and other non-Communist countries, thereby contributing directly to the breakup of the NATO alliance.
- "Sow distrust and create grounds for subversion and revolt against the United States in the Western Hemisphere and among the new nations of Africa and Asia."[18]

In recent years, the term "disinformation" has been used widely and inaccurately. It differs from "misinformation" in that the latter refers simply to erroneous information ("Oh, I was just misinformed about that"). "Disinformation" is not nearly as innocent a term, and it refers to something that is created as a falsehood from the start, something that is intended to generate a response. Sometimes the disinformation message can be packaged within a larger message of true information with the intention that the recipient will believe the disinformation as well as the true facts.

THE BIG LIE

Nazism died with the fall of the Third Reich in 1945, yet one of Adolf Hitler's principal tools has lived on: the big lie. Hitler said it best when he concluded, "The broad mass of a nation . . . will more easily fall victim to a big lie than to a small one."

There is no limit to the size of the big lie. Dictators will use any number of techniques to support it. The biggest examples of the big-lie technique often involve the nature of the regime itself.

To cite one example, according to John Lenczowski, a Soviet expert on the Reagan National Security Council (NSC), the Soviets tried to perpetuate the big lie that the "Soviet Union is not Communist."[19] Moscow calculated that if it could convince Western policy makers and opinion shapers that this was the case, it would go a long way to erase the "image of the enemy." The one U.S. policy maker who bought this idea was Ambassador Joseph Davies (see chapter 3), who demonstrated a breathtaking degree of gullibility, but other high-level U.S. officials also accepted this lie in varying degrees up through the 1980s.

In this regard, the Soviets perpetuated some subthemes to support the big lie. One was that the Soviets did not believe in their ideology anymore. You could not accept seriously what they said in their propaganda outlets.

Another supporting subtheme was that there was competition between factions of the leadership ("hawks and doves"). U.S. policy makers should therefore be careful not to antagonize the hawks in the Soviet leadership and should try to work with the doves in the Politburo and the Central Committee. During the late 1940s some U.S. policy makers even went so far as to urge presidents to get along with Joseph Stalin, for there were allegedly even *more* menacing Bolshevik leaders than Stalin whom we might have to deal with. Arnaud de Borchgrave, speaking in Washington in 1985, noted that Averill Harriman conveyed this message in 1947: "Help Stalin; if you don't there are more sinister forces waiting in the wings."[20]

The Soviets tried to convey the idea that some of their leaders were liberals beneath their Leninist exterior. The most spectacular case involved the packaging of Yuri Andropov as a "closet" liberal. This effort involved a large stretch of credulity, for Andropov was one of the most orthodox and doctrinaire of all seven heads of the USSR since the revolution and had headed the KGB for fifteen years before his elevation to general secretary of the CPSU. During his tenure at the KGB, Soviet policies became ever more repressive.

To perpetuate the idea that the Soviets were not Communist anymore, some Soviet propagandists made use of the structural deceptions built into the Soviet system. These included a constitution, a parliament (the Supreme Soviet), elections, churches, trade unions, freedoms of the press and speech, and the right of republics to secede from the USSR.

Throughout the 1970s and 1980s there were variations of this theme. It was preferable to portray some pro-Communist groups that

51

were vying for power in the Third World as "Robin Hood reformers" rather than as threatening Communists. The Sandinista regime in Nicaragua—when it was contending for power—was often given a free pass by many in the American media. Instead of hard-core Communists, the Sandinistas were portrayed by some as "agrarian reformers." Returning misty-eyed from a 1985 trip to Nicaragua, Senators Tom Harkin and John Kerry described Daniel Ortega as a "misunderstood democrat rather than a Marxist autocrat" in 1985.[21]

By the same token, apologists have defended Saddam Hussein's regime in some innovative ways. Few could argue with a straight face that it was not a police state, but many did advance the idea that Saddam had done nothing wrong.

The big lie is relevant here because some U.S. organizations of the Far Left disguise their own radical orientation or origins. At first glance (at their Web sites usually), it is often impossible to find this information altogether; it is not spelled out. One can easily get the erroneous idea that these organizations were formed as a kind of spontaneous gathering of "concerned" citizens.

LEADING MASSES FROM HARD-CORE ELEMENTS

This is a principle that has been a fact of life in left-wing politics for decades. It was apparent in Central America in the 1980s, when some hard-core Communists became the leading and directing body of the Sandinista movement in Nicaragua. It has been evident more recently as some peace movements have effectively been taken over by a small group of organizers with Communist sympathies.

The foundation of this technique was set in place as early as the 1930s. Against the backdrop of a worldwide depression and financial chaos, extremist movements of the Far Right and the Far Left flourished. Not only was fascism in vogue in countries in Central and Eastern Europe, but pro-Communist groups were burgeoning in some of the leading capitalist countries of the West.

Circumstances called for the Communists to ally themselves with anti-fascist groups. Accordingly, the Comintern (Communist International) could draw on three masters of the game who emerged during the 1930s: Dmitri Manuilsky, Willi Muenzenberg, and Georgi Dimitrov.

Manuilsky was a noted Comintern official for many years. After World War II he was the USSR's first ambassador to the United Nations. Manuilsky is well known for his statement in the early 1930s, when he spoke to a group at the elite Lenin School in Moscow:

> War to the hilt between communism and capitalism is inevitable. Today, of course, we are not strong enough to attack. Our time will come. . . . To win, we shall need the element of surprise. The bourgeoisie will have to be put to sleep, so we shall begin by launching the most spectacular peace movement on record. There will be electrifying overtures and unheard-of concessions. The capitalist countries, stupid and decadent, will rejoice to cooperate in their own destruction. They will leap at another chance to be friends. As soon as their guard is down, we shall smash them with our clenched fist.[22]

Less outspoken and more diplomatic was another Comintern official, a German named Willi Muenzenberg. He was a brilliant and tireless propagandist and organizer. "In August 1933 Muenzenberg organized a meeting in Amsterdam to bring about a united front against fascism, a gathering that took place under the sponsorship of French writers Romain Rolland and Henri Barbusse." Rolland announced the meeting with a radical call to arms against fascism: "The Fatherland is in danger! Our international Fatherland . . . the USSR is threatened!" This meeting was endorsed by luminaries such as Albert Einstein, John Dos Passos, Upton Sinclair, George Bernard Shaw, H. G. Wells, and Theodore Dreiser.[23] Earlier, in June 1933, Muenzenberg had organized another anti-fascist gathering of intellectuals at the Salle Playel in Paris, and "ten days later the Salle Playel and the Amsterdam groups merged to form the Committee of Struggle Against War and Fascism." Muenzenberg's mobilization of intellectuals came to the United States when the American League Against War and Fascism held its first meeting in September 1933, "largely attended by Communists and front organizations."[24]

Georgi Dimitrov was chief of the Comintern during the mid-1930s and remained in that post until the group was dissolved in 1943. He later ruled Bulgaria after World War II, leading a regime installed by the Red Army. Dimitrov articulated the principle of using hard-core elements to penetrate and manipulate mass movements. In 1935 a change in the party line put Communists in position to work effectively with non-Communist groups. The real objective of the Communists was to discredit their new partners and take over these groups. In July 1935 the leadership of the Comintern ordered Communists everywhere to cooperate with all groups that opposed fascism. In a phrase that would become part of anti-Communist lore, Dimitrov told the delegates that they should use mass organizations as Trojan horses to "penetrate the very heart of the enemy's camp."[25]

THE LONG MARCH THROUGH THE INSTITUTIONS

This term refers to the long-term plan of Communists, radicals, and their supporters to work their way into vital establishments that shape opinions. Once again we turn to the work of another foreign Communist, an Italian Marxist named Antonio Gramsci, who was active during the 1930s. He "pondered the historic inability of Communist parties to mobilize workers to seize the means of production and overthrow the capitalist ruling class," which Lenin had envisioned. "Gramsci's new idea was to focus the attention of radicals on the means of intellectual production as a new lever of social change." He urged radicals to acquire "cultural hegemony," meaning to "capture the institutions that produced society's governing ideas." This, he believed, would be the key to controlling and transforming society itself.[26]

In this respect, the radicals have succeeded beyond anyone's wildest dreams, for the administrations of American universities have fallen into the hands of individuals who generally profess liberal and radical ideas. Liberals and radicals have captured academia to a far greater extent than any of the other institutions. This control exceeds even that of their influence over the print and broadcast media.

Some former members of the Weather Underground Organization (WUO, or Weathermen) now occupy positions of authority on major campuses. Former domestic terrorists such as Bernardine Dohrn (Northwestern University) or Bill Ayers (University of Illinois at Chicago) come to mind. Besides them, there are thousands of other former activists, radicals, and far leftists who have risen to prominent positions within academia. The stakes are higher and the atmosphere is more politicized at the most prestigious universities.

The "march" began long before many people think, and the left-wing takeover of American universities is not a new story. As early as the 1930s Irving Kristol recalled that City College of New York (CCNY) was so radical that "if there were any Republicans at City—and there must have been some—I never met them, or even heard of their existence."[27] Moreover, many campuses were already radicalized by the mid-1960s. Among those most in the news were Berkeley, Columbia, Wisconsin, and Michigan. Today, campus leftism is not merely prevalent, but is "radical, aggressive, and deeply intolerant," according to Jeff Jacoby.[28] Not only are most college professors fashionably liberal, but "most faculties have a strong contingent of hard leftists whose views are extreme and whose concentrated numbers make it possible for them to dominate (and even define) entire academic fields," according to David Horowitz.[29]

Some academics freely admit that when they were in control of university faculties in the 1960s, they opened the doors to the hiring of radicals in the name of diversity. However, the leftists tenured after the 1960s first transformed the colleges and universities into political battlegrounds and then redefined them as "agencies of social change." In the process, according to Horowitz, "they first defeated and then excluded peers whom they perceived as obstacles to their politicized academic agendas."[30]

Of all the various institutions the leftists could target, they have done the most by far in academia. Richard Rorty has summarized this achievement: "The power base of the left in America is now in the universities, since the trade unions have largely been killed off. The universities have done a lot of good work by setting up, for example, African-American Studies programs, Women's Studies programs, and Gay and Lesbian Studies programs. They have created power bases for these movements."[31] Rorty is a professor of philosophy at the University of Virginia and a powerful voice who celebrated the conversion of colleges into political "power bases." This attitude is typical of many other academics as well.

David Horowitz points out that there is an organic connection between the political bias of the university and that of the press. "It was not until journalists became routinely trained in university schools of journalism that mainstream media began to mirror the perspectives of the adversary culture."[32] Seen in this way, there has been a steady process of graduates of distinguished J-schools such as Columbia University or the University of Missouri into the mainstream media, a process that has deepened the leftist tendencies in mainstream media. Bernard Goldberg noted that only two out of two hundred students at Columbia's J-school admitted to being "right of center."[33]

The bias in universities shows up in the following ways:

- Professors frequently commenting on politics in class, even though the political topic has nothing to do with the course.
- One-sided presentations on political issues.
- Using the classroom to present their personal political views.
- Perhaps most important, a self-perpetuating, entrenched group of radicals and liberals who—sitting on tenure and search committees—are ready to blackball any candidates with a conservative bent.

The result has been smugness, complacency, ideological blindness, and a condition of groupthink. Conservative viewpoints and values are grossly underrepresented in the curriculum, and conservatives themselves are relegated to second-class citizenship. As such, many students are likely to graduate without ever having a class taught by a professor with a conservative viewpoint. The result is that some students are conditioned to accept leftist viewpoints as "mainstream."

The unbalanced and biased selection process in the hiring of college faculty has been proved in research by the Center for the Study of Popular Culture. This research examined more than 150 departments and upper-level administrations at 32 elite colleges and universities. The key findings: The overall ratio of Democrats to Republicans at the 32 schools was "more than 10 to 1," or a total of 1,397 Democrats to 134 Republicans.[34] And not a single department at any of the 32 schools managed to achieve a reasonable parity between the two parties, even though, in the United States as a whole, registered Democrats and Republicans are roughly equal in number. The closest to parity was at Northwestern University, where registered Democrats outnumbered registered Republicans by a 4-to-1 ratio. Brown scored a 30-to-1 ratio; Bowdoin and Wellesley showed ratios of 23 to 1; while Columbia and

Yale demonstrated ratios of 14 to 1. At Columbia University, the researchers could not find "a single Republican in the history, political science, or sociology departments." At Cornell University the departments of English and history had no Republicans.[35]

INTIMIDATION AND PHYSICAL VIOLENCE

If all else fails, according to the hard-line radical mind-set, there is always the resort to physical violence and intimidation. This was displayed in spectacular fashion in the streets of Washington DC in 1971 during operations that the Far Left called Dewey Canyon III and May Day (that actually lasted for several days). Cora Weiss once called for storming the gates of the White House and issued a "call for chaos" to bring new enthusiasm to the antiwar movement. Her colleagues Tom Hayden and David Dellinger had once planned "tactics of prolonged direct action" to end the Vietnam War.

Consider also Gael Murphy of CodePink, a strident supporter of Saddam's Iraq. After giving aid and comfort to Saddam's regime, she returned to south Florida to attend a demonstration against a Broward County military recruiting office. She was described by a conservative Web site: "A seasoned protester, Gael employed many classic leftist tactics, such as shouting out that we were violating her right to free speech by exercising our own right to free speech. It did not take long before Gael resorted to the leftist tactic of physical intimidation."[36]

In recent years we have witnessed violent displays in campaigns against the World Trade Organization (WTO) and the World Bank. The campaign in Seattle in 1999 was one of the most violent in recent memory.

The most common displays of force have been the everyday attempts of the Far Left to control the dialogue. Those on campuses have encountered "speech codes" that are most often targeted against any kind of "offensive" speech (which often happens to be conservative in nature). Usually this takes the form of ridicule, with conservative message-bearers being labeled as "lunatics," "racists," or "hatemongers." Some conservative speakers on campuses—if they are invited at all—have been shouted down, heckled, or physically prevented from reaching the lectern.

IT HAS ALL HAPPENED BEFORE

CHEERLEADERS FOR HITLER

During the 1930s there was ample hysteria throughout radical right-wing circles in the United States. Much of it was directed against Franklin D. Roosevelt, his supposed "Jewish" heritage, and his alleged willingness to advance the cause of world Jewry and Communism. This led to some influential figures on the Far Right becoming enamored with Adolf Hitler and his goals in Germany. Some Americans copied Hitlerian tactics to achieve power.

THE BUND

Fritz Kuhn became the unquestioned leader of a group known as the Bund. In the early 1930s it was known as the League (*Bund*) of the Friends of the New Germany, and it changed its name in 1936 to the German American People's League.[1] One of its main goals was to convert people to the idea that Nazi Germany was a friendly power. This group had some sixty-five hundred activists as well as fifteen thousand to twenty thousand sympathizers in 1938. Most of the members were first- or second-generation Americans. Some two-thirds were male, and most lived in large cities in the East and Midwest. The Bund also featured a youth organization and girls' league. It operated some summer camps, which included Camp Sutter in Los Angeles, Camp Nordland in New Jersey, and Camp Siegfried in Yaphank, Long Island.[2]

Hitler had many admirers among Bund members. One unidentified follower stated, "Hitler is showing us a way to take care of people who get in our way, and we can do the same thing here."[3] In an infamous moment at Madison Square Garden in 1939, the Bundists and their friends pledged allegiance to the United States while giving the Hitler salute. One of the group's newspaper headlines claimed GERMAN BLOOD OUR PRIDE—A BETTER AMERICA OUR GOAL!

Upon returning from a meeting with Hitler in late 1936, Kuhn vowed to defeat Roosevelt's bid for reelection. The Bund's violence-laden rhetoric led to demonstrations and clashes with those who opposed them. The Bund promoted two themes, Americanism and anti-Communism, both of which contained much anti-Semitism. The Bund taught that Americanism and Nazism were compatible. Three individuals who received respectful attention in the Bund's camps and training halls were George Washington, Abraham Lincoln, and Horst Wessel (a Nazi "martyr" who was murdered in 1930). Yet the Bund worked on behalf of an anti-American foreign power.[4] Finally, convicted of grand larceny and forgery, Fritz Kuhn, the American *bundesfuehrer,* headed off to Sing Sing Prison.

SILVER SHIRTS

William Dudley Pelley headed an organization known as the Silver Shirts. He turned himself into a radical Anglo-Saxon protector of threatened American values and found ample opportunity to rave against the Jews. Pelley believed that Hitler's success in Germany demonstrated that anti-Semitic propaganda could lead to power and fame. Evidently with an eye toward becoming the American Hitler, Pelley stated, "I intend to lead to fight to rid our country of the Red Jewish menace."[5] Pelley charged that the Jews in America were taking their orders from Moscow, while FDR (a "Dutch Jew" whose real name was "Franklin D. Rosenfelt") was working in cahoots with Leon Trotsky.[6] Through marches, leaflets, and the acquisition of guns and munitions, the Silver Shirts worked toward the ultimate slaughter of the Jews and their allies.

At their peak, the Silver Legion had between ten thousand and fifteen thousand active members, although some estimates placed the number as high as twenty-five thousand card-carrying members and seventy-five thousand fellow travelers.[7]

FATHER CHARLES E. COUGHLIN

Father Charles E. Coughlin, the priest at the Church of the Little Flower in Royal Oak, Michigan, was also known as the "radio priest" and was influential throughout the 1930s. He spoke regularly over the radio and had a large, faithful audience (believed to be about thirteen million) that listened to him every Sunday evening and contributed millions of dollars to his cause. Coughlin also appeared at large rallies, where he would work himself into a frenzy. Some of those who answered his call for righteous violence joined a group called the Christian Front, many of whom anticipated the day when a Christian "Aryan" army would take over the United States.[8] Coughlin was known for anti-Semitic diatribes and was much admired in Berlin.

He was drawn to Hitler at least in part because Hitler liquidated the largest Communist party in the West and had destroyed the rest of the German Left as well. He believed that some type of Hitler-like "new order" in the United States could destroy "Jew-Bolshevism" as well. He could envision a "corporate-Christian America which would suppress Jews and radicals of every stripe, along with atheists, Masons, international bankers and plutocrats, and all others against who he had been inveighing for the past 12 years."[9]

By the late 1930s Father Coughlin drew even closer to the fascist powers, whose achievements thrilled him. He wholeheartedly endorsed the Nazi conquest of Czechoslovakia, Francisco Franco's occupation of Madrid, Benito Mussolini's invasion of Albania, and even Japan's seizure of further Chinese territory. In April 1939 he reminded his audience, "It should never be forgotten that the Rome-Berlin axis is serving western Christendom is a peculiarly important manner."[10]

By 1940 he became an unfailing apologist for Hitler. "He welcomed the fall of France and the advent of the puppet Vichy regime. He condoned the Luftwaffe's attempt to bomb England into submission. He applauded the new dispensation that the Axis powers were bringing to

Europe and Asia." However, these views—along with his well-known hyperbole—were more than most of his radio audience could stomach, and radio stations began dropping his program. By the end of 1940 his radio voice was stilled.[11]

FATHER GERALD B. WINROD

Reverend Gerald B. Winrod of Kansas found himself attracted to Hitler and his aims. Head of the Defenders of the Christian Faith, he noted, "Germany stands alone in her attempt to break Jewish control." Winrod was another die-hard FDR-hater and traced his "radicalism" to the president's supposed Jewish genes. According to Winrod, FDR was descended from the "Rosenvelt" line. Publishing a fake genealogy, Winrod ascribed FDR's allegedly pro-Soviet, pro-international banker stance to his advocacy of "Jewry's world program."[12]

CELEBRITIES

Famous aviator Charles A. Lindbergh Jr. was an outspoken isolationist and had some troubling relationships with the Nazis as well. He had visited Germany during the interwar period, toured German aircraft plants, and returned with glowing descriptions of German industry and the Luftwaffe. He had accepted a military medal from Hermann Goering, which made him vulnerable to accusations of being a Nazi sympathizer. The collapse of the Allied effort in France and Belgium was—according to him—the concern of the British, not the Americans. As the most prominent spokesman of the America First Committee, he believed that the United States should refrain from meddling in purely European conflicts. In July 1941 Interior Secretary Harold Ickes called Lindbergh a "Nazi mouthpiece." In September 1941 Lindbergh accused "the British, the Jews, and the Roosevelt administration of pushing the nation into war."[13]

Lindbergh was not alone in being won over by the German dictator. A well-known favorite of the silver screen in the 1930s, Mary Pickford, was a guest in Germany. She commented, "Hitler seems to be a great fellow for the Germans. Things certainly are marvelous now in Germany."[14] Well-known radio commentator Doug Brinkley also swooned over him. Hitler, he stated, was "a simple man for the common man and a great idealist." Brinkley noted, "Hitler treated Jews well; and concentration camps were pleasant places, as 'one influential Jew told me.'"[15]

In his time Hitler cast his spell over a wide range of influential figures. The Duke and Duchess of Windsor were photographed with him and may have been in line to return to power in a Nazified Great Britain. Joseph P. Kennedy Sr., the U.S. ambassador to the United Kingdom, was at least initially sympathetic to Hitler as well. Kennedy and his friend Viscountess Astor saw Hitler as a "welcome solution to [the] world problems" of Communism and Judaism in Europe. Kennedy told his Nazi counterpart in London that Roosevelt was "the victim of Jewish influence," and the German ambassador reported to Berlin that Kennedy was "Germany's best friend in London."[16]

Hitler's ally Mussolini also had a following in the United States. Angelo Rossi, the mayor of San Francisco, was an admirer, and the San Francisco police department had many supporters of the *Duce*. Governor Philip F. LaFollette of Wisconsin was another admirer. Henry Morgenthau, the secretary of the treasury, respected the way in which Mussolini restored the economic health of Italy. In addition, another Mussolini admirer was a certain "Colonel" Art J. Smith, who commanded a small legion of some thirty to one hundred "Khaki Shirts."[17]

ASSESSMENT: SO WHY DID THEY DO IT?

The 1930s brought about an astonishing array of radical right-wing groups. There were the Silver Shirts, the White Shirts, the Black Shirts (mostly Italian Americans), and the Bund, or the equivalent of the Brown Shirts (mostly German Americans), not to mention a large number of sects. All of them modeled themselves on the paramilitary outfits that Hitler and Mussolini used in their countries.

Many of these people admired Hitler and Mussolini in the belief that fascism represented an acceptable alternative to democracy. Many were dismayed at the huge and growing number of people left jobless and, in some cases, homeless by the Depression. In desperate economic times, people often look for desperate political solutions to the problems. Those individuals on the Far Right were convinced that they had a fighting chance that the American people would turn to them, everything else having failed, "just as the German and Italian people turned to Mussolini and Hitler out of desperation, each of them having also been scoffed at and ridiculed when they began their astonishing crusades."[18]

Even today, a look at advanced industrial countries in Europe indicates that economic hard times often bring authoritarian movements to the forefront. The best-known cases are those European countries where productivity and industrial growth are stagnant that have growing right-wing movements.

Many of these individuals were looking for scapegoats, and the Jews emerged as ideal scapegoats. The individuals in Far-Right movements saw Jewish plots where none existed and Jewish control over the key levers of power in the United States.

Some likely were overjoyed to read a book such as *Mein Kampf*, which offered a rationale for persecution of the Jews. As of 2006 some Muslim immigrants to European countries and to the United States have been singled out as scapegoats as well. In some cases, there are reasons for this, and in some cases not.

Some who fell under the fascist spell were simpletons while others were well-educated people who knew how to pull the levers of power and use their skills at verbal persuasion and manipulation. Few people, if any, could accuse Father Coughlin of stupidity, although some of his followers probably were.

CHEERLEADERS FOR STALIN

In the 1920s some Americans visited the newly formed USSR and returned gushing about what they had seen. Journalist Lincoln Stevens set the pace in 1919, then he came back to state, "I have been over into the future, and it works!" Jane Addams called the Russian Revolution "the greatest social experiment in history."[19] A number of other influential people saw the Soviet Union as a paradise under construction: George Bernard Shaw, H. G. Wells, Theodore Dreiser, Paul Robeson, Sidney and Beatrice Webb, Harold Laski, and Louis Fischer.[20] In some articles for the *New Republic* in 1928, famous educator John Dewey offered some misty-eyed enthusiasm for the USSR: "I have never seen anywhere in the world such a large proportion of intelligent, happy, and intelligently occupied children."[21]

The various trip reports by American intellectuals likely helped to shape the ideology behind President Roosevelt's New Deal. All of this—combined with the views of his close advisers—likely convinced him to adopt the approach to the Soviet Union that he did: diplomatic recognition in 1933 and constant accommodation until his death in 1945.

JOSEPH DAVIES

And then there was Joseph Davies. He served as U.S. ambassador to the USSR for seventeen months in 1937 and 1938. During this time he was repeatedly deceived by Soviet representatives, and he took a number of positions that reflected Moscow's viewpoint and that put the Soviets in the best possible light.

Davies was a corporation lawyer and a diplomat later in his life. He had been a supporter of FDR since 1920. In 1935 he married Marjorie Merriweather Post, the General Foods heiress. It was said that his wedding present to his bride would be to make her an ambassador's wife. Davies could well afford this, as proved by his contribution of $17,500 to FDR's reelection campaign. Apparently nobody thought it significant that Davies knew nothing about Russian history and politics and did not speak the language.[22] Davies's major task from FDR could be summed up in the simple sentence: Get along with the Russians. According to William Corson and Robert Crowley, "He was prepared to swallow any improbability as long as it emanated from an elevated Soviet source."[23] Davies soon began to report back what he thought the president wanted to hear. Kenneth Davis states, "He continued to do so, with great emphasis, in utter disregard of his own embassy staff. . . . and of many signs that his reported 'facts' and conclusions were probably untrue."[24]

Davies attended the purge trials of 1937 and 1938, perhaps the only envoy in Moscow to do so every day. He did so, however, in a state of bewilderment and concluded that the defendants were guilty. His book *Mission to Moscow* contains many passages in which he quotes other diplomats and correspondents who concluded that the accused were actually guilty of anti-state activities; some of these diplomats and correspondents are mentioned by name, but others are not. Davies threw himself enthusiastically into justifying the most improbable distortions as evidence in the purge trials, and never once did he call into question the nature of the evidence presented in court. *Mission to Moscow* is a sustained apologia for all of Stalin's excesses, and all criticism of the Soviets is stifled in the book.[25]

When Davies left Moscow in June 1938, his friend Maxim Litvinov, a foreign commissar, gave him a farewell dinner and asked him to pass on the "unbiased judgments" of his studies of Soviet life. President Mikhail Kalinin told Davies that he and his associates "much regretted" that Davies was leaving his post.[26] The last statement is arguably one of the most truthful things that Soviet officials told him during his sorry tenure in Moscow.

Mission to Moscow is a very useful tool to assess Davies's mind-set, perceptions, and vulnerabilities. The book is a record of his dispatches to the State Department, official and personal correspondence, diary and journal entries, with notes and comments up to 1943. A detailed content analysis of this book reveals—to be most diplomatic—an exotic interpretation of Soviet realities of the late 1930s. To judge from the statements therein, Davies lived in a world of sublime unreality during his tour there. His book reveals an abysmal and even stupefying degree of ignorance about Stalin, the Soviet political system, and the nature of the purge trials under way at the time.

There is no critical, reflective analysis of what the Soviets told Davis. He was told by the Soviets and by others that the defendants in the show trials were guilty, but nowhere did his legal-trained mind probe for evidence. He was told that the Soviet government "had gone out of its way to extend particular consideration" to the U.S. government, but did he once stop to consider why?[27] He echoed the Soviet line on the provisions of the 1936 Constitution, the purge trials, and other aspects of Soviet life. Is it any wonder that the Soviets were genuinely sorry to see him leave Moscow?

Davies had influence with President Roosevelt, who repeatedly sought his opinions. Davies's access was such that he lunched twice with him in April 1937, and FDR asked to meet with him again in December 1937.[28] In June 1938 Roosevelt told Davies he had "always heard" that the Soviets "had lived up to their agreements and were particularly scrupulous as to their given word."[29]

Davies's influence with the White House may well explain a calamitous reorganization within the State Department shortly after his appointment as ambassador. Under unidentified pressures from the White House, the Russian division within the department was abolished, and its unique collection of material on the USSR was ordered to be dismantled and destroyed. Treasury Secretary Henry Morgenthau and Interior Secretary Harold Ickes actively thwarted State Department officials who took a hard line toward Moscow, and they may have been involved in the breakup of the Russian division. No reason was ever given for this bizarre action, but it seems that the division chief, Robert F. Kelley, "tended to recommend firmer attitudes in the face of Soviet truculence than seemed wise to certain people."[30] This episode smelled of some pro-Soviet influence in the highest reaches of the U.S. government.

Davies also was close to others high up in the foreign policy establishment. He had a close friendship with Secretary of State Cordell Hull, Harry Hopkins, and Ambassador Joseph P. Kennedy among others. Clearly Hull relied on Davies substantially for viewpoints on the Soviet Union. Hull also attempted to accommodate the Soviets, and there is evidence that when they got a chance to negotiate with him, they fed his illusions.

One American authority, Dennis Dunn, has examined the role of the first five U.S. ambassadors to the USSR, and his work has generated a most revealing analysis of Davies's behavior. According to Dunn, "Davies thought that the Soviets were essentially Russian-speaking Americans who were quickly developing into democratic capitalists. This was his view when he arrived in Moscow, and it was still his opinion when he departed in June 1938."[31]

Davies ignored the advice of experts such as William Bullitt, Loy Henderson, George Kennan, and Charles "Chip" Bohlen. The experts did not respect the ambassador, and he had no use for their anti-Stalin disposition, despite their knowledge. Davies's main companions—besides military attaché Col. Philip Faymonville (called the "Red Colonel" and known for delusional pro-Stalin views)—were newsmen. This circle included Walter Duranty and Harold Denny of the *New York Times* ("who were notoriously pro-Stalin"), Joseph Barnes and Joseph Phillips of the *New York Herald-Tribune*, Charles Nutter and Richard Massock of the Associated Press, Normal Deuel and Henry Shapiro of the United

Press, James Brown of the International News, and Spencer Williams of the *Manchester Guardian*.[32] Some of these Western journalists supported Davies's idyllic view and deliberately portrayed a false image of Stalin's Russia in the United States.[33]

The communications channel went from Davies to Secretary of State Cordell Hull. In a telegram to Hull on April 1, 1938, Davies reiterated his point: "Many fine things are being done under the present regime. Many noble enterprises have been projected which arouse sympathy and inspire intense admiration."[34] There is no evidence that Hull took issue with these conclusions. Also, such views were warmly received at the White House, for adviser Harry Hopkins had also shown no interest in wanting to curb Stalin's "insatiable appetite for power and control."[35]

Of the first five U.S. envoys to Moscow, Davies was the least successful and most destructive representative from the viewpoint of America's interests. According to Dennis Dunn, Davies greatly exaggerated Russia's industrial development; totally misrepresented the purge trials, Communism, and Stalinism; fabricated facts and offered fanciful and preposterous interpretations of Stalin's crimes; and dismissed terror in Soviet society as a necessary consequence of rapid modernization.[36] According to Robert Williams, Davies and his wife did not comprehend "that they were, in part, pawns in a deadly game, a game in which Stalin was eager to manipulate Western opinion while destroying real and imagined enemies at home."[37]

The consequences of FDR's error in appeasing Stalin were costly and tragic. On one level it led to the Soviets' making life more difficult for other U.S. representatives in Moscow. At a higher level, this approach also enabled Stalin to separate Roosevelt and Winston Churchill and to adopt a demanding tone toward Roosevelt. Moreover, FDR's policy also contributed to the spread of Soviet rule abroad and strengthened Stalinism in the Soviet Union. Specifically FDR overlooked Stalin's expansionist moves in parts of Europe (moves against the Polish government in exile and plans to annex the three Baltic states as well as parts of Romania, Finland, and Poland).[38]

This case also shows political manipulation as well as a mismatch of the personalities of Davies and Stalin: the mind-set of an altar boy matched up with that of a crime boss. Not once did Davies ascribe to Stalin or his lieutenants the possibility of their playing an elaborate game of deception. Davies's mind screened out the possibility of deception because of his tendency to "mirror-image," or ascribe to the Soviets those values and goals that Americans possessed. He remarked that it was the purpose of the Soviet leaders "to promote the brotherhood of man and to improve the lot of the common people."[39] He was not the only American official who has mirror-imaged in this way, but he was one of the most influential persons to have done so for so long and with so profound an effect.

There is no evidence to suggest that Davies was recruited by Soviet intelligence. In fact, the Soviets were content to allow him to function in this way without approaching him to become a complicit agent of influence. Moscow was much more concerned with results than with the distinction between a witting and unwitting participant in its plans.

WALTER DURANTY

Davies was especially close to Walter Duranty of the *New York Times*, a longtime correspondent in the USSR. The Davies-Duranty association may have begun as early as January 1937, when the correspondent sailed with Davies on board the ship *Europa* to take up his post in Moscow. Content analysis of the Davies book reveals that Duranty's name is several times mentioned first among all others when Davies refers to the Moscow correspondents, those "unofficial colleagues" of "inestimable value" to him. Davies calls them a "brilliant group" and states that he came to rely upon them. Most tellingly, Davies states, "I shall always feel under a special obligation to Walter Duranty who told the truth as he saw it and has the eyes of genius."[40]

Others have taken a different view of him. According to William Corson and Robert Crowley, Duranty achieved his preeminence as Stalin's favorite foreign correspondent "by his willingness to report Bolshevik blather with scrupulous attention to detail."[41] Duranty attained an infamous reputation by steadfastly refusing to report on a famine in the southern USSR, a tragedy of immense proportions that Stalin fostered and exacerbated. Stalin praised Duranty's reporting and stated to the journalist, "You have done a good job in your reporting" about the USSR because "you tried to tell the truth about our country and explain it to your readers."[42]

Not surprisingly, Duranty had praise for *Mission to Moscow,* which he called a "good and true story" written with "exceptional vision and courage."[43] Duranty also played the critical role of gatekeeper to Soviet officials, as he entertained the Moscow press corps and ensured that the more deserving of them received cordial receptions from Soviet officials and the less deserving did not. After Duranty received a Pulitzer Prize, he became—according to the conventional wisdom of the day—the West's foremost "Soviet expert." Thus he was prepared to advise FDR directly and did so at length shortly after Roosevelt was elected.[44]

Walter Duranty was desperate to maintain his access to Stalin and consistently portrayed his regime in sympathetic tones. Unfortunately, Duranty's influence was as pervasive on Davies as it was on his newspaper readership. Duranty's help to Stalin came at a critical time, when the Soviets first tried to collectivize agriculture in the late 1920s during the first Five-Year Plan. There was considerable resistance from the peasantry, and it was in Ukraine—forcibly brought into the USSR—that collectivization met its greatest resistance. To break this resistance, and to campaign against Ukrainian national culture as well, Stalin issued unreasonable delivery quotas for grain that could not be met without the peasants themselves dying of starvation—a deliberate use of starvation as a weapon. Stalin later authorized seizures of the peasants' grain to meet the targets.

In November 1932 Duranty claimed, "There is no famine or actual starvation nor is there likely to be." In June 1933 he reported, "The 'famine' is mostly bunk," at the very time when it was pervasive and deadly throughout Ukraine. He later wrote in August 1933, "Any report of a famine in Russia is today an exaggeration or malignant propaganda."[45]

Malcolm Muggeridge, who tried to report the truth about the famine in Ukraine, called Duranty "the greatest liar of any journalist I have met in fifty years of journalism."[46] Duranty was not ignorant of events and knew exactly what was happening; this much is known from his private comments to others. He actually guessed correctly at the number of deaths from the forced collectivization of agriculture and the famine—about 9.5 million in all (according to sources from now-opened Soviet archives). At least 5 million perished in Ukraine alone, a number that does not include casualties in other Soviet republics from the forced collectivization.

Duranty won not only a Pulitzer Prize in 1932 but also praise from the *Nation*. That magazine—far left even then—praised him for his work in "the most enlightening, dispassionate and readable dispatches from a great nation in the making which appeared in any newspaper in the world."[47]

Robert Conquest, who has chronicled Stalin's terror campaigns masterfully, cited one Communist as saying that the USSR could hope to attract support around the world for its Marxist system only if the human costs of its policies were kept from the public eye.[48] Duranty obediently played his part in denial and deception masterfully, as the *New York Times* readers never gained an inkling of the great human tragedy unfolding in the early 1930s.

MICHAEL PARENTI

There are modern-day disciples of Davies and Duranty. Take, for example, the works of Michael Parenti, a modern-day apologist or tacit supporter of Stalin and Stalinism. In his book *The Anticommunist Impulse* (1969), the jacket statement is significant: "An expression of how our obsession with anticommunism 'has warped our national commitments to freedom and prosperity, immobilized us in our efforts to remedy national ills, and caused the pursuit of a foreign policy that has led to the death and maiming of hundreds of thousands of young Americans.'" Parenti states that anti-Communism "is an outgrowth of our loftiest messianic visions and our crudest materialistic drives and as such it tells us more about ourselves than about the world we inhabit." Individuals such as Parenti have gone so far in their crusade against anti-Communism that they claim, since anti-Communists live in a delusional world all their own, anything they might say about Communism should be dismissed out of hand.[49]

Some of Parenti's assertions can only be called "howlers. " As pointed out by Richard Gid Powers:

> Had anticommunists charged Stalin with murdering millions? Laughable. "That Stalin could have maintained such popular devotion among

the masses while so decimating their ranks is, to say the least, highly questionable." The Gulag was another fiction: "When the camps were abolished after Stalin's death, there was no sign of twenty million half-starved victims pouring back into Soviet life. Labor camp inmates numbered in the thousands." The idea that Russians could not change their jobs, or move about freely in their own country, Parenti derived as another anticommunist myth.[50]

The sad fact is that these claims occurred many years after former Soviet leader Nikita Khrushchev himself revealed the scope of Stalin's crimes in 1956, and heroic figures such as Alexander Solzhenitsyn and Andrei Sakharov were persecuted for telling the truth about Soviet mass murders and labor camps.

Parenti continues on the loose, spewing his toxic waste to the present day. He received his Ph.D. in political science from Yale University and has taught in a number of colleges and universities. According to his Web site, he is the author of 18 books and 250 articles and appears of radio and television talk shows. He lectures on college campuses before a wide range of audiences in North America and abroad, and "his books are enjoyed by both lay readers and scholars." His Web site claims that his works have been translated into 17 languages, including Chinese, Greek, Korean, Persian, Serbian, and Turkish. Among the topics he treats are "imperialism and U.S. interventionism," "political bias in the U.S. news media," and "fascism: past and present."[51]

ASSESSMENT: SO WHY DID THEY DO IT?

The available evidence suggests that ego-weakness, not stupidity, accounts for the actions of people such as Davies, Duranty, or Parenti. Davies had advanced academic and judicial degrees, and one cannot say that stupidity led to his perceptions and behavior. But he was described as "ignorant, conceited, and arrogant," traits that affected his judgment. The evidence also suggests Davies had a propensity for wishful thinking, an intolerance of opposing points of view, and an inability to weigh evidence and draw impartial conclusions.

By the same token, Duranty accomplished much and could not have remained in his position in Moscow had he been stupid. He was well aware of how to play the system, to include his role as gatekeeper for other journalists in Moscow. There is little doubt that he was self-important and felt a need to influence others (including a sitting president) by his actions.

In addition, Parenti clearly does not suffer from stupidity. Anyone who can attain a doctorate from Yale, teach in various universities, and publish as he has cannot be called stupid. His more recent behavior is in some respects more puzzling than those figures from the 1930s, given the overwhelming evidence of the vast scale of human suffering and misery involved in the building of a socialist society in the Soviet Union. All of his actions suggest a willingness and choice to screen out any information that would conflict with his half-baked opinions.

CHEERLEADERS FOR HO CHI MINH

During the 1960s and 1970s there was no shortage of American supporters of Ho Chi Minh, his regime, and his cause. Many chanted Ho's name in the streets and on campuses and marched under North Vietnamese or Vietcong flags. There is no doubt that the U.S. antiwar movement was large and diverse. The majority of all who participated simply wanted the war to end. A minority within that group, however, clearly was rooting for the North Vietnamese and Vietcong to win the war. The latter group would do whatever it could to offer aid and comfort to the North Vietnamese regime and the Vietcong—usually in the form of active collaboration or delivery of material aid.

TRAVELERS

Until Hanoi opens its archives and records from the Vietnam War, we will have an incomplete picture of the full extent of this collaboration between selected Americans and the North Vietnamese regime. For the present time, one way to determine who was the most active—and useful to the enemy—is to see who traveled abroad to meet North Vietnamese or Vietcong representatives. But the complete list of Americans who did so is not yet available in any public forum. Still, there is ample evidence about the most prominent Americans who traveled abroad to meet with the North Vietnamese or Vietcong. A substantial number of officials of the antiwar or "social justice" movements went to North Vietnam, and some met with enemy officials in various countries abroad.

There was never a shortage of misty-eyed effusion after these trips. Many of the pilgrims returned raving about the heroic "resistance fighters" battling the American "imperialists" against heavy odds.

- After meeting with North Vietnamese and Vietcong officials in Bratislava, Czechoslovakia, in 1967, Tom Hayden was reported to gush, "Now we're all Vietcong."[52]

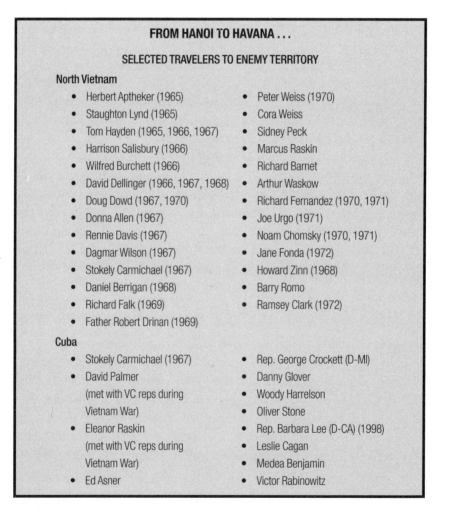

FROM HANOI TO HAVANA . . .

SELECTED TRAVELERS TO ENEMY TERRITORY

North Vietnam

- Herbert Aptheker (1965)
- Staughton Lynd (1965)
- Tom Hayden (1965, 1966, 1967)
- Harrison Salisbury (1966)
- Wilfred Burchett (1966)
- David Dellinger (1966, 1967, 1968)
- Doug Dowd (1967, 1970)
- Donna Allen (1967)
- Rennie Davis (1967)
- Dagmar Wilson (1967)
- Stokely Carmichael (1967)
- Daniel Berrigan (1968)
- Richard Falk (1969)
- Father Robert Drinan (1969)

- Peter Weiss (1970)
- Cora Weiss
- Sidney Peck
- Marcus Raskin
- Richard Barnet
- Arthur Waskow
- Richard Fernandez (1970, 1971)
- Joe Urgo (1971)
- Noam Chomsky (1970, 1971)
- Jane Fonda (1972)
- Howard Zinn (1968)
- Barry Romo
- Ramsey Clark (1972)

Cuba

- Stokely Carmichael (1967)
- David Palmer
  (met with VC reps during
  Vietnam War)
- Eleanor Raskin
  (met with VC reps during
  Vietnam War)
- Ed Asner

- Rep. George Crockett (D-MI)
- Danny Glover
- Woody Harrelson
- Oliver Stone
- Rep. Barbara Lee (D-CA) (1998)
- Leslie Cagan
- Medea Benjamin
- Victor Rabinowitz

- Upon returning from a 1967 trip to North Vietnam, Donna Allen stated, "When you come back, you've dedicated your life."[53]
- On the heels of a trip to North Vietnam in 1971, Joe Urgo stated that his trip "had an enormous impact on me in convincing that I was on the side of the Vietnamese *now*."[54]

These trips evidently led to the suspicion that the peace movement was directed from abroad. A CIA study of the U.S. antiwar movement as part of the infamous Operation CHAOS (ordered by President Lyndon

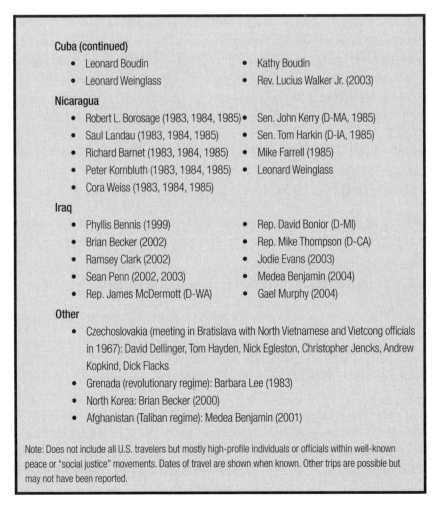

Cuba (continued)
- Leonard Boudin
- Leonard Weinglass
- Kathy Boudin
- Rev. Lucius Walker Jr. (2003)

Nicaragua
- Robert L. Borosage (1983, 1984, 1985)
- Saul Landau (1983, 1984, 1985)
- Richard Barnet (1983, 1984, 1985)
- Peter Kornbluth (1983, 1984, 1985)
- Cora Weiss (1983, 1984, 1985)
- Sen. John Kerry (D-MA, 1985)
- Sen. Tom Harkin (D-IA, 1985)
- Mike Farrell (1985)
- Leonard Weinglass

Iraq
- Phyllis Bennis (1999)
- Brian Becker (2002)
- Ramsey Clark (2002)
- Sean Penn (2002, 2003)
- Rep. James McDermott (D-WA)
- Rep. David Bonior (D-MI)
- Rep. Mike Thompson (D-CA)
- Jodie Evans (2003)
- Medea Benjamin (2004)
- Gael Murphy (2004)

Other
- Czechoslovakia (meeting in Bratislava with North Vietnamese and Vietcong officials in 1967): David Dellinger, Tom Hayden, Nick Egleston, Christopher Jencks, Andrew Kopkind, Dick Flacks
- Grenada (revolutionary regime): Barbara Lee (1983)
- North Korea: Brian Becker (2000)
- Afghanistan (Taliban regime): Medea Benjamin (2001)

Note: Does not include all U.S. travelers but mostly high-profile individuals or officials within well-known peace or "social justice" movements. Dates of travel are shown when known. Other trips are possible but may not have been reported.

B. Johnson) concluded that there was no significant evidence of Communist control or direction of the U.S. peace movement or its leaders, an assertion that LBJ and other administration officials did not believe or wish to believe. Yet the study also noted that the only extensive government contacts maintained by peace activists were with Hanoi.[55]

FONDA AND CLARK

Jane Fonda and Ramsey Clark made two of the most publicized trips to North Vietnam in 1972. Jane Fonda toured the country July 8–22. She was photographed on a North Vietnamese antiaircraft artillery gun mount—a picture that no liberal or radical group wants you to see these days—and toured bomb-damaged parts of the country. After talking with American POWs, she made a special report over the radio in which she testified to the good treatment of the prisoners and called on the U.S. airmen to halt the bombing. Her broadcast provoked unmitigated furor in the United States, and the State Department, veterans organizations, and conservative politicians condemned her, and some members of Congress charged her with treason.[56] Fonda's efforts on behalf of the North Vietnamese earned her the nickname "Hanoi Jane." The storm centered on her one well-publicized trip to North Vietnam, and it is not commonly known that her husband, Tom Hayden, made three such trips.

Ramsey Clark was well known by 1972, having served as President Johnson's attorney general from 1967 to 1969. He and other Far-Left leaders had previously formed the Citizens Committee for the Amendment to End the War, designed to mobilize grassroots support for withdrawal by a fixed date.[57] Clark surveyed bomb damage in the countryside from July 29 to August 12 as part of an international commission to assess the war damage in North Vietnam. Clark's hand-wringing statements clearly indicate that he was distressed by what he saw. He said afterward that he had seen "more apartments, villages, dikes and sluices destroyed than I ever want to see again." The country "has now been bombed back into the 17th century," he stated, and seeing the survivors of the bombed villages was "almost unbearable." John Mitchell, Clark's successor as attorney general, said that Clark had been "unwittingly duped into playing Hanoi's wretched game of using POWs as bargaining chips." Mitchell also called Clark a "megaphone for Communist propaganda."[58]

INTERNATIONAL WAR CRIMES TRIBUNAL

The year 1967 also featured a bizarre episode that benefited Ho Chi Minh's cause: the infamous International War Crimes Tribunal (IWCT) sponsored by ninety-four-year-old British philosopher Bertrand Russell. The IWCT began meeting in Sweden and later met in Denmark. Its major sessions took place in May and November 1967. The United States was accused of "aggression, civilian bombardment, the use of experimental weapons, the torture and mutilation of prisoners and genocide involving forced labor, mass burial, concentration camps and saturation bombing of unparalleled intensity." Naturally, the United

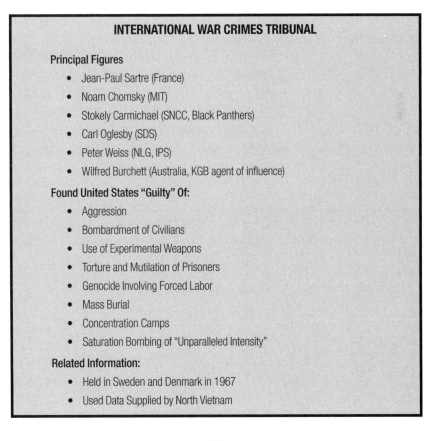

INTERNATIONAL WAR CRIMES TRIBUNAL

Principal Figures
- Jean-Paul Sartre (France)
- Noam Chomsky (MIT)
- Stokely Carmichael (SNCC, Black Panthers)
- Carl Oglesby (SDS)
- Peter Weiss (NLG, IPS)
- Wilfred Burchett (Australia, KGB agent of influence)

Found United States "Guilty" Of:
- Aggression
- Bombardment of Civilians
- Use of Experimental Weapons
- Torture and Mutilation of Prisoners
- Genocide Involving Forced Labor
- Mass Burial
- Concentration Camps
- Saturation Bombing of "Unparalleled Intensity"

Related Information:
- Held in Sweden and Denmark in 1967
- Used Data Supplied by North Vietnam

States was found guilty on all counts. The tribunal made widespread use of gut-wrenching testimony and data supplied by the North Vietnamese. The tribunal was so skewed and one-sided that even CBS News and the *New York Times* recognized it as a farce and a propaganda ploy.[59]

One of the few Americans to take part was Carl Oglesby, a veteran SDS operative and convert to radical causes. He claimed that the evidence at the tribunal "got to you."[60] Oglesby had worked closely with Sidney Blumenthal in the 1960s, and Blumenthal later went on to the Clinton White House.[61] The IWCT was supported by the leading Marxist intellectuals in Europe and the United States, notably French philosopher Jean-Paul Sartre, who had worked with the Soviet-backed World Peace Council, and Noam Chomsky. Chomsky went to North Vietnam where—among other things—he "negotiated" POW releases as a propaganda ploy to show the "benefits" of cooperating with the North Vietnamese. Also on the tribunal were Stokely Carmichael, Peter Weiss, and Wilfred Burchett, an Australian journalist and notorious KGB agent of influence working for the pro-Vietnamese Dispatch News Service. (The Dispatch News Service provided Seymour Hersh's story of U.S. war crimes at My Lai to the *New York Times* in November 1969.)[62]

Nor was there ever any doubt that the North Vietnamese and Vietcong valued such help. As early as 1965, the Hanoi regime placed great importance on the U.S. antiwar movement, and Norman Morrison (who burned himself fatally in front of the Pentagon) was then already a national hero in North Vietnam.[63]

COMMUNIST VIETNAM SAYS "THANK YOU"

We would like to thank the communist parties and working class of the countries of the world, national liberation movements, nationalist countries, peace-loving countries, international democratic organizations, and progressive human beings, for their wholehearted support, and strong encouragement to our people's patriotic resistance against the U.S. for national salvation.

Wall plaque inside the War Remnants Museum (originally the War Crimes Museum) established in 1975 in Ho Chi Minh City (formerly Saigon). The quote is from an excerpt from a report of the Vietnamese Communist Party Central Executive Committee, December 1976. Source: John E. O'Neill and Jerome R. Corsi, *Unfit for Command: Swift Boat Veterans Speak Out Against John Kerry* (Washington, DC: Regnery, 2004), photo following page 88.

ASSESSMENT: SO WHY DID THEY DO IT?

It is difficult to fathom all the reasons for this type of collaboration. The reasons were likely as complex and numerous as the various strands of the American antiwar movement itself. Some who met with the North Vietnamese and Vietcong probably were well meaning, wishing to bring the war to a rapid conclusion. Others were more inclined to cheer for the other side and even wish for an American defeat. These were the ones who delivered whatever assistance they could to the cause of Ho Chi Minh. Some who went to meet with the North Vietnamese and Vietcong probably had a combination of motives to do what they did.

None of the individuals seemed to suffer from a lack of self-importance, and all believed that—for whatever reasons—they had an inside track to the appropriate corridors of powers or communications channels. To cite one example, Cora Weiss was described as having "tremendous dedication and almost as tremendous self-importance."[64] They would sometimes say, "They'd never lie to *me*," or "I've been there and *really* understand them and their situation." The sense of self-importance comes through in their statements, and with that sentiment often come self-righteousness and self-delusion. Probably none who went believed that they could be deceived or led around by their noses— although this is precisely what occurred time after time.

GET THE
RIGHT TOOLS

A PROJECT SUCH AS this needs a healthy mix of books as well as sources found on the World Wide Web. These sources are listed in the back of this book in the bibliography.

BOOKS

As for books, it is necessary to look at conservative, liberal-radical, and impartial works. Books by some well-known conservative authors have helped to frame the argument here and point out some transgressions of the Far Left. Books by liberal and radical sources are necessary as well, such as those that give a history of the U.S. antiwar movement during the Vietnam years. Books by George Soros and Bill Moyers have been useful in illustrating the points made here, as I have taken words directly from the pens of those authors.[1] Books that have described the media have been useful as well, including those by Richard Viguerie and David Franke as well as former CBS News insider Bernard Goldberg.[2]

WEB SITES

Given the fluid and dynamic nature of American politics, it is essential to use the many Web sites out there. This includes conservative, liberal-radical, and impartial Web sites as well. Several dozen Web sites proved especially useful in this work and are cited in the endnotes. I cannot refer to all of these Web sites as "recommended" (especially those of some of the targeted groups here). However, they clearly are "related" for they point out how these groups see themselves, the issues, and those who stand in their way.

The Internet is arguably the most promising of the various alternative media used by conservatives today. On the most-visited Web sites, some twenty-four are on the Right and eleven are on the Left.[3] The Internet news audience is growing steadily as well. In 1999 only 6 percent of people got their news via the Internet, but this figure had jumped to 19 percent in 2003. Most of these are young people.

By the account of Viguerie and Franke (*America's Right Turn*), the big breakthrough for the Internet occurred in January 1998. At that time, Matt Drudge had outed Monica Lewinsky as President Bill Clinton's sex partner. Only ten days later First Lady Hillary Clinton used the term "Vast Right Wing Conspiracy" to Matt Lauer of NBC. Her staffers then assembled a stunning 331-page "enemies list," in which those who plied their trade on the Internet were big culprits.[4]

Some conservative Web sites have proved especially valuable:

- Accuracy in Media (www.aim.org)
- Discoverthenetwork.org: A Guide to the Political Left (www.discoverthenetwork.org)
- Front Page (www.frontpagemagazine.com)
- National Review Online (www.nationalreview.com)
- World Net Daily (www.worldnetdaily.com)

Moreover, there are quite a few Web sites that take no particular position but are sources of ample data to back any robust research project. Those Web sites frequently can answer questions about the sources and flow of political money. Many of them were especially useful during the presidential election of 2004 and remain useful to the present day.

ANALYTICAL TOOLS

This work highlights different analytical tools. These include the time-tested approaches of link analysis, content analysis, matrix analysis, time-event charting, and analysis of competing hypotheses. Also included are two other approaches that I call shades-of-gray analysis and Gemini analysis.

LINK ANALYSIS

The principal tool used in this book is link analysis, which seeks to join up different elements into an interrelated set. This approach tries to demonstrate the interrelationships between various groups or actors. By presenting a unified set of groups or actors, the relationships between them can be readily understood.

Link analysis is not a new tool, as law enforcement and intelligence bodies have used it for many decades. It goes back to at least the 1920s, when it was a useful device to examine the connections among organized-crime figures. Link analysis can be used to connect individuals with one another or individuals to a certain movement or event.

Example Task: Examine some of the relationships that accounted for the influence of Mark Lane, a radical lawyer and conspiracy theorist who emerged during the 1960s.

Solution: Draw the connections between Lane and three individuals: Jane Fonda, philosopher Bertrand Russell, and Soviet official Genrikh Borovik. Then factor in other influential figures who interacted with those three individuals.

First-order analysis: (A) Fonda had turned against the Vietnam War while she was living in Paris between 1965 and 1969. Shortly thereafter Lane brought her into contact with the Vietnam Veterans Against the War (VVAW). Lane also worked with Fonda on the Winter Soldier Investigation (WSI), a kangaroo court "war crimes" tribunal. (B) British philosopher Bertrand Russell, ninety-four years old when he sponsored the effort to investigate U.S. "war crimes" in Vietnam, supported Lane's publishing efforts and arranged funding for him as well. (C) Lane had regular contact with Genrikh Borovik, a Soviet media figure, KGB official, and head of the Soviet Committee for the Defense of Peace (SCDP)—one of Moscow's most influential fronts of the 1960s and 1970s.[5]

Second-order analysis: (A) Fonda was married to Tom Hayden, the founder of the Students for a Democratic Society (SDS) and one who

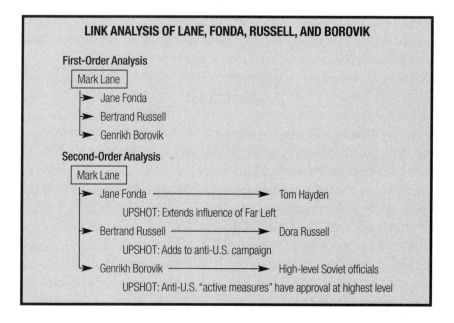

LINK ANALYSIS OF LANE, FONDA, RUSSELL, AND BOROVIK

First-Order Analysis

> Mark Lane
> > Jane Fonda
> > Bertrand Russell
> > Genrikh Borovik

Second-Order Analysis

> Mark Lane
> > Jane Fonda ⟶ Tom Hayden
> > UPSHOT: Extends influence of Far Left
> > Bertrand Russell ⟶ Dora Russell
> > UPSHOT: Adds to anti-U.S. campaign
> > Genrikh Borovik ⟶ High-level Soviet officials
> > UPSHOT: Anti-U.S. "active measures" have approval at highest level

has devoted his adult life to campaigning against the United States and its policies. (B) Bertrand Russell's wife, Dora, was also instrumental in the effort to "try" the United States for "war crimes" and added much to her husband's effort. (C) Genrikh Borovik was well connected to the upper echelons of the Soviet leadership as well as to media circles, as he was a journalist, novelist, playwright, and television presenter who had worked in the United States. The Soviets believed that Lane's conspiracy theory (that the CIA had killed President John F. Kennedy) worked to their advantage. Therefore, second-order analysis adds greatly to our understanding of the primary linkages.

CONTENT ANALYSIS

Content analysis is often a useful tool when trying to ascertain the meaning of a written work. Simply put, content analysts seek to assess the nature of a given work (an article or book) by examining the terminology or the frequency with which certain themes are raised or terms are used.

Content analysis is used to a certain extent here, specifically in examining the nature of various Web sites of certain groups. This is one way to throw light on these groups by revealing what they say about themselves, the issues they are tackling, why they believe these issues matter, and the various obstacles that stand in their way.

Example Task: Examine specific evidence that some U.S. clergymen willingly provide material aid as well as significant moral and psychological assistance to the regime of Fidel Castro in Cuba.

Solution: Look closely at the actions of the group called IFCO–Pastors for Peace as well as the speeches of its founder, the Reverend Lucius Walker Jr. The content of the IFCO/PFP Web sites clearly states that the group has delivered material aid to Cuba on many occasions. By mid-2005 this group had delivered fourteen caravans of material aid to Cuba and had dispatched many delegations and work brigades. The first Friendshipment Caravan carried fifteen tons of milk, medicines, Bibles, bicycles, and school supplies to Cuba in November 1992. The fourteenth Friendshipment of July 2003 involved "caravanistas" to celebrate the fiftieth anniversary of the beginning of the Cuban Revolution. Meanwhile, Lucius Walker Jr.—the head of IFCO/PFP—addressed a throng in Havana's Plaza of the Revolution on May 1, 2003. The content analysis of his speech revealed his willingness to join Cuba in its struggle against "U.S. terrorism." It revealed his plea for the United States to stop its "hypocritical lies and distortions about Cuba's human rights record." And he urged the Cubans, "Hold on to your revolution."[6] This was only several weeks after some dissidents were given draconian sentences of up to twenty-eight years in prison, so perhaps he advocated an even tougher crackdown on domestic opposition to Castro. In short the content analysis of his actions revealed treachery of the lowest order, and made it abundantly clear what his organization stood for. (See the appendix for various quotes from Reverend Walker.)

MATRIX ANALYSIS

Matrix analysis attempts to see what features certain individuals or groups may have in common. The data is presented on a grid, with the individual or groups usually listed on the vertical axis and the measuring or assessment data presented on the horizontal axis. Matrix analysis can be either very simple or extraordinarily involved.

Example Task: Assess and evaluate the interlocking relationships between the heads of some of the most prominent radical groups in the

INTERLOCKING LEADERSHIP OF SEVERAL GROUPS

(UFPJ, GLOBAL EXCHANGE, CODEPINK, IOW)

	UFPJ	GE	CP	IOW
Medea Benjamin	X/f	X/h	X/f	X/b
Leslie Cagan	X/fs			X/b
Jodie Evans			X/f	
Andrea Buffa	X/s	X	X	
Gael Murphy	X/s		X/e	X/b

Key: f = founder; h = head; s = steering committee; e = executive committee; b = board

United States. These groups include United for Peace and Justice (UFPJ), Global Exchange, CodePink, and Iraq Occupation Watch (IOW).

Solution: Matrix analysis of the heads of these organizations clearly reveals the close connections at the upper leadership levels. Specifically, several of these women belong to two or more of these groups. Medea Benjamin is a high-ranking member of all four. Leslie Cagan heads UFPJ and is on the board of IOW. Andrea Buffa is on the Steering Committee of UFPJ and is also a member of Global Exchange and CodePink.

Gael Murphy occupies leadership positions at UFPJ, CodePink, and IOW. In this case, matrix analysis displays this relationship better than any other tool.

TIME/EVENT CHARTING

This is a straightforward way to present data in a historical or chronological context. Often this kind of analysis is used to present "what occurred when." Time/event charting is frequently used in the news media in efforts to simplify some series of events, and often involves the presentation of time lines.

Example Task: Depict the order of formation of the various radical/liberal groups over the twentieth century and early twenty-first century.

TIME LINE OF FORMATION OF MAJOR GROUPS

Pre-1960

1917	AFSC (American Friends Service Committee)
1920	ACLU (American Civil Liberties Union)
1923	WRL (War Resisters League)
1936	NLG (National Lawyers Guild)
1958	WWP (Workers World Party)

1960–99

1963	IPS (Institute for Policy Studies)
1966	CCR (Center for Constitutional Rights)
1966	NACLA (North American Congress on Latin America)
1969	CEP (Council on Economic Priorities)
1974	CNSS (Center for National Security Studies)
1975	RCP USA (Revolutionary Communist Party, USA)
1977	Mobilization for Survival
1981	PFAW (People for the American Way)
1983	DSA (Democratic Socialists of America) *
1986	FAIR (Fairness and Accuracy in Reporting)
1987	Refuse and Resist
1987	SANE/FREEZE **
1988	IFCO/PFP (Interreligious Foundation for Community Organization/Pastors for Peace)
1988	Global Exchanges
1992	IAC (International Action Center)
1993	Peace Action
1998	MoveOn.Org

2000–2005

2001	International ANSWER (Act Now to Stop War and End Racism)
2002	NION (Not in Our Name)
	Progressive Donor Network
	UFPJ (United for Peace and Justice)
	CodePink
	IOW (Iraq Occupation Watch)
2003	MMA (Media Matters for America) web site

*Formed from the merger of the Democratic Socialist Organizing Committee and the New American Movement

**Formed from the merger of the Committee for a SANE Nuclear Policy and the Nuclear Weapons Freeze Campaign. In 1993 SANE/FREEZE was renamed as Peace/Action.

Some conflicting data on formative years for some groups

Solution: Construct a time line that begins with World War I and extends to the present. Find the year that each of the groups was formed, and chart it on this time line. Because this covers such an extended length of time, divide the time line into three distinct periods. This time line shows which groups were formed at a very early stage (pre-1960) and which have developed in more recent years. This particular time line is the basic conceptual tool used in chapters 5, 6, and 7.

ANALYSIS OF COMPETING HYPOTHESES

The analysis of competing hypotheses is a relatively advanced analytical tool, sometimes used to seek explanations for things that are otherwise perplexing or bewildering. The technique here involves establishing a series of hypotheses on the vertical axis, and setting out possible explanations on the horizontal axis.

Example Task: Try to make sense out of this statement by Arthur Ochs Sulzberger Jr., the co-chairman of the *New York Times,* who spoke at the Poynter Institute in Tampa in February 2005. He was asked a question about his newspaper's liberal bias and replied, "I hear more complaints that the newspaper is in the pocket of the Bush administration than that it is too liberal."[7]

Solution: Construct a matrix that can show the various hypotheses for this perplexing statement. Set out the hypotheses along the left side of the matrix, on the vertical axis—possible explanations why he made such a statement. Along the top edge of the matrix on the horizontal axis, put in things that would support each of those hypotheses (items of evidence, for example).

There are at least six hypotheses why Sulzberger would make this statement: (a) he hears things very selectively; (b) he is parroting the big lie about "right-wing media bias"; (c) he is surrounded by leftists who tell him this kind of thing on a regular basis; (d) he is out of touch with reality; (e) he is in denial, or (f) he believes his audience is stupid and gullible. On the horizontal axis are possible explanations that might support some of these hypotheses: (a) his own leftist background causes him to say this; (b) his current job causes him to say this; or (c) his statement actually reflects the actual situation, that the *New York Times* is in the Bush administration's pocket.

ANALYSIS OF COMPETING HYPOTHESES AND SULZBERGER STATEMENT			
Hypotheses:	background	job	actual situation
Selective hearing	X		
Big lie: "right-wing bias"		X	
Surrounded by leftists		X	
Out of touch	X		
In complete denial	X		
Thinks audience stupid	X?	X?	

There are no easily identified solutions to this issue, but the preliminary evidence suggests that it is either Sulzberger's own left-wing background or his current job that leads him to make this statement. His statement in no way reflects the actual situation, as the *New York Times* has not endorsed a Republican for president since Dwight D. Eisenhower's day. The paper has taken repeated stands against the initiatives of the Bush administration, as well as conservative U.S. presidents before George Bush. And—tellingly—the paper continues to employ a host of Far-Left ideologues such as Maureen Dowd, Paul Krugman, and their ilk.

SHADES-OF-GRAY ANALYSIS

This type of analysis attempts to discern various levels of commitment or involvement of selected individuals or groups. It is one answer to the problem of lumping individuals or groups into a single, homogeneous category—an approach that often oversimplifies the issues. This tool is useful in differentiating hard-core true believers from casual participants. It seeks to determine the differences between the dangerous radical and the moderate liberal, and even seeks to find some middle ground between them.

Example Task: Make some kind of distinction between die-hard, committed radicals and more casual liberals.

Solution: Set out some criteria for separating the groups into two distinct camps.

As a start, ask whether this person did or did not: (a) travel at any time to North Vietnam, Cuba, or Saddam's Iraq; (b) devote twenty-five years or more of his/her life to the radical cause; or (c) give material aid or moral/psychological support to a foreign terrorist or foreign terrorist group. If the answer to any of these questions is "yes," then it's safe to place that person in the column of a die-hard committed radical. This guideline is used in this book as well. (See pages 74–75 for this graphic.)

David Horowitz has done pioneering work by using this approach in his own work. In order to avoid typecasting all leftists into one large group, he employs five distinct categories: totalitarian radicals, anti-American radicals, leftists, moderate leftists, and affective leftists. These run the gamut to hard-core, totally committed radicals such as Brian Becker to the casual leftists such as entertainers Katie Couric or Robin Williams.[8]

GEMINI ANALYSIS

This is a little-known analytical approach that is quite simple. Rather than look at just one individual or group, it is sometimes useful to examine a pair of individuals or groups as to assess the interaction between them. It matters that liberal policy makers Clark Clifford and Paul Warnke once were law partners in Washington DC. It matters that Cora Weiss and the Reverend William Sloane Coffin Jr. worked closely together at the Riverside Church in New York City. And it certainly matters that George Soros and Morton Halperin work together to channel money to various causes. This approach often leads to more sophisticated assessments than examining just one individual or group.

Example Task: Examine how President Bill Clinton's foreign policy or national-defense decisions may have been affected by the orientation of his two national security advisers, Anthony Lake and Samuel "Sandy" Berger.

Solution: Build a graphic that lays out the apparent political orientation of both these individuals and also depicts their relationship with one another. This type of graphic would show the relevant background items in each person's life before the White House job, that person's apparent orientation while on the job as national security adviser, or relevant events afterward.

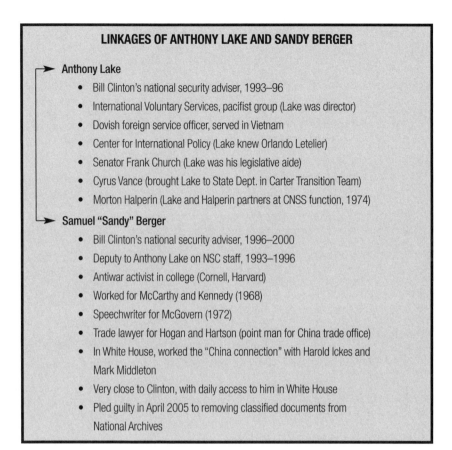

LINKAGES OF ANTHONY LAKE AND SANDY BERGER

Anthony Lake

- Bill Clinton's national security adviser, 1993–96
- International Voluntary Services, pacifist group (Lake was director)
- Dovish foreign service officer, served in Vietnam
- Center for International Policy (Lake knew Orlando Letelier)
- Senator Frank Church (Lake was his legislative aide)
- Cyrus Vance (brought Lake to State Dept. in Carter Transition Team)
- Morton Halperin (Lake and Halperin partners at CNSS function, 1974)

Samuel "Sandy" Berger

- Bill Clinton's national security adviser, 1996–2000
- Deputy to Anthony Lake on NSC staff, 1993–1996
- Antiwar activist in college (Cornell, Harvard)
- Worked for McCarthy and Kennedy (1968)
- Speechwriter for McGovern (1972)
- Trade lawyer for Hogan and Hartson (point man for China trade office)
- In White House, worked the "China connection" with Harold Ickes and Mark Middleton
- Very close to Clinton, with daily access to him in White House
- Pled guilty in April 2005 to removing classified documents from National Archives

GROUPS, LEADERS, AND THEIR LINKAGES

BEFORE 1960

I N THE EARLY PART of the twentieth century, there was only a small hand-
ful of social justice or antiwar groups. As such, there was nothing like
the network of linkages that is apparent today. However, those groups
that did form then have shown remarkable staying power and resiliency.

THE AMERICAN FRIENDS SERVICE COMMITTEE (1917)

Founded in 1917 for the ostensible purpose of assisting European
refugees and those affected by World War I, the American Friends Service Committee (AFSC) provided a home for conscientious objectors.[1]
Although the AFSC repeatedly denied it, the group had close associations with the Communist Party USA and various socialist revolutionary
groups.

The AFSC gave assistance to the Soviet Union in order to allow a
degree of "relaxed domestic control" as well as to "achieve greater benefits through peaceful co-existence" than it could through war. In the
1930s the AFSC refused to criticize the USSR because the establishment
and development of personal ties "seemed to be the only way to diffuse
hostilities." The AFSC later claimed that "the real threat to world stability was the United States."[2]

Year after year, the AFSC has attempted to sell itself as the logical extension of traditional Quakerism and the concept of social justice while simultaneously offering tangible support and material assistance to "some of the most brutal, repressive, and corrupt regimes in world history." It has perpetually criticized the United States while turning a blind eye to the excesses and brutality of the Vietnamese Communists, the Palestine Liberation Organization (PLO), and the Cambodian Khmer Rouge of Pol Pot. In the 1970s the AFSC claimed that the massacres of Pol Pot were the product of "American misinformation" and also noted that the North Vietnamese victors were carrying out the task of reconstructing Vietnam with "extraordinary humaneness" (ignoring the summary executions and confinement to labor camps of South Vietnamese officials).[3]

The AFSC's primary goal is to agitate for the unilateral disarmament of the United States, compelling the United States to withdraw economically and militarily from foreign posts around the globe. Moreover, the AFSC has taken a "strong stance against laws that would apprehend and punish illegal immigrants to the United States," as it recognizes no justification for the United States to guard its borders more diligently.[4]

THE AMERICAN CIVIL LIBERTIES UNION (1920)

The American Civil Liberties Union (ACLU) was formed in 1920 and was first known as the Civil Liberties Bureau. "It took the side of aliens threatened with deportation by Attorney General Alexander Palmer for their radical views." The ACLU also opposed attacks on the Industrial Workers of the World (IWW, also known as the Wobblies) and other labor unions to organize and meet.

In 1925 the ACLU persuaded John T. Scopes to defy Tennessee's anti-evolution law to provoke a court test. Clarence Darrow, a member of the ACLU's National Committee, headed the Scopes legal team. In the end, Scopes was found guilty and fined $100. Subsequently, the Tennessee Supreme Court reversed the case but not the conviction. In 1942, a few months after Pearl Harbor, ACLU affiliates on the West Coast sharply criticized the U.S. government's policies regarding enemy aliens and U.S. citizens descended from enemy ancestry. This included the relocation of Japanese-Americans, internment of aliens, and prejudicial curfews.[5]

Early in its history, the ACLU was singled out for criticism for its apparent pro-Communist stance. In 1931, for example, the Special House Committee to Investigate Communist Activities noted that the ACLU is "closely affiliated with the Communist movement" in the United States and that "fully 90% of its efforts are on behalf of Communists who have come into conflict with the law." The House committee noted that while the ACLU claimed to stand for the freedom of speech, the press, and assembly, it is "quite apparent that the main function of the ACLU is an attempt to protect the Communists." Moreover, the committee stated, "Since its beginnings, the ACLU has waged war against Christianity."[6]

During the long history of the ACLU, many critics have claimed that it has sought to advance a liberal agenda, going far beyond its stated goal of defending constitutional rights. Some have pointed to its opposition to the death penalty and further note that the ACLU has not been consistent in protecting all civil liberties. It has not protected the right to bear arms, as provided for in the Second Amendment. On the religious front, the ACLU has been accused of attempting to remove all references to religion from American government—pushing the concept of separation of church and state far beyond its original meaning. This issue appears each Christmas season, as one or another ACLU chapter inveighs against the display of religious symbols in public places. The ACLU has also been accused of promoting a radical form of Islam called Wahhabism (most recently through its association with the Council on American-Islamic Relations, or CAIR).

The ACLU has also taken stands on other issues. Today it supports "reproductive rights, including the right to choose an abortion." It supports "full civil rights for homosexuals, including government benefits for homosexual couples." It supports affirmative action (government-sanctioned reverse discrimination). In addition, it opposes the criminal prohibition of drugs and supports the legalization of drugs such as heroin, cocaine, and marijuana.[7]

THE WAR RESISTERS LEAGUE (1923)

The War Resisters League (WRL) was formed in 1923 by those who had opposed World War I. "Many of its founders had been jailed during the war for refusing military service." This group was formed from the Fellowship of Reconciliation when many Jews, suffragettes, social-ists, and anarchists combined to form the more secular WRL.

The WRL continued its activities in subsequent decades. During World War II many of its members were imprisoned. In the 1950s the WRL was active in the U.S. civil rights movement and also "organized protests against nuclear weapons testing and civil defense."

In the 1960s the WRL was the first pacifist organization to call for an end to the Vietnam War. In the 1970s and 1980s its "opposition to nu-clear weapons was expanded to include opposition to nuclear power." The group has also been active in feminist and anti-racist causes.[8]

NATIONAL LAWYERS GUILD (1936)

The National Lawyers Guild (NLG) was founded in 1936 by members of the Communist Party USA (CPUSA) and liberal fellow travelers. This organization of radical lawyers adopted a benevolent pose as a "profes-sional organization that functions as an effective social force" in the ser-vice of the common people. In fact, it has consistently embraced its Communist heritage.[9]

During the late 1940s and early 1950s the NLG represented the Hollywood Ten, spies Julius and Ethel Rosenberg, and thousands of what it calls "victims of anti-Communist hysteria." The NLG claims that it was unjustly labeled as subversive by the U.S. government.[10]

The NLG remains an outpost of the International Association of Democratic Lawyers (IADL), which itself was one of a complex of thir-teen interlocking front groups of the Soviet Communist Party. The IADL had its headquarters in Brussels and was formed in 1946 to sup-port Soviet propaganda, to issue legal statements and appeals for Soviet political priorities, and to condemn non-Communist causes. For a time the NLG had some twenty-five thousand members in eighty countries.[11]

All of these groups reported to the International Department (ID) of the CPSU's Central Committee. The purposes of the ID's front groups were to appeal to a broad range of opinion, to support Soviet propa-ganda themes, to conceal connections between the USSR and the Soviet Communist Party, to attack the West, and to never criticize the USSR.[12] Some of the most active front groups during the cold war were the

96

World Peace Council (WPC), the World Federation of Trade Unions (WFTU), the Women's International Democratic Federation (WIDF), and the World Federation of Democratic Youth (WFDY).

Some of the front groups also created "fronts of fronts," groups to address particular issues and to put further distance between them and Moscow. One example was Generals for Peace, a front of the World Peace Council. The U.S. affiliate of the World Peace Council is the U.S. Peace Council, which played a prominent role in the cold war.

In recent years the NLG has sought to legally represent persons and groups that have attacked the United States. The NLG was been at the forefront of various efforts to weaken U.S. intelligence and security agencies. It has opposed the proposed Domestic Security Enhancement Act (DSEA), also known as Patriot Act II, and has endorsed the Civil Liberties Restoration Act (CLRA), designed to roll back security policies that were adopted after the terrorist attacks of 9/11. Moreover, the NLG advocates open borders and mass immigration. The group is the "spearhead of the Open Borders Lobby," and its National Immigration Project consists of a network of lawyers and legal workers.[13]

THE WORKERS WORLD PARTY (1959)

The Workers World Party (WWP) is a Communist-socialist party in the United States founded by Sam Marcy. The WWP claims to embrace Marxism-Leninism, but others characterize it as being Stalinist. Ideologically the group is made up of different streams of Communist thought. In origin it is a Trotskyite group, but describes itself as Marxist-Leninist (a term rarely used by Trotsky followers). Yet the WWP continues to sell the writings of Trotsky, Stalin, and Mao Zedong. In practical terms, it supports the remaining Communist nations of Cuba, North Korea, and China. It also supports countries that it sees as victims of "American imperialism," such as Libya and Iraq.[14]

The WWP was formed as a splinter group from the Socialist Workers Party in 1958 over some long-standing differences. Some of these differences included Marcy's support for the Chinese Revolution led by Mao Zedong as well as his support for the brutal Soviet armed intervention in Hungary in 1956—an event that alienated many Communists worldwide. The WWP also supported the Soviet invasion of Czechoslovakia in

1968 and its invasion of Afghanistan in 1979—other events that put the USSR and the WWP on the wrong side of the "self-determination" issue.

At first the WWP was confined to the Buffalo, New York, area, but it expanded in the 1960s. The party's youth movement, called Youth Against War and Fascism, attracted support for its campaigns against the war in Vietnam.

The WWP has been active in U.S. presidential elections since 1980. Its candidate of 1984 and 1988, Larry Holmes, remains a powerful force within the WWP to this day. The WWP has opposed both Persian Gulf wars and has sometimes been an important ally of Third World solidarity movements in the United States. The group also supported China's brutal crackdown in the Tiananmen Square protests of 1989. Moreover, the group has defended Saddam Hussein as well as Serbian dictator Slobodan Milosevic.

The WWP split in 2004, and a new group—the Party for Socialism and Liberation—was formed by several WWP members.[15] The long-term effects of this split remain unclear.

More significantly, the WWP has been a guiding and leading force in two movements: the International Action Center (IAC), a WWP front formed in 1992, and International ANSWER (ANSWER for short), formed in 2001.[16] The most prominent members of the WWP today are Brian Becker and Larry Holmes (both members of the party's secretariat) as well as Teresa Gutierrez, Sarah Sloan, and Sara Flounders. All of these persons appeared at a rally sponsored by ANSWER in 2003, although they were not identified as WWP members.

ALL IN THE FAMILY

Many of the foundations of today's Far-Left movement were set in place during the 1930s. Against the backdrop of a worldwide depression and financial chaos, extremist movements of the Far Right and the Far Left flourished. Not only was fascism on the rise in countries in Central and Eastern Europe, but pro-Communist groups were also growing in some of the leading capitalist countries of the West.

In some cases the parents of today's figures in "progressive" movements were quite active during the 1930s, 1940s, and 1950s. It is logical to assume that the formative experiences of public people during that time have carried over into attitudes of their offspring through the process known as political socialization.

The family issue is now increasingly important because the second generation is inheriting their parents' causes. The second generation includes progressive names that have become prominent in recent years: Cockburn, Rubin-Weiss, Boudin, Ickes, Thomas, Soros, Moyers, and Richards.

COCKBURN CONNECTION

One example is that of Claud Cockburn (1904–81). The son of a diplomat, Cockburn (pronounced ko-burn) was born in China. He was a socialist author and journalist as well as a sympathizer of Joseph Stalin. He wrote for the *Daily Worker* under the pseudonym of Frank Pitcairn from 1935 to 1946. He served as a war correspondent for that Communist paper in Spain in the 1930s, acting on assignment from the head of the British Communist Party. At that time he gained a reputation for spreading fabrications. He later wrote under the name of James Helvick when he authored the novel *Beat the Devil* in 1951. Educated at Oxford as well as universities in Budapest and Berlin, Cockburn received his start as an unofficial correspondent in Berlin in the 1920s. He later wrote for the *Times* of London as a correspondent from New York and Washington DC from 1929 to 1932. His stint at the *Times* overlapped that of Graham Greene (the darling of Havana and Moscow), who was a subeditor there, and he was also a close friend of Malcolm Muggeridge. Cockburn also contributed to the *New Statesman*, the *Daily Telegraph*, *Private Eye*, the *Saturday Evening Post*, and the British humor magazine *Punch.* Cockburn's most ambitious effort was his newsletter, called *The Week*, a recurring tip sheet of politics that he published between 1933 and 1946. Cockburn broke with the Communist Party after World War II and moved with his family to Ireland in 1948, but he continued to contribute to various newspapers and journals.[17]

During the time he was most active, Cockburn maintained close contact with Mikhail Koltsov of the Soviet Embassy in London. Koltsov was both an editor of *Pravda* as well as a Stalinist agent in Spain.

Cockburn has had three sons—Alexander, Andrew, and Patrick— all of whom remain active journalists to the present day.

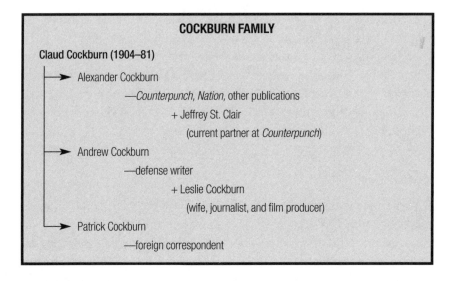

COCKBURN FAMILY

Claud Cockburn (1904–81)

➤ Alexander Cockburn

—*Counterpunch, Nation,* other publications

+ Jeffrey St. Clair

(current partner at *Counterpunch*)

➤ Andrew Cockburn

—defense writer

+ Leslie Cockburn

(wife, journalist, and film producer)

➤ Patrick Cockburn

—foreign correspondent

Alexander Cockburn is the proud heir of the family tradition and was the closest to his father before Claud died in 1981. He was born in Scotland in 1941 and grew up in Ireland. Another Oxford graduate, he has lived in self-described exile in the United States since 1972, where he has worked as a syndicated or contributing columnist. Since that time he has managed to defend the Soviet invasion of Afghanistan as well as the regime of Muammar Abu Minyar al-Qadhafi in Libya. He has spoken strongly against the United States and its policies of "terror" during the civil war in Nicaragua. He has been a regular contributor to the *Nation,* although his work has also appeared in the *Wall Street Journal,* the *Village Voice, House and Garden,* and the *Los Angeles Times.*

In 1987 he wrote a book entitled *Corruptions of Empire: Life Studies and the Reagan Era.* One reviewer noted the "same disrespect of his father for the truth was also evident in this book which defended every anti-American tyrant and regime in the Third World."[18] More recently, Alexander has been a strident opponent of U.S. ventures in Afghanistan and Iraq. He now teams with Jeffrey St. Clair to co-edit the journal *Counterpunch.*[19]

Andrew Cockburn was born in Scotland in 1947, grew up in Ireland, and also lives in the United States. Another Oxford man and author, he has specialized in defense issues and international relations over the past three decades. He produced a special on the Red Army for PBS and wrote a book called *The Threat: Inside the Soviet Military Machine* in 1983. The book was an effort to debunk the "big threat" picture of the Soviet armed forces and made a case for moral equivalency in stating that both the U.S. and Soviet military systems were large, inefficient, wasteful bureaucracies, each inflating the threat posed by the other for its own selfish purposes.[20] He has been a contributing editor of *Defense Week* and contributes regularly to *Counterpunch*.[21]

Andrew is married to Leslie Cockburn, a journalist and CBS news producer.[22] In 1987 she wrote a book entitled *Out of Control: The Story of the Reagan Administration's Secret War in Nicaragua, the Illegal Arms Pipeline, and the Contra Drug Connection*. Leslie recognized the help of her husband in compiling her book.

Patrick Cockburn also was born in Scotland and grew up in Ireland. He had earlier worked as a correspondent for the *Financial Times* in Moscow. Patrick later worked in Baghdad during the first Persian Gulf War and has also served in Jerusalem for the *Independent*. Filing from Iraq, three of Patrick's articles appeared in Alexander's *Counterpunch* in late 2003, each with a distinctly anti-U.S. title. Patrick's most recent book is *Out of the Ashes: The Resurrection of Saddam Hussein*, which he wrote with his brother Andrew.[23] (Perhaps a second resurrection is in order now.)

RUBIN-WEISS CONNECTION

Samuel Rubin (1901–78) is responsible primarily for the initial surge of funding to major left-wing organizations. His parents brought him from Russia to America as a child. He was a registered Communist Party member, although he had business talent and decided to operate like a good capitalist. Rubin was also a friend and business associate of Armand Hammer, a longtime supporter of Lenin. In 1930 Rubin founded the Spanish Trading Corporation, but he closed it when Francisco Franco took power in Spain. In 1937 Rubin founded Faberge Perfumes and "built it from a small specialty shop into a major cosmetics firm." In 1959 he established the Samuel Rubin Foundation from his personal wealth. "In 1963 Rubin sold Faberge for $25 million and gave a portion to his foundation." This foundation has funded "legions of left-wing

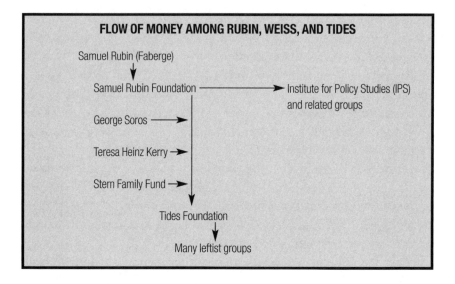

FLOW OF MONEY AMONG RUBIN, WEISS, AND TIDES

Samuel Rubin (Faberge)

Samuel Rubin Foundation ⟶ Institute for Policy Studies (IPS) and related groups

George Soros ⟶

Teresa Heinz Kerry ⟶

Stern Family Fund ⟶

Tides Foundation

Many leftist groups

causes" since then; the Institute for Policy Studies (IPS) is among the leading recipients.[24]

Cora Weiss, née Rubin, is the daughter of Samuel Rubin and has been the director of the Samuel Rubin Foundation from its founding. "She was also instrumental in the funding decision" to create the Institute for Policy Studies (IPS). Her husband, Peter Weiss, was the first chairman of the IPS board of directors. The couple selected Marcus Raskin and Richard Barnet as co-directors of the IPS. Cora gained notoriety as a leader of the Vietnam War–era coalitions who traveled to Paris and Hanoi for repeated meetings with Communist leaders.[25] She has been active in a variety of radical causes for at least four decades.

Peter Weiss, born in 1925 in Vienna, Austria, is the senior partner of the law firm Weiss, David, Fross, Zelnick, and Lehrman in New York City. His firm specializes in trademark, copyright, and international law. Weiss is a "prominent member of the National Lawyers Guild (NLG)" and has served many other Far-Left causes. He was chairman of the IPS board of directors until the 1990s.[26]

BOUDIN CONNECTION

Leonard Boudin was a prominent radical lawyer. He was especially active in the 1960s and 1970s and died in 1989. He was the brother-in-law of the radical journalist and Soviet agent I. F. Stone. Stone had a newsletter called *I. F. Stone's Weekly*, which was comparable to the Cockburn newsletter in the United Kingdom in the 1930s and 1940s. Stone considered himself "American to the core and radical to the end." (Only the first part of that phrase is somewhat questionable.) Boudin was the law partner of Victor Rabinowitz, who once defended Fidel Castro, Benjamin Spock, and Daniel Ellsberg. Moreover, Boudin hired Leonard Weinglass, a leader of the NLG, who himself defended the Symbionese Liberation Army (SLA) as well as cop-killer Mumia Abu-Jamal. In addition, Weinglass has defended Boudin's daughter, Cathy Boudin.[27]

Cathy Boudin became even better known thanks to her involvement with the Weather Underground Organization (WUO), or "Weathermen," and its violent activities. In 1984 she and Bernardine Dohrn were sent to prison for participating in a bank robbery in which a policeman was killed. Cathy Boudin has a host of connections and links to other radical

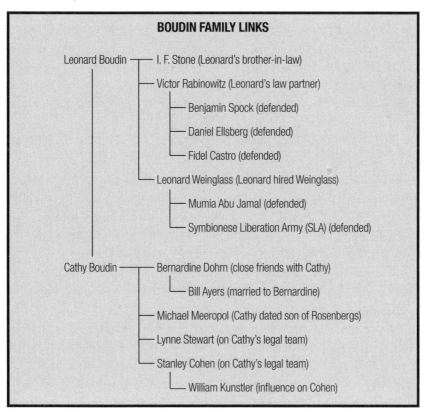

BOUDIN FAMILY LINKS

Leonard Boudin
— I. F. Stone (Leonard's brother-in-law)
— Victor Rabinowitz (Leonard's law partner)
— Benjamin Spock (defended)
— Daniel Ellsberg (defended)
— Fidel Castro (defended)
— Leonard Weinglass (Leonard hired Weinglass)
— Mumia Abu Jamal (defended)
— Symbionese Liberation Army (SLA) (defended)

Cathy Boudin
— Bernardine Dohrn (close friends with Cathy)
— Bill Ayers (married to Bernardine)
— Michael Meeropol (Cathy dated son of Rosenbergs)
— Lynne Stewart (on Cathy's legal team)
— Stanley Cohen (on Cathy's legal team)
— William Kunstler (influence on Cohen)

figures. She became acquainted with Bernardine Dohrn in the late 1960s, and the two remained close for years after that. Dohrn worked for the NLG in Manhattan where she was involved in draft-resistance counseling. Dohrn married Bill Ayers, a veteran organizer of the Students for a Democratic Society (SDS). She received money from actor Jon Voight, and for a time she and Ayers lived on Voight's houseboat in California. Boudin had also dated Michael Meeropol, the son of executed spies Julius and Ethel Rosenberg. In addition, Boudin had a strong connection to radical lawyers Lynne Stewart and Stanley Cohen; they both joined her legal team in the early 1980s. Stewart has a connection with Dohrn through the NLG and is involved with several other radical organizations herself. Cohen is a protégé of radical lawyer William Kunstler, who founded the Center for Constitutional Rights (CCR).[28]

ICKES CONNECTION

Harold Le Claire Ickes (1874–1952) served as Franklin Roosevelt's secretary of the interior between 1933 and 1945. Ickes held leftist political views, and in 1932 he played an important role in persuading "progressive" Republicans to support FDR in the election. He claimed that the "business administrations" of three Republican presidents "had ruined virtually everybody in the country."[29]

In 1933 FDR picked him as his secretary of the interior. This job involved running the Public Works Administration (PWA), which spent some $6 billion on large-scale projects over the next six years. Ickes worked closely with the National Association for the Advancement of Colored People (NAACP) to establish quotas for black workers in PWA projects. In a profile of Ickes in 1934, the *New York Times* noted that he "knows all the rackets that infest the construction industry."

Ickes controlled a private investigative group, unbeknownst to the general public. One effort of this group was dedicated to exposing Nazi propaganda efforts in the United States, and it uncovered startling information about German connections with the Silver Shirts, Father Charles Coughlin, and groups such as the Christian Mobilizers. Ickes turned this material over to the attorney general, and "during the next year very bad things happened to the subjects of the investigations."[30] FDR remained aware of what Ickes was up to, at least in general. Ickes assembled an able committee of "helpers" to combat subversive fascist propaganda. His circle included Dorothy Thompson, pollster George Gallup, Henry Luce, and theologian Reinhold Niebuhr.[31] Ickes grew adept at leaking information when it suited his and FDR's purposes.

Ickes was a member of a Stalinist front called the League for Peace and Democracy.[32] Moreover, he took an active role against anti-Soviet officials in the State Department. According to Dennis Dunn, President Roosevelt, Treasury Secretary Henry Morgenthau, and Interior Secretary Harold Ickes told Soviet ambassador Constantine Oumansky emphatically that anti-Soviet officials in the State Department would be thwarted.[33] Ickes's involvement was peculiar, for it was far outside the bounds of his job as secretary of the interior.

Ickes did not get along with Harry Truman and resigned from the government in 1946. In his final years Ickes wrote a syndicated newspaper column and contributed regularly to the *New Republic*. He wrote several books, including his memoirs, *The Autobiography of a Curmudgeon* (1943). Ickes died in Washington in 1952.

His son, Harold M. Ickes, was deputy chief of staff in the Clinton White House between 1994 and 1996. As a student at Stanford, Ickes fell under the influence of Professor Allard Lowenstein, who seduced many idealistic young students into the New Left. Ickes later traveled to the Dominican Republic in 1965, evidently to assist a socialist president who was deposed, but his role in this event remains obscure to this day. "Ickes met Bill Clinton while both were working on Operation Pursestrings, a grassroots lobbying effort aimed at pushing through the Hatfield-McGovern amendment to cut aid to South Vietnam."[34]

As a labor lawyer, Ickes represented many corrupt unions controlled by organized-crime families. He worked on behalf of labor racketeers and gangsters, which brought him perilously close to prosecution. Bill and Hillary Clinton later found many uses for Ickes's peculiar talents.[35] Hillary Clinton "placed Ickes in charge of a special unit within the White House Counsel's office, dedicated to suppressing Clinton scandals." Because so many of his jobs involved damage control at that time, Ickes referred to his role as "Director of Sanitation." Former Clinton adviser Dick Morris noted that whenever there was something that Bill Clinton thought required ruthlessness or vengeance or skullduggery, "he would give it to Harold."[36]

By 1996 federal investigators began zeroing in on Ickes's involvement in numerous Clinton scandals. These included the illegal commandeering of more than one thousand secret FBI files on potential Clinton foes as well as the spilling of military and technological secrets to China in exchange for campaign contributions. Ickes became a liability and was fired by President Clinton shortly after his reelection in 1996.

Ickes ran the successful Senate campaign of Hillary Clinton in 1999–2000 and has remained an influential force in Democratic circles. After passage of the McCain-Feingold Act in March 2002, Ickes helped George Soros put together—with various activists and left-wing Democrats—an effort to circumvent the soft-money ban instituted by the McCain-Feingold Act.[37] He personally helped to launch groups such as America Coming Together (ACT), America Votes, the Center for American Progress (CAP), Joint Victory Campaign 2004, the Thunder Road Group, and the Media Fund.

One of Ickes's major accomplishments was creating the Media Fund. It received more than $28 million from left-wing labor organizations: Service Employees International Union (SEIU) and the American Federation of State, County, and Municipal Employees (AFSCME). The Media Fund was extremely active in creating and airing attack ads against George W. Bush during the 2004 presidential campaign.[38]

As of late 2004, various sources indicate that Ickes is with his old law firm, Meyer, Suozzi, English, and Klein, as well as with the Ickes and Enright Group. To this day, Ickes remains one of the most important persons in the Democratic Party.

THOMAS CONNECTION

Norman Thomas (1884–1968) was the son of a Presbyterian minister and studied political science under Woodrow Wilson at Princeton University, from which he was graduated in 1905. "Influenced by the writings of the Christian Socialist movement in the United Kingdom, Thomas became a committed socialist. He was ordained in 1911 and became pastor of the East Harlem Presbyterian Church in New York City." A pacifist, Thomas believed that World War I was an "immoral, senseless struggle among rival imperialisms."[39]

Thomas joined with several others to form the Fellowship of Reconciliation (FOR), a group from which a faction later split off in 1923 to become the War Resisters League (WRL). Moreover, in 1917 Thomas joined with Crystal Eastman and Roger Baldwin to establish the National Civil Liberties Bureau (NCLB). In 1920 Thomas joined with Jane Addams, Elizabeth Gurley Flynn, and Upton Sinclair to establish the American Civil Liberties Union (ACLU). As such, Thomas was intimately involved with two organizations that continue to the present. Thomas served as associate editor of the *Nation* in 1921–22 and was codirector of the League of Industrial Democracy from 1922 to 1937.

After the death of Eugene V. Debs, Thomas because the Socialist Party's candidate for president in 1928, 1932, and 1936. Although he was easily beaten each time, "Thomas had the satisfaction of seeing FDR introduce several measures that he had advocated."

Thomas helped to form the America First Committee (AFC) in 1940, with one of its goals being to keep America out of the war. This committee was dissolved four days after the attack on Pearl Harbor. Thomas was the Socialist Party candidate in 1940, 1944, and 1948, thus running a total of six times. He denounced rearmament and the development of the cold war. He also campaigned against poverty, racism, and the Vietnam War.

The grandson of Norman Thomas, Evan Thomas has long been the assistant managing editor of *Newsweek* magazine. The magazine has maintained a consistent liberal (though not radical) slant throughout its existence.

SOROS CONNECTION

George Soros is a Hungarian-born American businessman. Born in 1930, he is famous as an investor, currency speculator, and philanthropist. He is chairman of Soros Fund Management and the Open Society Institute (OSI). Soros is known primarily for donating huge sums of money to organizations that sought to defeat President George W. Bush in 2004.[40]

Soros learned his craft at a young age, trading currencies on the black market in Hungary during World War II. He left Hungary for the

United Kingdom in 1947 and graduated from the London School of Economics in 1952. In 1956 Soros moved to the United States. He stated that he intended "to earn enough on Wall Street to support himself as an author and philosopher." At one time, Soros's net worth reached an estimated $11 billion, but it is now believed to be closer to a paltry $7 billion.

In 1970 he founded the Quantum Fund with Jim Rogers. This fund "returned more than 4,000 percent" over the next ten years and created the bulk of Soros's fortune. Soros plays the currency markets through this fund, which is registered in Curacao, Netherlands Antilles—a tax haven cited as one of the most important centers for money laundering. By using Curacao, "Soros not only avoids paying taxes but also hides the nature of his investors and what he does with their money."

Soros had earlier stated that removing George W. Bush from office was the "central focus of my life" as well as "a matter of life and death" for which he would willingly sacrifice his entire fortune. Soros gave some $3 million to the Center for American Progress (CAP), $5 million to MoveOn.org, and $10 million to America Coming Together (ACT). According to the Center for Responsive Politics, in 2004 Soros

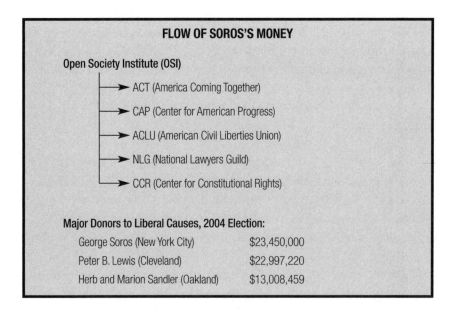

FLOW OF SOROS'S MONEY

Open Society Institute (OSI)

➤ ACT (America Coming Together)

➤ CAP (Center for American Progress)

➤ ACLU (American Civil Liberties Union)

➤ NLG (National Lawyers Guild)

➤ CCR (Center for Constitutional Rights)

Major Donors to Liberal Causes, 2004 Election:

George Soros (New York City)	$23,450,000
Peter B. Lewis (Cleveland)	$22,997,220
Herb and Marion Sandler (Oakland)	$13,008,459

donated $23,581,000 to various 527 groups dedicated to defeating President Bush.[41]

Soros also donates to other causes that he deems worthy. For example, in 2002, he contributed $20,000 to the defense committee of radical lawyer Lynne Stewart.

This information surfaced from records filed with the IRS and was reported in February 2005. This was about the same time that a New York jury found Stewart guilty of helping her terrorist client, "blind sheikh" Omar Abdel Rahmanm, communicate with his Islamist followers from prison. Stewart was found guilty of all counts against her, including conspiring to provide and providing material support to terrorists.[42]

Soros blames many of the world's problems on the failures inherent in market fundamentalism. In 1997 he predicted the imminent collapse of the global capitalist system. His writings also include a healthy dose of blame-America-first. This is illustrated by a look at his book *The Bubble of American Supremacy* (2004): "The reckless pursuit of American supremacy has put us and the rest of the world in danger." So he claims that the only way we can "extricate ourselves" is by rejecting President Bush. "How can we escape from the trap that the terrorists have set for us?" he asks. "Only by recognizing that the war on terrorism cannot be won by waging war." We must, he notes, "correct the grievances on which terrorism feeds." He claims that the war on terrorism as pursued by the Bush administration cannot be won "because it is based on false premises."[43]

A personal dislike for George Bush comes through loud and clear. For example, he asserts, "Being a reformed substance abuser and born-again Christian, he had personal acquaintances with the devil." Soros is much better at lobbing verbal grenades at George Bush than in predicting the future, as he stated in 2003, "I am confident that he will be rejected in 2004."[44]

Now in his midseventies, Soros is likely contemplating the building of a dynasty. He has five children, three by his first wife, Annaliese, and two by his second wife, Susan. He has recently placed his two oldest sons—Robert and Jonathan—in charge of his empire and the day-to-day investment decisions. Forty-two-year-old Robert currently serves as chief investment officer, and thirty-five-year-old Jonathan is acting as deputy chairman.

Robert is focusing on state-level politics at present. He and his wife gave some $100,000 to the New York State Democratic Campaign Committee in 2004.[45] Jonathan is an activist with MoveOn.org. He also financially sponsors other groups. Occasionally commentators refer to this network of independent, nonprofit issue groups controlled by the Soros, Ickes, and other families as the Shadow Party. David Horowitz and Richard Poe have concluded that this Shadow Party is "here to stay" and will continue to grow. Already, they note, "Shadow Party control of Democrat fund raising has given Soros and his minions influence over the party's platform, strategy and candidate."[46]

MOYERS CONNECTION

Bill Moyers, born in 1931, is a journalist, advocate, and financier for liberal causes. He is influential in several different spheres and has been adept at portraying himself as a "moderate" to U.S. audiences. Moyers was deputy director of the Peace Corps during the Kennedy administration, as well as special assistant to President Lyndon B. Johnson from 1963 to 1967. His association with LBJ goes back to 1954, when he first worked for him as a summer intern. Others who worked in the Johnson administration include Ramsey Clark and Morton Halperin.

During the 1964 election campaign, Moyers was the instigator of

---

JOHNSON INSIDERS, THEN AND NOW

Ramsey Clark
> THEN: Attorney General, 1967–69
>
> NOW: International Action Center (IAC), Act Now to Stop War and End Racism (ANSWER), and many other liberal causes

Bill Moyers
> THEN: Special Assistant to President Johnson, 1963–67
>
> NOW: Believed retired after serving many liberal causes

Morton Halperin
> THEN: Deputy Assistant Secretary of Defense for Policy Planning and Arms Control, 1967–69
>
> NOW: Head of Washington DC office of Open Society Institute (OSI)

---

the "daisy girl" commercial that purported to show that Barry Goldwater was a dangerous influence who could lead the nation into nuclear war. He ordered from the Madison Avenue firm of Doyle Dane Bernbach an unforgettable ad that had a little girl plucking petals from a daisy while an off-camera voice counted down to a final image of a nuclear blast and mushroom cloud. It closed with the words, "These are the stakes: To make a world in which all of God's children can live, or to go into the dark. We must either love each other, or we must die. Vote for President Johnson on November third. The stakes are too high for you to stay home."[47] This ad is still remembered as one of the most negative ads ever shown on national television.

Moyers has been in broadcast journalism sine 1971. He was once executive editor of the public television series *Bill Moyers Journal.* He was then a CBS News correspondent and senior news analyst for that network. In 1986 he formed his own independent production company, Public Affairs Television, Inc., based at WNET in New York.[48] Moreover, Moyers was a trustee of the Rockefeller Foundation for twelve years and more recently served as president of the Florence and John Schumann Foundation. He has been prominently featured on Public Broadcasting Service (PBS), which he has often used as a platform for liberal pronouncements.

Moyers has been known to pay advocates to come up with an anti-corporate, anti-capitalist message, and then report the totally biased outcome on PBS television. In March 2001 PBS stations nationwide aired a ninety-minute report on the chemical industry titled *Trade Secrets: A Moyers Report.* The report portrayed the chemical industry in a "cold, calculated cover-up of deadly health effects," and "implied that the chemical industry was guilty of premeditated murder of its own employees." In the thirty-minute panel discussion that followed, Moyers hosted two activists who had advance knowledge of the show's subject matter. One anti-industry panelist had previously received $325,000 in grants from the Schumann Foundation. "The chemical industry was represented by two men who had no advance knowledge of the show's content."[49]

Moyers's philosophy is summed up in his own words. He told the Environmental Grantmakers Association on October 16, 2001, "True believers in the god of the market would leave us to the ruthless cruelty of unfettered monopolistic capital where even the law of the jungle breaks down."[50]

Moyers's son John is the executive director of the Florence and John Schumann Foundation, known for its support of National Public Radio (NPR), PBS's *Frontline,* and the *Columbia Journalism Review.* John Moyers is also as executive director of the Florence Fund, a nonprofit corporation based in Washington DC. TomPaine.com is a Web site project of the Florence Fund.[51]

RICHARDS CONNECTION

Ann Richards was born in 1933 and attended the University of Texas at Austin. At that time she became politically active, working for "critical social causes," according to one favorable biographic sketch. She was a former Texas state treasurer, a county commissioner, a teacher, and "activist." Richards came upon the national scene with a keynote address to the 1988 Democratic National Convention. She entered the 1990 gubernatorial campaign and was elected the forty-fifth governor of Texas. One favorable review of her service noted her as a "longtime advocate of civil rights and economic justice" who created "the most representative and inclusive administration in Texas history."[52]

George W. Bush defeated her decisively in the 1994 race for governor, which effectively ended her career as a candidate for elected office. As such, both Richards and her daughter, Cecile, have pursued a personal vendetta against Bush ever since. In 1998 Richards was a senior adviser with the Washington DC–based law firm of Verner, Lippfert, Bernhard, McPherson, and Hand. During the 2004 campaign she made appearances in many states to attack George Bush's reelection effort.

Cecile Richards is the president of America Votes and also serves on the board of America Coming Together (ACT). America Votes was launched "to help coordinate the activities of a growing number of nonprofit groups within the Shadow Party." In July 2003 a number of Democratic Party heavyweights launched America Votes and appointed Cecile as its first president. She is hard set against the so-called Christian Right. "After her mother's 1994 defeat, Cecile founded the Texas Freedom Network, a grassroots organization" aimed at countering the influence of "conservative Christians," especially on local school boards.[53]

GROUPS, LEADERS, AND THEIR LINKAGES
1960–99

THE CONFRONTATIONAL DECADE OF the 1960s set the stage in many ways for the ideological divide that continued throughout the remainder of the twentieth century. Many of those who marched, demonstrated, pontificated, or otherwise stood against U.S. policy in Vietnam continued their opposition to most—if not all—U.S. policies in the 1970s, 1980s, and 1990s. The ideological cast of the 1960s was the mold into which later generations of the Far Left were poured.

There has been a *wall* separating those for and against U.S. policies in Vietnam, and the term is not an exaggeration. Since the mid-1960s there has been a polarization between the extremes of both camps, with both sides continuing to lob volley after volley of precision-guided insults and scattershot stereotypes, with neither side seeing much in common with the other.

In many respects it makes sense to divide this period into two, the 1960s–1970s and the 1980s–1990s. The confrontational issues of the 1960s—Vietnam more than any other—continued well into the 1970s, and many groups that took a stand on these issues spanned both of those decades. By the same token, there was some continuity of issues from the 1980s into the 1990s as well, and many of those groups described here operated in both decades. In general, those groups that opposed President Ronald Reagan's conduct of the cold war also stood against U.S. efforts to intervene in Iraq in 1990–91 and in the Middle East and South Asia later on.

Set against this backdrop is the emergence of an alliance opposed to U.S. interests, a development that has attracted little attention from the media. Since the mid-1970s Muslim and other Islamic radical leaders have initiated a tactical entente with leftist movements otherwise composed of "godless unbelievers" such as Marxist or pro-Communist groups. Some thirty years ago, professional revolutionary Ilich Ramirez Sanchez (also known as Carlos the Jackal) converted to Islam. The letters he sent to his lawyer from La Sante prison in Paris underline his dedication to a coming Muslim revolution. In addition, the Iranian organization Mujahideen al-Khalq (MEK) amalgamates socialism and Islam.[1] Seen in this context, it is no surprise to find Muslim groups and those defending Islamic radical causes to be joined in the same coalitions as pro-Communist groups. The membership of coalition groups such as United for Peace and Justice (UFPJ) bears this out. A Washington DC demonstration in January 2005 brought together an official of the Arab-American Institute with the usual suspects of the Workers World Party (WWP)–International Action Center (IAC)–ANSWER triad.

THE RADICALIZED CAMPUS

The formative experiences of many activists occurred during their college days. The recollection of a three-year stint at the University of Michigan in Ann Arbor (1969–71) brings back a host of vivid memories:

- The presence of Vietcong and North Vietnamese flags on campus.
- Burning of American flags or using them for picnic blankets.
- The chant, "Ho, Ho, Ho Chi Minh . . . the NLF is gonna win!"
- University President Robben Fleming denouncing the war in a packed auditorium just as classes resumed in the fall of 1969.
- A lopsided ratio of Democrats on the staff of the social sciences departments, with many of those Democrats on the Far Left (the history department was said to have a 50-to-1 Democrat-Republican ratio).

- The hectoring and condescending style of radical professors who never passed up a chance to slam any U.S. foreign or military venture, to indoctrinate students to a Hard-Left point of view, or to determine grades according to student's conformity with their own political views.
- The invitations by some professors to allow radical student spokesmen to come in and lecture classes while professors stood to the side.
- The very effective use of "guerrilla theater" to disrupt classes or lectures in auditoriums. One of the most dramatic involved two students playing the roles of U.S. authorities dragging away a "drafted" student to the army; the former were most effective in playing the role of Nazi-like bullies, while the draftee loudly shrieked, sobbed, and howled as he was dragged away to fight in the unpopular war.
- A periodic parade of convoys or buses from Ann Arbor and Detroit to Washington DC, usually for the demonstration of the month—whatever it might be.
- The permeating smell of marijuana at large gatherings, and the city of Ann Arbor's imposing a token $5 fine if police caught anyone in possession of marijuana for personal use.
- The early days of academic "speech codes" to prevent anyone from saying anything "offensive" about left-wing, homosexual, or minority movements on campus. The same protection from offensive speech did not apply to those on the other side of those movements.
- The successful intimidation tactics used by radical groups such as the SDS or the black student movement. This included sit-ins, building occupations, shouting down any opposing voices, and a panoply of street tactics.

KEY EVENTS

Even today, the images of the late 1960s and early 1970s loom vividly in the mind's eye, especially of those "who were there." So return with us to those thrilling days of yesteryear! The following noteworthy events marked a turbulent era:

- June 1965: Some fourteen National Guardsmen are called out during a riot at Watts, a black ghetto in south Los Angeles. A total of thirty-four die, four thousand are arrested, and the area is in ashes after five days.
- January 31, 1966: Students demonstrate nationwide against the Vietnam War.
- June 1967: Detroit race riots end after eight days, with forty-three dead.
- July 1967: Newark, New Jersey, race riots end after six days, with twenty-six dead.
- August 1967: In response to President Lyndon B. Johnson's persistent interest in the extent of foreign influence on domestic unrest, the CIA develops Operation CHAOS. Meanwhile, the FBI begins its Operation COINTELPRO against black nationalists.
- October 21, 1967: Antiwar protesters make a night march on the Pentagon.
- April 1968: Black militancy increases on campuses. The president of San Francisco State University resigns as black instructors urge black students to bring guns on campus.
- May 9, 1968: FBI begins COINTELPRO operations against the New Left.
- August 26, 1968: Yuppies lead major riots at the Democratic National Convention in Chicago.
- April 20, 1969: A group of black students armed with machine guns takes over a building at Cornell University and then leaves after negotiations with the administration.
- October 15, 1969: National Moratorium antiwar march.
- November 15, 1969: Second and larger National Moratorium antiwar march.
- January 20, 1970: U.S. Army's domestic surveillance program is revealed.
- March 6, 1970: A Greenwich Village townhouse in New York is destroyed by an explosion in what is believed to be a bomb factory of the Weathermen; later three bodies are found.
- May 9, 1970: Nearly one hundred thousand students demonstrate in Washington DC. President Richard M. Nixon, unable to sleep, goes to the Lincoln Memorial to address them.

- April 27, 1971: FBI's COINTELPRO operations are ended in response to disclosure about the program in the press.
- June 13, 1971: The *New York Times* publishes the first installment of the Pentagon Papers, a secret, classified history of American involvement in Vietnam since World War II.
- July 2, 1971: John Erlichman forms the Plumbers group at President Nixon's request. Less than a year later, this group is implicated in the Watergate break-in and scandal.[2]

According to Richard Gid Powers, the 1960s also saw a "rebirth of the old united front refusal to exclude anyone on the Left from the radical movement." In 1963 Dagmar Wilson of the Women's Strike for Peace opened that group to Communists. Other groups that welcomed Communist participation included the Fair Play for Cuba movement, the Berkeley Free Speech movement, and the black Student Nonviolent Coordinating Center (SNCC). The Students for a Democratic Society (SDS) denounced "unreasoning anti-Communism" at its 1962 organizational meeting at Port Huron, Michigan. The SDS claimed, "Communists were less dangerous to the country than their anti-Communist persecutors."[3] More than forty years later the liberal acceptance of the Communist presence and sponsorship of events has continued.

INSTITUTE FOR POLICY STUDIES (1963)

The Institute for Policy Studies (IPS) may be considered the poster child of the various groups established during the 1960s. It is "America's oldest left-wing think tank" and has long supported anti-American causes around the world. In 1963 two former government officials—Richard Barnet and Marcus Raskin—organized the group. Barnet had been a Soviet specialist with the Arms Control and Disarmament Agency (ACDA), while Raskin had once been a legislative assistant to radical Congressman Robert Kastenmeier (D-WI). Raskin quickly began to organize the Liberal Project, a mini-caucus of twelve leftist congressmen who wished to bring about some utopian—if not radical—changes in U.S. defense policies. The IPS was founded as a tax-exempt 501(c)(3) organization, and the institute's seed money came from the Rubin Foundation and Cora Weiss.[4]

"By 1965 Barnet and Raskin had greatly intensified IPS's organizing efforts against U.S. defense and foreign policies," and they "dropped the pretense of scholarship for the production of blatant propaganda." A partnership emerged between the IPS and a host of radicals and liberals, as they worked together to support the goals and causes of nearly every revolutionary and terrorist movement backed by the USSR, Cuba, or North Vietnam. The IPS also conducted "major efforts to present a favorable image" of the terrorists of the Palestine Liberation Organization (PLO), the Soviet-dominated Popular Liberation Movement of Angola (MPLA), and the African National Congress (ANC) of South Africa, not to mention several Latin American terrorist or guerrilla groups.

The IPS claims that it is a source of "radical scholarship," but former IPS director Robert L. Borosage (who has also served as president of the Washington DC chapter of the National Lawyers Guild) admitted that the institute's "scholarship" is "not academic" and "does not adhere to academic disciplines." Instead, IPS members are expected to teach projects and organize experiments that put into operation radical alternative programs "devised by IPS's pro-Communist fellows and associates." In short, IPS acknowledges that it operates as a training center for radical organizers and serves as a transmission mechanism for radical programs.[5]

The IPS has had remarkable continuity since its founding—unstinting and unwavering opposition to U.S. policies in every part of the world. In the 1960s and 1970s it championed antiwar activities and advanced a host of left-wing causes (including those of the Cuban and North Vietnamese regimes). In the 1980s it fought the efforts of President Reagan to roll back Communism abroad and joined the vanguard of the so-called anti-corporate globalization movement in the 1990s. Most recently it has resisted U.S. policies vis-à-vis Iraq.

Two of its spin-offs are noteworthy. In 1966 the IPS spawned the North American Congress on Latin America (NACLA), described as a radical intelligence-gathering organization. Its affiliate in the Netherlands, the Transnational Institute (TNI), is a major source of anticapitalist propaganda. Other spin-offs include the Center for National Security Studies (CNSS), founded in 1974, which strove to compromise the effectiveness of U.S. intelligence agencies. The mastheads of two anti-U.S. intelligence publications were heavy with IPS members.[6]

The IPS is also linked to a phalanx of left-wing antiwar groups, either through funding or leadership. These include the Committee for a Sane Nuclear Policy (SANE) and the Fellowship of Reconciliation. Significantly, the IPS is a member organization of the United for Peace and Justice (UFPJ) coalition and has many links to the Tides Foundation, a major source of funding for leftist groups.

Often IPS takes an active hand in interacting with policy makers. In 1985, as President Reagan pressed Congress to assist the Contras in Nicaragua, IPS fellow Peter Kornbluth arranged for Senators John Kerry (D-MA) and Tom Harkin (D-IA) to meet with Sandinista leaders in Managua. "Convinced by the Kerry-Harkin team about the allegedly happy atmosphere in Managua, Congress denied the funds" to the Contras, although it reversed itself later when Sandinista chief Daniel Ortega flew to Moscow to meet with his Soviet sponsors.[7]

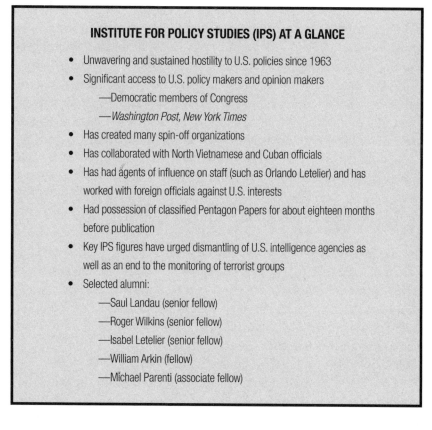

INSTITUTE FOR POLICY STUDIES (IPS) AT A GLANCE

- Unwavering and sustained hostility to U.S. policies since 1963
- Significant access to U.S. policy makers and opinion makers
    —Democratic members of Congress
    —*Washington Post, New York Times*
- Has created many spin-off organizations
- Has collaborated with North Vietnamese and Cuban officials
- Has had agents of influence on staff (such as Orlando Letelier) and has worked with foreign officials against U.S. interests
- Had possession of classified Pentagon Papers for about eighteen months before publication
- Key IPS figures have urged dismantling of U.S. intelligence agencies as well as an end to the monitoring of terrorist groups
- Selected alumni:
    —Saul Landau (senior fellow)
    —Roger Wilkins (senior fellow)
    —Isabel Letelier (senior fellow)
    —William Arkin (fellow)
    —Michael Parenti (associate fellow)

IPS professes unyielding opposition to free markets and to capitalism in general. It opposes the trinity of capitalism, big corporations, and globalization. The latter brings in its opposition to the World Trade Organization (WTO) and to the North America Free Trade Association (NAFTA).

Moreover, the IPS has worked with the Congressional Black Caucus and the Progressive Caucus in efforts to hamstring U.S. foreign policy. In the past, the IPS has had the support of such luminaries as the late Les Aspin (D-WI, and former secretary of defense under Bill Clinton), John Conyers (D-MI), George Crockett (D-MI), Ron Dellums (D-CA), Tom Harkin (D-IA), Leon Panetta (D-CA), Patricia Schroeder (D-CO), and Robert Toricelli (D-NJ).[8]

Currently leading IPS spokesmen are making the case for a more vigorous European opposition to U.S. policy, because they believe that the United States is a rogue nation. At the same time, the IPS professes faith in the righteousness of the United Nations and touts a U.S. foreign policy that is attuned to the edicts of the UN rather than to U.S. national interests. Since 1996, according to its Web site, the IPS has been working toward the goal of "crafting a new kind of UN-centered, democratic and people-based internationalism." One component of this effort is the "challenge to U.S. unilateralism and military interventionism, especially in the wake of the September 11th terrorist attacks." Project director Phyllis Bennis has appeared on many different forums: National Public Radio, *The Phil Donohue Show*, and Commonwealth media outlets (including the BBC, CBC, and the Australian ABC).[9]

CENTER FOR CONSTITUTIONAL RIGHTS (1966)

Just as Cora Weiss was instrumental in the development of the IPS, her husband, Peter Weiss, has been one of the key players at the Center for Constitutional Rights (CCR), which was established in 1966. For fifteen years Peter Weiss had been a leader of the CCR, a "tax-exempt litigation group of National Lawyers Guild (NLG) activists." Peter Weiss is also a direct funder of the Council on Economic Priorities (CEP, described below) as well as a prominent member of the NLG.[10]

The CCR is a "civil rights legal advocacy nonprofit organization" based in New York City. It grew out of the Law Center for Constitutional Rights, developed with lawyers representing civil-rights activists in Mississippi who saw a need for a center to support litigation. Among its four founding lawyers is William Kunstler. Significantly, founder Kunstler and co-counsel Leonard Weinglass played a leading role in the case of the Chicago Seven and were themselves charged with thirty-eight counts of contempt for their "vigorous defense." The CCR also provided advocacy to U.S. servicemen evading the draft during the Vietnam War. Since that time, the CCR has handled high-profile cases, representing Philip Agee (former CIA officer and traitor), Castroite parties, and support groups for foreign terrorist movements.

Recently the CCR has filed lawsuits on behalf of those detained at Guantanamo Bay and has "sought criminal investigation in Germany of U.S. officials, notably Secretary of Defense Donald Rumsfeld, for alleged war crimes in the Abu Ghraib prison."[11]

NORTH AMERICAN CONGRESS ON LATIN AMERICA (1966)

The North American Congress on Latin America (NACLA) formed in 1966 after the Tricontinental Congress in Havana, which was attended by individuals affiliated with Students for a Democratic Society (SDS). NACLA stated it was recruiting "men and women, from a variety of organizations and movements, who not only favor revolutionary change in Latin America, but also take a revolutionary position toward their own society." SDS leaders called NACLA the "intelligence-gathering arm" of the radical movement. Subsequently NACLA "planted or developed covert sources in government agencies and private companies," and its materials have been used in a number of anti-U.S. Cuban publications.[12]

NACLA's particular targets have included U.S. defense, counterinsurgency, and antiterrorist programs, companies that provide arms and police equipment to Latin America, and U.S. companies involved in Latin America. In the British edition of his book *Inside the Company: CIA Diary,* Philip Agee acknowledged that agencies of the Cuban government and Cuban Communist Party provided "special assistance" and that three individuals of NACLA obtained vital research materials in New York and Washington DC. NACLA veterans include Michael Klare, an IPS associate who also lectures on U.S. arms sales, antiterrorist, and counterinsurgency programs at the University of Havana; and Michael

Locker, who is also on the staff of the Cuba Resource Center, a nonprofit, tax-exempt pro-Castro corporation in New York City.[13]

NACLA refers to itself as an "independent, nonprofit organization" that provides information on a "range of political, social, and economic issues in the Americas." "With a critical eye on U.S. foreign policy, we continue to examine the interrelationships between multiple forms of social exclusion—class, race, gender, ethnicity, sexuality—that are at the heart of ongoing militarism, human rights violations, environmental destruction and poverty that plague the region." All of this has a purpose, it states, for "NACLA was born of the belief that through careful study, the 'elements and relationships' of injustice could be revealed, and once revealed, opposed by an informed public."[14]

The core of the group's work is a bimonthly magazine called *NACLA Report on the Americas.* About half of its revenue comes from the sale of the magazine, with some 25 percent from grants and the other 25 percent from donations from church groups, family foundations, and individuals. Through this publication and various seminars and conferences, NACLA's mission is "to reveal, to document, and to analyze the structures of exploitation." The group is "still dedicated to uncovering the truth about the impact of U.S. and transnational institutions on the peoples of the Americas." The only hint of NACLA's ties to other groups is its statement that "we have working relationships with a number of progressive, policy-oriented, Washington-based research groups who help us evaluate the directions of U.S. policy," evidently a guarded reference to the IPS and its spin-off organizations.[15]

NACLA's interests have evolved even though its orientation has not. In the cold war days, it was greatly focused on arms, the military, and the CIA. Today the group is focusing on topics such as NAFTA and the financial struggles of many Latin American nations. Its publication has become the bible for U.S. leftists interested in Latin America, and it is popular with professors who use it as "evidence" that an "alternative vision" for the region exists in the United States. The group's executive director, Fred Rosen, makes no pretense that the publication is objective. "We don't publish any center-right or any right-hand opinions. That's not our mission." Although the publication seldom features Cuba, it did run an article in 2002 written by a Cuban political scientist that was "anything but critical of the regime."[16]

COUNCIL ON ECONOMIC PRIORITIES (1969)

The Council on Economic Priorities (CEP) was founded in 1969 by Alice Repper-Marlin, who is executive director, editor in chief, and president ex-officio of the board of directors. It is another nonprofit, tax-exempt 501(c)(3) foundation. IPS stalwart Richard Barnet was listed as one of CEP's first advisers and consultants in 1970, and from 1977 to 1980 he was a CEP trustee.

In 1981 the CEP unveiled one of its typical projects in a briefing to the National Press Club in Washington DC. The study was entitled *The Iron Triangle: The Politics of Defense Contracting.* This effort was a four-year $100,000 research project financed by several organizations and individuals with close ties to the IPS, including NACLA. The study "focused on the type of classified information to which these groups have access" that was related to research and development (R&D) programs for new U.S. weapons. This was an in-depth survey and analysis of eight key defense firms. The CEP study targeted the R&D process "in the production of new weapons and defense systems," in effect calling for the end to U.S. secrecy in the development of new weapons, tactics, and military policies. CEP appeared unconcerned that there are legitimate national security reasons as to why long-term weapons-development programs and military-policy meetings are kept secret.

CEP credits its success to the extensive national press coverage it receives. Its reports have been covered in the *New York Times, Washington Post,* and other newspapers, and numerous television and radio programs have reported on the CEP's work.

The group's stated goals are "significant improvements in both the quality of corporate performance" as well as "the quality of governmental performance as it interacts with the corporate establishment."[17] Beyond that bland statement, rest assured that the CEP's goals do not include greater or wiser spending on national defense.

CENTER FOR NATIONAL SECURITY STUDIES (1974)

The Center for National Security Studies (CNSS) was founded in1974 as a "non-governmental advocacy and research organization" to cite the group's Web site.[18] In its early days, the staff of CNSS "included a significant number of persons drawn from the Institute for Policy Studies (IPS) and the National Lawyers Guild (NLG)." The staff drawn from IPS have included "David Cortright, a former organizer of anti-Vietnam War GIs at Fort Bliss, Texas; Courtland Cox, a former activist with Student Nonviolent Coordinating Center (SNCC); and Mark Ryter" of IPS. Those prominent in the NLG group have included Robert L. Borosage, Susan Kaplan of the NLG San Francisco chapter, and Judy Mead, who was NLG's national treasurer in 1977. Other staff and consultants have come from the North American Congress on Latin America (NACLA).[19]

The advisory committee of the CNSS, as listed in a 1975 newsletter, included two leading NLG figures. One was Peter Weiss, who was also chairman of the IPS board of trustees. Another was former NLG president Thomas Emerson; in 1956 Emerson's name was included in a list of eighty-two most active "sponsors of Communist front organizations" by the Senate Internal Security Subcommittee. In addition to NLG ties, the CNSS is very closely tied to the American Civil Liberties Union (ACLU).[20]

In many ways, the story of CNSS is the story of Morton Halperin. In 1974 Halperin became the center's first director and served in that post

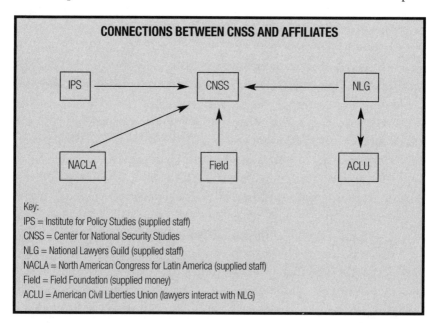

CONNECTIONS BETWEEN CNSS AND AFFILIATES

Key:
IPS = Institute for Policy Studies (supplied staff)
CNSS = Center for National Security Studies
NLG = National Lawyers Guild (supplied staff)
NACLA = North American Congress for Latin America (supplied staff)
Field = Field Foundation (supplied money)
ACLU = American Civil Liberties Union (lawyers interact with NLG)

until 1992. He has long been a prominent figure in a host of causes. Throughout his long stint in the Washington area, Halperin affiliated himself with many organizations in his unceasing attempts to promote his radical views and cripple U.S. defenses against external and internal enemies. He has been associated at different times with the Brookings Institution, the Rand Corporation, the Hudson Institute, and the Institute for Defense Analysis.[21] He has also been affiliated with the International Movement for Atlantic Union, Freedom House (a center for anti-anti-Communism), and other groups.

Halperin served in three administrations, those of Lyndon B. Johnson, Richard M. Nixon, and Bill Clinton. In the 1960s Halperin served in a high position in the Defense Department and was dovish on the Vietnam War, calling for a halt to the bombing of North Vietnam. From 1967 to 1969 he was deputy assistant secretary of defense on policy planning and arms control.[22] Under Nixon, Halperin joined the National Security Council staff, where he was a senior assistant under Henry Kissinger. This appointment was immediately criticized by Gen. Earle Wheeler, chairman of the Joint Chiefs of Staff, FBI director J. Edgar Hoover, and Senator Barry Goldwater. Halperin and Kissinger were colleagues at Harvard in the 1950s—which may have led to his appointment—although Kissinger soon lost faith in him. Halperin was under suspicion for a leaked story to the *New York Times* on the bombing of Cambodia, and he was also suspected to have a connection with Daniel Ellsberg and the leaking of Pentagon Papers. By this time, Halperin had gained a prominent spot on Nixon's enemies list.

Before Halperin took his position at the CNSS in 1974, he headed the Project on National Security and Civil Liberties, sponsored jointly by the tax-exempt Fund for Peace (FFP) and the ACLU. Between 1984 and 1992 Halperin "also directed the Washington office of the ACLU, where he was responsible for its first national legislative program."[23] As such, for an eight-year period, he held leading positions with the CNSS as well as the ACLU. From 1998 until 2001 Halperin was the head of the policy planning staff at the Clinton State Department.

Significantly, Halperin is now the director of the Washington DC office of George Soros's Open Society Institute (OSI) as well as the Open Society Policy Center. As such, he is Soros's key man in Washington, with close and continuing access to radical and liberal organizations coupled with an insider's knowledge of policy within the State and Defense Departments where he once worked.

According to the current CNSS Web site, the center was founded "to work for control of the FBI and CIA and to prevent violations of individual liberties in the United States." The CNSS works to strengthen the public's right of access to government information, to combat excessive government secrecy, to assure effective oversight of intelligence agencies, and to protect the right of political dissent, among other stated goals.[24] It is fair to say that through the combined efforts of organizations such as the CNSS and its close allies in the NLG, ACLU, and IPS, the net effectiveness of U.S. intelligence and security agencies has been diminished. These groups have maintained a barrage of lawsuits, discovery proceedings, and public broadsides against the FBI, CIA, and other intelligence agencies. Should these groups have their way, U.S. intelligence and security agencies would become toothless.

One interesting link is a partnership between the CNSS and People for the American Way (PFAW). The latter group is a co-plaintiff and co-counsel in *CNSS v. Department of Justice*, which contends that the Justice Department's refusal to release information on the "mass detention" of the fall and winter of 2001 violated the Freedom of Information Act. The lawsuit was filed on December 5, 2001. In November 2002 a federal district court issued a favorable decision ordering release of the names and other information on detainees. But the U.S. Court of Appeals reversed that ruling in June 2003 and upheld the withholding of the information. The plaintiffs filed a petition for review by the U.S. Supreme Court, but that petition was denied in January 2004. According to the PFAW Web site, PFAW and CNSS are consulting on "other avenues to pursue the information."[25]

REVOLUTIONARY COMMUNIST PARTY, USA (1975)

The Revolutionary Communist Party, USA (RCP USA), which was known originally as the Revolutionary Union, is a Maoist organization that was formed in 1975. The RCP USA claims that U.S. imperialism will never change peacefully, and the group believes the only way for the "oppressed masses" to ever liberate themselves is through waging a people's war and building a socialist society on the ashes of capitalism.

The RCP USA was formed by former members of the Revolutionary Youth Movement II (or RYM II) faction of the Students for a Democratic Society (SDS) after that group disintegrated in 1968. Beginning in the Bay Area of Northern California, Bob Avakian teamed with H. Bruce Franklin and Stephen Charles Hamilton to form the Revolutionary Union (RU). This group expanded nationally with great speed. Of the various groups that emerged from the SDS, "it was the first to seriously attempt to develop itself at the theoretical level" (with the publication of *Red Papers 1*) and the first to try to make a connection with working-class communities. It was "able to absorb a series of similar local collectives" that had developed out of SDS.[26]

As a result of criminal indictments in 1981 stemming from a demonstration at the White House against Chinese leader Deng Xiaoping, RCP USA national chairman Bob Avakian and other RCP USA leaders "fled the United States and have been living in France and England ever since." The RCP USA remains active in both the United States and Western Europe and "is considered by its critics to be a very centralized and authoritarian group."[27]

The group has staged a number of provocative actions. It raised a red flag over the Alamo in San Antonio. Damian Garcia, who raised the flag, was eventually killed, and the RCP USA claims that "his murder was the result of his actions." A member of the RCP USA's youth organization, the Revolutionary Communist Youth Brigade, burned a U.S. flag at the Republican National convention in 1984. This resulted in a U.S. Supreme Court case known as *Texas v. Johnson.*

The RCP USA is a participant in the Revolutionary Internationalism Movement (RIM), which is a "grouping of revolutionary Maoist parties and organizations" around the world. These groups include the Shining Path group of Peru—known for brutal terrorist tactics—and the Communist Party of Nepal (Maoist).[28]

Following the reelection of George W. Bush in 2004, the RCP USA released a statement called "The Battle for the Future." The statement labeled Bush a "Christian Fascist" and calls on the masses to resist. This document also touts Bob Avakian as a great leader.[29]

A few of the group's leaders are known to the public. Carl Dix was earlier noted to be a national spokesman, and Joe Urgo—an old-time North Vietnam visitor (1971)—is also a prominent member. C. Clark

Kissinger—a former math teacher with an affinity for Lenin caps—has been affiliated with the RCP USA for at least twenty-five years. He is a former national officer of SDS in the 1960s, a veteran of the 1968 Chicago riots, and a lifelong Maoist. Mary Lou Greenberg is also a prominent member of the RCP USA.

Most significantly, the RCP USA has been instrumental in the establishment of two other groups. C. Clark Kissinger founded the antiwar group called Refuse and Resist! in 1987, and Mary Lou Greenberg is a well-known member of that organization. Moreover, Kissinger and Greenberg are both prominent in Not in Our Name (NION), which was founded in 2002. Greenberg is a director of NION, while Kissinger is a spokesman of NION and also partly directs the group.

MOBILIZATION FOR SURVIVAL (1977)

This group clearly has its roots in Communism. It includes among its constituent organizations the Communist Party USA (CPUSA), the U.S. Peace Council (an arm of the World Peace Council), Women for Racial and Economic Equality, and the Southern Organizing Committee for Racial-Economic Justice.

The initial momentum of the Mobilization for Survival (MFS) came primarily from the Vietnam-era antiwar movement. After a campaign to stop the B-1 bomber, people from various peace organizations came together in early 1977 "to discuss the potential of organizing a mass movement around the issues of nuclear weapons, conventional arms, and their economic and social consequences." In the summer of 1977 the goals of the MFS were established: "zero nuclear weapons, ban nuclear power, stop the arms race, fund human needs."[30]

The group claims to mark the coming together of two major streams of popular involvement and action against the nuclear menace: the peace movement (which previously concentrated on nuclear weapons) and the environmental movement (opposed to nuclear power plants). The MFS also sought to unite not only the peace and environmental movements but also labor, third world, black, women, and public-interest groups "in an effort to isolate the proponents of nuclear technology, capital-intensive energy and military superiority."[31]

The MFS can best be understood by examining its two founders,

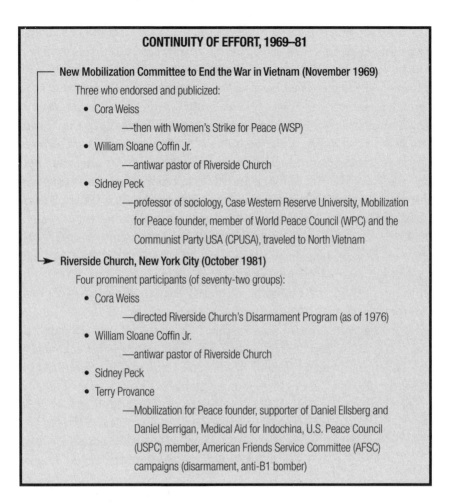

CONTINUITY OF EFFORT, 1969–81

New Mobilization Committee to End the War in Vietnam (November 1969)

Three who endorsed and publicized:

- Cora Weiss
  - —then with Women's Strike for Peace (WSP)
- William Sloane Coffin Jr.
  - —antiwar pastor of Riverside Church
- Sidney Peck
  - —professor of sociology, Case Western Reserve University, Mobilization for Peace founder, member of World Peace Council (WPC) and the Communist Party USA (CPUSA), traveled to North Vietnam

Riverside Church, New York City (October 1981)

Four prominent participants (of seventy-two groups):

- Cora Weiss
  - —directed Riverside Church's Disarmament Program (as of 1976)
- William Sloane Coffin Jr.
  - —antiwar pastor of Riverside Church
- Sidney Peck
- Terry Provance
  - —Mobilization for Peace founder, supporter of Daniel Ellsberg and Daniel Berrigan, Medical Aid for Indochina, U.S. Peace Council (USPC) member, American Friends Service Committee (AFSC) campaigns (disarmament, anti-B1 bomber)

Sidney Peck and Terry Provance. Sidney Peck is a "former functionary of the CPUSA" and has been "active in the World Peace Council," a well-known Soviet front. His roots go back to the Vietnam War, when he was a prominent member of the New Mobilization Committee to End the War in Vietnam in 1969. His involvement included a pilgrimage to North Vietnam in 1969. He is a professor of sociology at Case Western Reserve University. Peck had also been appointed as the director of international relations for nongovernmental organizations that participated in a Soviet-directed disarmament offensive at the United Nations; this was the Second Special Section on Disarmament that was held in New York City during June and July 1982.[32]

Terry Provance, the current spokesman for the MFS, has been active in a number of organizations. He is a former supporter of Daniel and Philip Berrigan, who were charged with conspiracy to kidnap Henry Kissinger. Provance then went to work for the defense committee for Daniel Ellsberg. "He was also connected with Medical Aid for Indochina, a group formed following the appeals of the World Peace Council for aid to North Vietnam in 1973." Provance was also director of the American Friends Service Committee's (AFSC) national campaign to stop the B-1 bomber. Provance's statements found their way into the Communist press in articles on disarmament and the dismantling of NATO. "In 1976 he was a delegate to the World Peace Council conference in Helsinki." He participated in a Washington DC rally with a Dutch Communist Party activist and the head of the East German Peace Council. In 1981 he was a featured speaker at an anti-NATO rally in Bonn, "organized by the Communist Party and the World Peace Council."[33]

MFS has participated in a number of demonstrations at many nuclear power plants, the Rocky Flats nuclear weapons plant in Colorado, the Trident submarine base in Washington, and could be counted on the make an appearance (to generate collective U.S. guilt) someplace on Hiroshima Day and Nagasaki Day—August 6 and 9.[34] It is most telling that the group refers to those days as examples of U.S. "terrorism."

PEOPLE FOR THE AMERICAN WAY (1981)

People for the American Way (PFAW) was founded in 1981 as a liberal advocacy group. Its founder was Norman Lear, the creator of the television series *All in the Family.* PFAW has shown remarkable resiliency and staying power after nearly twenty-five years. According to its history, the organization has advanced the same basic themes: "embracing America's diversity, respecting Americans' rights, defending liberty, democracy and the American way." PFAW claims to advance the causes of "pluralism, individuality, freedom of thought, expression and religion," but its actions are often directly opposed to those platitudes.[35]

According to the group's history, PFAW began when Lear searched for an "appropriate response" to what he perceived as a new and "disturbing" political movement in the United States. The Religious Right, he claimed, was determined to impose a radical and extremist agenda, one that acknowledged only its leaders' religious beliefs and sought to diminish Americans' religious freedoms. Those who dared dissent, the Religious Right called atheistic, anti-Christian, and anti-family. Lear particularly singled out individuals such as Jerry Falwell and Pat Robertson as well as groups such as the Moral Majority.[36]

Evidently PFAW depends heavily on the Hollywood axis. One of its co-chairmen, David E. Altschul, resides in Encino, California. A Google search reveals that a David E. Altschul is a partner of Altschul and Olin, LLP, a law firm for the entertainment industry. (Confirmation that the two Altschuls are the same person is unavailable.) The other co-chairman is Lara Bergthold of Beverly Hills, who had served as John Kerry's liaison with Hollywood and was named a deputy political director of that campaign in 2004. Lear himself resides in Beverly Hills.[37]

One of the stars of *All in the Family,* Rob Reiner ("Meathead"), is not a known member of PFAW, but he is an activist and supports MoveOn.org. In mid-2004 Reiner's name was linked to an effort to produce television ads for that group that were designed to smear President Bush and denigrate the war on terror. This program was overseen by Laura Dawn, an entertainer behind MoveOn.Org's contest that challenged members to shoot their own anti-Bush commercials; this resulted in the Web site posting two ads comparing George Bush with Adolf Hitler.

Members of the PFAW board of directors include actor Alec Baldwin, radical priest Father Robert Drinan, and Anthony T. Podesta (of Clinton White House notoriety). These very same individuals are on the board of directors for the PFAW Foundation, along with Bianca Jagger and John Moyers (Bill's son).[38]

PFAW is headquartered in Washington DC, and its current president is Ralph G. Neas. Neas received a J.D. from the University of Chicago Law School and has taught at several universities. He earlier served as executive director of the Leadership Conference on Civil Rights (LCCR). In 1987 he led a successful effort by LCCR and its members—including PFAW—to block the nomination of Robert Bork to the U.S. Supreme Court. Senator Ted Kennedy described Neas as "the

101st Senator for Civil Rights." He is also responsible for much of the subsequent battle against Clarence Thomas, who was later confirmed for the Supreme Court.[39]

Neas has been president of PFAW and the PFAW Foundation since 2000, and since then its membership has increased from 300,000 to 675,000. He has led a national effort to "challenge the far-right movement to reverse decades of social justice progress." In addition, PFAW's Web site states that Neas has built coalitions to block a permanent and massive tax cut, to amend the USA PATRIOT Act, and to "defend and reform our nation's public schools." Reading between the lines, this means weakening the USA PATRIOT Act and opposing any voucher programs for private schools. According to Kay Daly, "When Neas isn't litigating to block minority children from participating in school-choice voucher programs, he is in the courtroom trying to make the Internet a safe haven for pornographers and pedophiles."[40]

Just a few days before the November 2, 2004, election, PFAW and Neas were "orchestrating the activities of more than ten thousand" Democratic lawyers in the battleground states. The lawsuits in Florida began before the election, and some two thousand lawyers were "dispatched to that state alone."[41] This PFAW program was named Election Protection. PFAW has also been involved in efforts to register black and Hispanic voters. Both efforts are clearly aimed at a greater turnout for Democrats in local and national elections.

It is more accurate to describe PFAW as a liberal—rather than radical—organization. Yet it has partnered with radical groups, such as Morton Halperin's CNSS (the lawsuit filed against the Department of Justice in late 2001). A look at its board of directors clearly reveals those who have supported radical causes. Moreover, it has embraced Noam Chomsky, the notorious MIT professor. PFAW's annual Christmas eBay auction and fund-raiser featured two autographed Chomsky books. As part of this effort, PFAW described Chomsky as a "crucial voice of an alternative way of looking at the actions of the military-industrial complex" that drives American politics. Significantly, PFAW placed the catchphrase "military-industrial complex" at the locus of U.S. policy.[42] Chomsky, it should be noted, believes that the United States is a leading terrorist state that got what it deserved on 9/11; his works are usually brimming with a pernicious hatred for the United States. This episode reveals more about PFAW's agenda than any flowery wording on the group's Web site.

INSIGHT: A WORD ABOUT LINGUISTIC DECEPTION

The use of the name *People for the American Way* bears examination. It implies that those who opposed what PFAW advocates are not for the American way. It further implies that there is only one "American way"—whatever PFAW deems it to be. The very name of the organization thus brings an inherent contradiction to the old liberal mantra of inclusiveness. Curious, isn't it?

Moreover, the use of *America* or *American* is often encountered in the names of these groups. The term is disarming, as it conveys a warm, fuzzy feeling—giving an indication that these are somehow patriotic groups. Consider the wide range of Hard-Left groups that use the names:

- America Votes (Cecile Richards, head)
- American Civil Liberties Union (ACLU)
- American Friends Service Committee (AFSC)
- America Coming Together (ACT; Minyon Moore, head)
- Campaign for America's Future (CAF; Robert L. Borosage, head)
- Center for American Progress (CAP; John Podesta, head)
- People for the American Way (PFAW)

The point here is that linguistic deception is as old as politics itself. Part of that linguistic deception centers around what names groups choose to adopt. Just the name *Students for a Democratic Society* could have evoked some general acceptance in earlier years. ("Oh, how nice. Those students are behind democracy.") But then people discovered what SDS really stood for. By the same token, the 1936 Constitution of the USSR under Joseph Stalin contained articles providing for freedom of speech and religion. American dupes enamored with Stalin and the Soviet experiment often pointed to those articles in efforts to explain that the Soviets were "just like us."

Other forms of linguistic deception are linked with the techniques like the big lie. For example, the group IFCO/Pastors for Peace refers to the five convicted Cuban spies as the "five Cuban heroes." Leslie Cagan of United for Peace and Justice (UFPJ) calls the United States the "world's foremost terrorist nation." Iraq Occupation Watch refers to the January 30, 2005, election as a "train wreck of an election." MoveOn.org is involved with "repudiating the torture of prisoners of war." (This implies that standard U.S. policy is torture and also that those captured terrorists deserve POW status—a double affront to one's intelligence.) Radical historian Howard Zinn notes that "war is terrorism," implying that anything we do to protect ourselves and hunt down terrorist groups is heinous. Sara Flounders of the WWP notes that "inspections are war," thereby giving Saddam Hussein a free pass for life. She also has stated that the United States has plans for a "criminal war of colonial conquest." The newspaper *Workers World* assures us, "Iraq has done absolutely nothing wrong." ("Well fine, then we don't have to go to war with Saddam!")

The longer you examine these groups and their language, the more examples of this may be found. It is comparable to falling down the rabbit hole, just like Alice in Wonderland, and finding that reality is turned upside down. But then again, the study of politics is sometimes more about perceptions than reality.

DEMOCRATIC SOCIALISTS OF AMERICA (1983)

The Democratic Socialists of America (DSA) is the "largest socialist organization in the United States" today. It was formed from a merger of Michael Harrington's Democratic Socialist Organizing Committee and the New American Movement (a coalition of writers and intellectuals with roots in both the Old Left and New Left). DSA is organized at the local level, although its nationwide campaigns are coordinated by its national office in New York City. DSA "works with labor unions, community organizations, and campus activists."[43]

Among DSA's most noteworthy members are actor Ed Asner (television's "Lou Grant"), feminist Gloria Steinem (founder of *Ms.* magazine), prominent black scholar and activist Cornel West, and anti-American academic Noam Chomsky. Some members of Congress have had ties to it as well, including Ron Dellums (D-CA) and Bernie Sanders (I-VT), who has spoken to DSA conferences.[44] Electoral politics are a secondary concern throughout the history of the DSA, for the main aim has been to promote socialist ideas in general. On electoral issues, DSA supports what it calls the "left wing of the possible" on a case-by-case basis.

Asner has taken his rightful place in the shrine of Hollywood Half-wits. In May 2003, when Pat Buchanan noted that Fidel Castro had denied Cubans free elections for forty years, Asner fired back, "We didn't have a free election in 2002." Asner also noted that "because of pressure by the United States, Fidel demonstrated his independence of the United States," claiming that the United States forced him into the sphere of Soviet influence.

Referring to President George Bush, Asner stated, "I have never seen him as a man with clarity and vision." Moreover, Asner stated that Bush's actions are "desecrating the America that I grew up in and believed in. . . . He is making us an imperialist government. He is choosing to replace heads of state and government he doesn't like."[45]

Asner's history of leftist political involvement dates well back at least twenty years. This makes him a contemporary of Norman Lear (as they both publicly joined leftist causes at about the same time), although the current status of their relationship is not certain. Asner has long supported Central American revolutionaries. His group, called Medical Aid, flew actor Mike Farrell "to Nicaragua to assist in the surgery" of a Sandinista leader who had previously killed fifteen Americans (including four marines). Another Asner group—the Committee of Concern for Central America—invited Daniel Ortega to the United States for a "nine-day propaganda tour." Naturally, Asner has visited Castro in Cuba and returned "singing his praises."[46]

FAIRNESS AND ACCURACY IN REPORTING (1986)

Fairness and Accuracy in Reporting (FAIR) is a watchdog group of the national media. It was founded in 1986 with the task of working against what it perceives as conservative media bias and erroneous reporting. The group's bimonthly magazine called *Extra!* often features claims of current media bias, censorship, and effects of media consolidation. FAIR also produces a half hour radio program called *CounterSpin*, which broadcasts nationally on more than 130 radio stations.[47]

According to its Web site, FAIR advocates greater diversity in the press and scrutinizes media practices that "marginalize public interest, minority and dissenting viewpoints."

"As a progressive group, FAIR believes that structural reform is ultimately needed to break up the dominant media conglomerates, establish independent public broadcasting, and promote strong, non-profit sources of information." Its Web site notes that the group "works with both activists and journalists," perhaps a nod to the idea that the activists supply most of the leftward party line that FAIR touts. Significantly, FAIR's Web site includes a media activist kit, which includes a number of tips on everything from how to organize demonstrations to how to communicate with media representatives effectively.[48]

About 30 percent of this group's funding comes from foundation grants, including grants from the Rockefeller Commission, the MacArthur Foundation, the Ford Foundation, and Bill Moyers's Schumann Foundation.[49]

As of early 2005, FAIR was engaged in image building for Dan Rather, who retired from CBS News on March 9, 2005. FAIR claims the notion that Rather has used his CBS platform to disseminate left-wing propaganda over the last two decades "does not hold up to scrutiny." At the same time, FAIR was readying a broadside against John Negroponte, the nominee for the position as director of national intelligence (DNI). The central theme: media omissions on Negroponte's role in human-rights abuses when he was ambassador to Nicaragua in the mid-1980s.[50]

The very existence of FAIR is proof that liberals and radicals keep attempting to promote and sustain one of the big lies of the modern era—that the media is actually dominated by conservatives and not liberals. In one respect, this group helps the Left play defense by adopting a good offense.

REFUSE AND RESIST! (1987)

Refuse and Resist! (R&R) was born in 1987, with the Revolutionary Communist Party USA (RCP USA) the key to its founding. Longtime key member C. Clark Kissinger founded this group, and RCP USA member Mary Lou Greenberg is a well-known member of R&R as well.

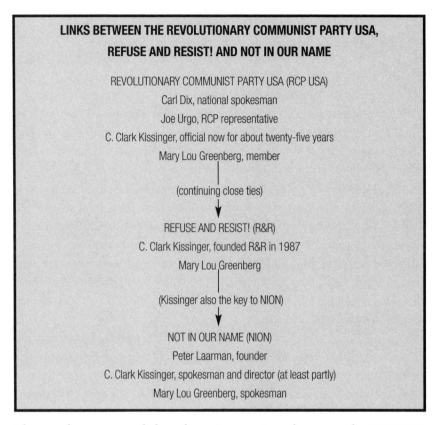

LINKS BETWEEN THE REVOLUTIONARY COMMUNIST PARTY USA, REFUSE AND RESIST! AND NOT IN OUR NAME

REVOLUTIONARY COMMUNIST PARTY USA (RCP USA)

Carl Dix, national spokesman

Joe Urgo, RCP representative

C. Clark Kissinger, official now for about twenty-five years

Mary Lou Greenberg, member

(continuing close ties)

REFUSE AND RESIST! (R&R)

C. Clark Kissinger, founded R&R in 1987

Mary Lou Greenberg

(Kissinger also the key to NION)

NOT IN OUR NAME (NION)

Peter Laarman, founder

C. Clark Kissinger, spokesman and director (at least partly)

Mary Lou Greenberg, spokesman

The two have ensured that close ties continue between the RCP USA and R&R.

According to R&R's Web site, this is an organization "for everyone who refuses to go along with today's national agenda of repression and cruelty, poverty and punishment." The group's mission, the Web site claims, "is to build a climate, culture and community of resistance to defeat the whole reactionary agenda." The Web site reports that R&R was formed "by artists, lawyers, activists and others who saw an alarming trend in the United States toward greater state control and repression." It is interesting to note that this was at a time when President Reagan was advocating much less state control over individuals and local affairs. Still avoiding any mention about the RCP USA or Communists, the Web site notes that the group is a "non-partisan, national membership organization." It really appears to be made up of everybody, according to this claim: "We are students and teachers, youth, artists, working people, professionals and activists, well-known and 'ordinary' people."[51]

If anything, this group is resisting what it calls the Hard Right that is seeking to pack the courts and "rig the rules," with the target being democracy itself, as indicated on its Web site. Two of R&R's poster children at present are convicted cop-killer Mumia Abu-Jamal (whom they call a "political prisoner" and is still facing a death sentence) as well as radical lawyer Lynne Stewart (found guilty of assisting a terrorist in February 2005).[52]

In their never-ending quest for recognition, R&R activists have been engaged in a number of activities. They have disrupted sessions of the U.S. Supreme Court. They have occupied the offices of Rep. Henry Hyde (R-IL) and the National Right to Life Committee. They issued a "national warning" about the "Government's true purpose regarding the 1990 census," which is to "keep tabs on everyone, especially the undesirables." They have been arrested for climbing over the fences of hidden INS detention camps in Texas.[53]

In 1988 the group organized Resist in Concert! which featured dozens of "progressive artists," with Sinead O'Connor headlining the event. At this event the group presented the first national Courageous Resister Awards to persons who "just said no." The presenters included Susan Sarandon, Robbie Conal, and Philip Agee, former CIA officer-turned-arch-traitor.[54]

C. Clark Kissinger has continued his old ways. In 2001 he was released from federal prison after a six-month sentence for making a speech in support of Mumia Abu-Jamal. Kissinger's most noteworthy quote stems from his memories of Vietnam-era activism: "I think that the largest single failing that we made during that whole period was not sending a contingent to North Vietnam to fight on the North Vietnamese side."[55] This suggests a peculiar kind of guilt that he and others did not do more to kill U.S. servicemen and further aid our enemies.

Both the Revolutionary Communist Party USA (RCP USA) and Refuse and Resist! had a difficult time adjusting to the reelection of George W. Bush in November 2004. The following month the RCP USA ran a broadside on the Refuse and Resist! Web site, evidently authored by "Chairman" Bob Avakian (not "Chair" Bob?) or one of his close colleagues. The Web site noted that someone like Bob Avakian "comes along only very rarely." The broadside is an exercise in lunacy. Bush and his people are not just ordinary Republicans nor are they ordinary Christians, but instead they are "Christian Fascists." If this group gets its way, "society will be plunged into a high-tech Dark Ages." The RCP USA notes that "Bush is dismantling democratic rights" and suppressing ordinary protests with massive force, "including even tanks in the streets." As for Bush's mandate? Well, the "will of the people was NOT expressed in this election." Therefore, "There was no real fight, and people should not grant a shred of legitimacy to Bush." And waiting for yet another Democrat to disappoint and betray people four years later "is not only worthless—it may be way too late." The only way is for revolution, led by "Chairman Bob." The following says it all:

> People have made this kind of revolution before—first in Russia, then in China. And they accomplished amazing things. In the end, however, those revolutions were finally turned back and defeated by the guardians of the old order. But building on their tremendous accomplishments—and examining deeply and unsparingly their negative experiences—Bob Avakian has brought forward a radical new "model" and vision of what this socialist society must be all about.[56]

R&R has remained busy. In February 2005 the group held a rally for Mumia Abu-Jamal in Philadelphia, and in March 2005 it held a National Day of Appreciation for Abortion Providers. At present it remains unclear just how much influence this group has. It does not represent a threat to the survival of the republic; it looks more like a theater in which juvenile fantasies of "playing at revolution" can be acted out.

SANE/FREEZE (1987)

The SANE/FREEZE movement was formed in 1987 as a result of the merger between the Committee for a SANE Nuclear Policy and the Nuclear Weapons Freeze campaign. The combined group held its founding congress in Cleveland, Ohio, and Jesse Jackson's speech (who else?) at the event drew more than one thousand persons. The group joined the International Peace Bureau, a coalition of disarmament groups.

In 1957 the Committee for a SANE Nuclear Policy was founded and launched its first ad in (where else?) the *New York Times*. In 1959 the first meeting of Hollywood SANE occurred, hosted by Steve Allen. Other members "included Marlon Brando, Henry Fonda, Marilyn Monroe, Arthur Miller, Harry Belafonte, and Ossie Davis." In 1962 SANE organized a rally on "Cuba Sunday" to express "concern and outrage over the Cuban Missile Crisis"—although it is unlikely that the outrage was directed at Nikita Khrushchev for installing long-range missiles in Cuba and initiating the crisis in the first place. By 1965 the group was an early critic of U.S. intervention in Vietnam and was quite active, organizing a rally in Madison Square Garden as well as a march on Washington.[57]

SANE was arguably the first prominent leftist movement of the post–World War II era to attract celebrities. A rally in Madison Square Garden attracted Eleanor Roosevelt, Norman Cousins, and Norman Thomas. In the early 1960s Bertrand Russell and Benjamin Spock were noted as sponsors.[58]

The U.S. effort to enhance its arsenal quickly attracted the attention of SANE and gave this group a number of fashionable causes after the Vietnam War. In 1969 it stood against the U.S. effort to develop the anti-ballistic missile (ABM). In 1972 it argued for a congressional cutoff of funds for the Vietnam War, and the next year led the effort for Congress to pass the War Powers Act. In 1977 it campaigned against both the B-1 bomber and the neutron bomb. In 1981 it was active against any major U.S. weapons programs: the Pershing II missile, the cruise missile (due for deployment in Europe), and the MX ICBM.[59] Its opposition to U.S. force improvement in the face of a relentless Soviet military buildup spanned both the Carter and Reagan administrations.

The Nuclear Weapons Freeze campaign was born in the early 1980s. The first of many nuclear-freeze resolutions was approved in (where else?) western Massachusetts. In the following year the Nuclear Weapons Freeze campaign was founded in Washington DC. In 1982 the Kennedy-Hatfield freeze resolution was introduced in the U.S. Senate, and the resolution passed the House of Representatives the following year. In 1985 the group was active in direct-action protests at the Nevada nuclear test site, and the following year the movement began to merge with SANE. In 1990 SANE/FREEZE led a public resistance to the U.S. military buildup in the Persian Gulf after the Iraqi invasion of Kuwait. In 1991 SANE/FREEZE coordinated anti–Gulf War marches in Washington and also worked with the Riverside Church Disarmament Program (New York City) to "launch a campaign against conventional arms" (but evidently only U.S. conventional arms). In 1993 the SANE/FREEZE movement was renamed Peace Action.[60]

INTERRELIGIOUS FOUNDATION FOR COMMUNITY ORGANIZATION AND PASTORS FOR PEACE (1988)

Pastors for Peace (PFP) is a special ministry of the Interreligious Foundation for Community Organization (IFCO). IFCO was founded in 1967, but its more noteworthy creation, Pastors for Peace, was established in 1988 "to pioneer the delivery of humanitarian aid to Latin America and the Caribbean."[61] Since then, thousands of people ("caravanistas") have participated in caravans to Mexico and Central America, including fourteen caravans to Cuba between 1992 and 2003. Moreover, the group has sent delegations and "work brigades" to these countries, including Cuba. Pastors for Peace is in fact a pro-Communist activity and has been one of the most consistent supporters of the Castro regime.

This group states that the embargo of Cuba is an "immoral policy that uses hunger and disease as political weapons."[62] PFP works with Cuban organizations such as the Martin Luther King Jr. Memorial Center and the Cuban Council of Churches to deliver what it calls "U.S.-Cuba Friendshipments." These deliveries mitigate the impact of the U.S. embargo and mobilize thousands of U.S. citizens "in favor of an alternative." PFP claims that all too often, "our own government impedes the healthy development of our neighbors to the south. When this is the case, we define an alternative—the 'People's Foreign Policy.'"[63] In this case, the greatest beneficiary is the Castro government. Castro welcomes ever more presents from the "caravanistas," or more accurately, the "collaboristas."

Both IFCO and Pastors for Peace were founded by Reverend Lucius Walker Jr. He had served as associate general secretary of the National Council of Churches of Christ in the USA from 1973 through 1978. His creation, IFCO, is an "ecumenical agency whose mission is to help forward the struggles of oppressed people for justice and self-determination." In 1984 he became—and remains—pastor of the Salvation Church in Brooklyn, describing himself as "dedicated to preaching the social gospel."[64] He preached this social gospel to a giant throng gathered in Havana's Plaza of the Revolution on May 1, 2003, as he urged the Cubans to "hold on to your revolution." He also complimented them on remaining "disciplined and vigilant," and stated, "You must continue to take the high moral ground." In 2000 in Havana, Reverend Walker proclaimed, "Long live the creative example of the Cuban Revolution," and had words of praise for Castro's "wisdom and heartfelt concern for the poor of the world."[65]

This is a striking contrast to the courage of the late Pope John Paul II, who stood up to Communist rule in his native Poland and elsewhere and helped to bring about the ultimate downfall of Communism in the USSR and Eastern Europe.

Some clearly appreciate Walker's efforts. The Sandinista regime in Nicaragua decorated him with the Sandino Award. The Cuban government has awarded him the Carlos Findley Award as well as the Order of Friendship.[66] In addition to his ventures in Cuba, Walker reportedly traveled frequently to Iraq as well, usually with Ramsey Clark, dropping in on Saddam Hussein's regime in earlier days.

GLOBAL EXCHANGE (1988)

Global Exchange is a group with origins in San Francisco. It was founded by Medea Benjamin in 1988. Global Exchange has long devoted its resources and manpower to a wide variety of leftist causes. It has such an antiwar stance that—in the opinion of Benjamin—the U.S.-declared war on terrorism is itself a form of terrorism.

The real agenda of this group is hidden behind a much more bland self-description found on its Web site. Global Exchange is an international human-rights organization "dedicated to promoting political, social and environmental justice globally." The group "has been working to increase global awareness among the U.S. public while building partnerships around the world."[67] In this description, the major indicator phrase is *social justice*—often a code word for some type of radical orientation. In another self-descriptive phrase of the group, it states, "We have worked to increase the U.S. public's awareness of global issues while building progressive, grass-roots international partnerships."[68] Here the key code word is *progressive*, a surefire giveaway about the group.

Among other things, Global Exchange achieves its goals through major programs such as its "political and civil rights campaigns" (which includes campaigns to improve relations with some of our country's enemies) and its "social and economic rights campaigns," focused against the World Trade Organization (WTO), World Bank, and International Monetary Fund (IMF). The group also sponsors "reality tours," which include travel to Cuba, Vietnam, South Africa, and Mexico. These tours also serve as "human rights delegations" that observe and report on events in areas of conflict.[69]

Medea Benjamin has roots in the New York City area but also lived in Cuba and was once married to a Cuban. She was then deported from Cuba for writing an anti-government article in a Cuban Communist-run newspaper.[70] She was in San Francisco in the 1980s, and in 1988 she founded Global Exchange. In 1999 *San Francisco* magazine noted that she occupied their "power list" of the "Sixty Players Who Rule the

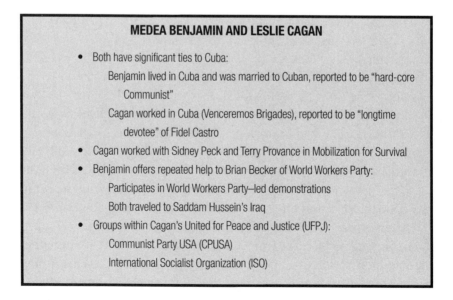

MEDEA BENJAMIN AND LESLIE CAGAN

- Both have significant ties to Cuba:
    Benjamin lived in Cuba and was married to Cuban, reported to be "hard-core Communist"
    Cagan worked in Cuba (Venceremos Brigades), reported to be "longtime devotee" of Fidel Castro
- Cagan worked with Sidney Peck and Terry Provance in Mobilization for Survival
- Benjamin offers repeated help to Brian Becker of World Workers Party:
    Participates in World Workers Party–led demonstrations
    Both traveled to Saddam Hussein's Iraq
- Groups within Cagan's United for Peace and Justice (UFPJ):
    Communist Party USA (CPUSA)
    International Socialist Organization (ISO)

Bay Area." In 2000 she ran for the Senate on the Green Party ticket from California.[71]

The deportation from Cuba evidently did not sour Benjamin on Cuba and Communism, for "many of the causes that she backs are Communist in nature." Most of the antiwar demonstrations in which she has participated have been led by the Workers World Party or its front groups, and in the 1980s she vehemently "opposed U.S. military aid to those who were fighting against Communist forces in Central America."[72] Benjamin has been described as a "hard-core Communist," and is also a "longtime comrade" of Leslie Cagan of United for Peace and Justice (UFPJ). In addition, Benjamin has enthusiastically joined Workers World Party (WWP) officials (such as Brian Becker) in shrill denunciations of U.S. policy at rallies on October 26, 2002, and January 19, 2003. She and Becker have both made the pilgrimage to Saddam's Iraq as well.

Passionately anti-capitalist, Benjamin is widely seen to be a chief organizer behind the 1999 Seattle riots in which some fifty thousand protesters did millions of dollars' worth of damage in an effort to shut down meetings of the WTO.[73]

Global Exchange has allied itself strongly with similar groups that emerged after 2000, including UFPJ and CodePink. In 2002 Benjamin went to Afghanistan to meet people with relatives who had died in the U.S. bombing there.[74] She had nothing to say about the Taliban's culpability in forcing the war by refusing to hand over Osama bin Laden and his henchmen—as President Bush had demanded in the weeks before the U.S. air strikes. This was an opportunity for her to weigh in against the U.S. effort and to urge Americans to examine the "root causes" of resistance to the United States in the Arab world.

In December 2004–January 2005, Benjamin was involved in a joint effort with CodePink to bring $600,000 in medical supplies and cash to the terrorists and their supporters who were fighting Americans in Fallujah, Iraq.[75] The choice of Fallujah is most revealing, as it has been the epicenter of the most violent resistance to the U.S. military in the country—one of the main points of the deadly Sunni Triangle. It is also the notorious city in which the bodies of four U.S. contractors were mutilated, burned, and hanged from a bridge. (That did not seem to bother Benjamin on her trip.) This aid to Fallujah was barely reported in the world's media, but it was reported that Rep. Henry Waxman (D-CA) had written a letter to the U.S. ambassador in Amman, Jordan, to help facilitate the transport of this aid to Iraq.

INTERNATIONAL ACTION CENTER (1992)

The WWP created the International Action Center (IAC) in 1992, and the IAC serves first and foremost as a front for the WWP and its activities. The IAC has two major offices, one in Boston and the other in San Francisco. The group's Web site says nothing substantive or revealing about its origins.

Ramsey Clark founded the WWP. The activities of this disgraced former U.S. attorney general alone would be enough to fill another book, but suffice to say that he has undertaken just about every possible action within his power to weaken or cripple the United States, to campaign on the side of its enemies, and to give whatever aid and comfort he can to anti-American regimes and causes. Clark returned to Baghdad in late 2005 to offer legal aid to Saddam Hussein at his trial. At present, two co-directors of the IAC are Brian Becker and Larry Holmes, who also sit on the secretariat of the WWP. Radical lawyer Lynne Stewart is also a member of the IAC.

Becker is one of the most notorious. In August 2002 he went to Iraq as part of a Ramsey Clark delegation. In an article in *Workers World,* he bitterly condemned the "lawless aggression" of the "imperialist" and "racist" U.S. air patrols enforcing the no-fly zone over Iraq. In early 2000 Becker went to North Korea to help build what he termed a "movement of genuine solidarity" with the brutal regime of Kim Jong-il. A writer from the WWP newspaper notes that the Becker party was deeply impressed by the North. The misty-eyed article in the WWP paper notes, "Wherever we went and whomever we spoke with, what impressed us the most was the unbreakable determination of the North Korean people to defend their socialist society against U.S. imperialism."[76]

Larry Holmes is cut of the same cloth. He was part of an IAC delegation at a Baghdad antiwar conference in September 2002—"in solidarity with Iraq," as he put it. While there he stated, "We know Bush and his clique want to divert attention away from rising joblessness, poverty and misery among our brothers and sisters. The capitalist crisis is very deep. Underneath there's a catastrophic capitalist crisis in the making." Holmes concluded an article about the trip with the telling words: "We not only want to stop the war; we want to bring the war home where it belongs."[77] Those words could easily be taken to mean opening up an Iraqi-supported military or terrorist action within the United States. It was a clear-cut throwback to the Vietnam phrase, "Bring the war home."

Seen in this light, there is no fundamental difference between Clark, Becker, and Holmes. Their sentiments appear to be nearly identical, and this troika appears to operate with a degree of coordination in their trips abroad to some of the world's most sinister regimes.

The IAC is an integral player in the constellation of present-day anti-war and anti-U.S. groups. For example, the IAC was a signatory to a February 2002 document composed by the radical group Refuse and Resist! This document condemned military tribunals and the detention of immigrants apprehended in connection with the post–9/11 investigations. The IAC is an integral member of United for Peace and Justice. The IAC has campaigned for increased wages and benefits to immigrant workers,

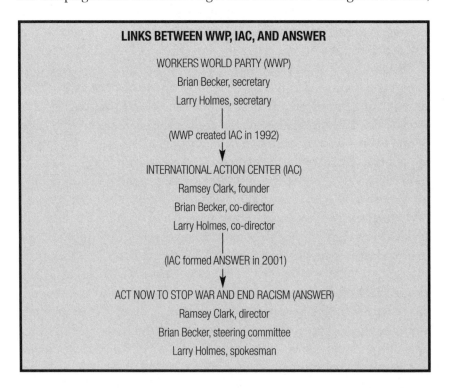

LINKS BETWEEN WWP, IAC, AND ANSWER

WORKERS WORLD PARTY (WWP)

Brian Becker, secretary

Larry Holmes, secretary

(WWP created IAC in 1992)

INTERNATIONAL ACTION CENTER (IAC)

Ramsey Clark, founder

Brian Becker, co-director

Larry Holmes, co-director

(IAC formed ANSWER in 2001)

ACT NOW TO STOP WAR AND END RACISM (ANSWER)

Ramsey Clark, director

Brian Becker, steering committee

Larry Holmes, spokesman

including those now living illegally in the United States; it has also advocated that women be given unrestricted access to taxpayer-funded abortions at any stage of pregnancy.

Just as the WWP "created the IAC," so the IAC created International ANSWER in 2001. As officials of the WWP and IAC who appear at ANSWER rallies and demonstrations are not identified by their true affiliation, it is impossible for most laymen to determine their true colors. Simply put, the IAC provides cover for WWP officials to operate. The three organizations work in lockstep, as there has been close coordination of their activities ever since the creation of ANSWER.[78]

PEACE ACTION (1993)

In 1993 SANE/FREEZE was renamed Peace Action (PA). By the following year it had already made its mark in the U.S. Congress. Rep. Cynthia McKinney (D-GA) and Senator Mark Hatfield (R-OR) introduced legislation that it created to restrict U.S. weapon sales to "dictators and human-rights abusers." In 1995 Peace Action led a "national dialogue" during America's Days of Collective Guilt, Shame, and Hand-Wringing, otherwise known as the anniversaries of the bombings of Hiroshima and Nagasaki.[79]

In 1997 Peace Action celebrated its so-called fortieth anniversary (actually the anniversary of SANE) with gala events in Boston, New York, and Washington DC. (There was no mention of such events in the South, Midwest, or other "flyover states" in the U.S. heartland.) Among the congressional darlings who spoke or who were honored at this august gathering were Rep. Ronald Dellums (D-CA), Senator Tom Harkin (D-IA), and Rep. Cynthia McKinney (D-GA).[80]

More recently, Peace Action staged the largest demonstration in the history of the Los Alamos National Laboratory in New Mexico on "Nagasaki Day." The demonstration was led by actor Martin Sheen, who managed to take time off from his pressing duties at *The West Wing*. Peace Action's Web site notes that the group responded to the terrorist attacks of September 11, 2001, "with a call for Justice not War." In 2003 Peace Action launched the Campaign for a New Foreign Policy, aimed at a foreign policy based on "human rights and democracy, nuclear disarmament and international cooperation."[81]

In 2004 Peace Action participated in the anti-Bush jihad, along with many other leftist groups. In March 2004, for the first time in the movement's history (which it dates back to 1957), the group "disendorsed" a presidential candidate, formally calling for his defeat. Kevin Martin, the executive director of the Peace Action PAC, stated, "George W. Bush's foreign policy is counterintuitive, radical and dangerous." Because of Bush's pursuit of security through aggression and unilateralism, its planned building of new U.S. nuclear weapons and its exportation of the weapons around the world, "Bush has pushed this country and the world towards a cataclysm rather than towards safety."[82] In June 2004 Peace Action joined with UFPJ and the Win Without War group in a series of marches, vigils, educational forums, and leaflet campaigns to "express the deep and growing opposition to Bush administration policies." For them it was a happy coincidence with the opening of Michael Moore's latest deceptive film *Fahrenheit 9/11*. Kevin Martin noted, "The June 30th 'transfer' of sovereignty is nothing but another deception by the Bush administration—a PR stunt."[83]

MOVEON.ORG (1998)

MoveOn.org (called MoveOn hereafter) is one of the best-known of liberal political groups to emerge in the current era. The key to its operation is its ability to organize and inform an online community that is estimated to number around two million people. Originally begun in 1998 as an e-mail group that petitioned Congress to "move on" past the impeachment proceedings against President Bill Clinton, "MoveOn grew to national prominence for its strong disapproval of the 2003 invasion of Iraq." Since then, it devoted much of its effort to defeating President Bush in November 2004 and beyond that to oppose any initiative that comes from the White House.

This group is made up of three distinct organizations: MoveOn.org, "a 501(c)(4) organization that primarily focuses on education and advocacy on important national issues"; MoveOn PAC, which exists primarily to help members "elect candidates who reflect the organization's values"; and MoveOn.org Voter Fund, one of the so-called 527 organizations that "runs advertising and other activities" to persuade voters.

In 2004 this last group ran many ads in the "battleground" states criticizing the Bush administration's policies.[84]

MoveOn uses e-mail as its "main conduit for communicating with members." Nearly every e-mail "encourages recipients to forward it to others who share an interest in the topic." The MoveOn Web site also uses multimedia, "including videos, audio downloads, and images." The group's Action Forum is like a blog in which members write on issues they think are important, thus establishing the group's priorities. In this way, the most popular ideas rise to the top. In short, the group is quite sophisticated on the Web. It has the addresses of all its members and can organize them to Zip Code-plus-four, which itself is a great asset for influencing campaigns. Also, the group has ample funds and is not dependent on foundations for its continued survival.[85]

There is no pretense of objectivity by any part of this group. The *Washington Post* notes that MoveOn has created pressure within the Democratic Party for a "vigorously liberal agenda" that goes "beyond simple opposition to the Bush administration."[86] MoveOn founder Wes Boyd rejects the advice of "centrists" such as the Democratic Leadership Council, who call for the party to moderate its position on foreign and domestic policies. Boyd noted in mid-2003, "The primary war to build trust is to consistently fight for things that people care about." This suggests that Boyd knows precisely what "the people" care about.

MoveOn does not operate in a vacuum. It is a member group of United for Peace and Justice (UFPJ) and collaborates with UFPJ on specific issues. In addition, MoveOn has collaborated with the ACLU, the Center for American Progress (CAP), and the Natural Resources Defense Council (NRDC).[87] Its cooperation with the UFPJ and ACLU says a great deal about MoveOn's true colors. It also benefits from George Soros's Open Society Institute (OSI); Soros gave MoveOn a large donation (cited as between $1.6 and $5 million) before the 2004 presidential election. The group has also benefited from donations from Peter B. Lewis, chief executive of the Progressive Corporation ($500,000).[88]

The command structure of MoveOn is made up of several individuals. Wes Boyd and Joan Blades, two former entrepreneurs in Silicon Valley, are the co-founders. Carrie Olson is chief operating officer, and Peter Schurman is the executive director. Zach Exley, the author of two anti-Bush Web sites, also joined this group. He was once associated

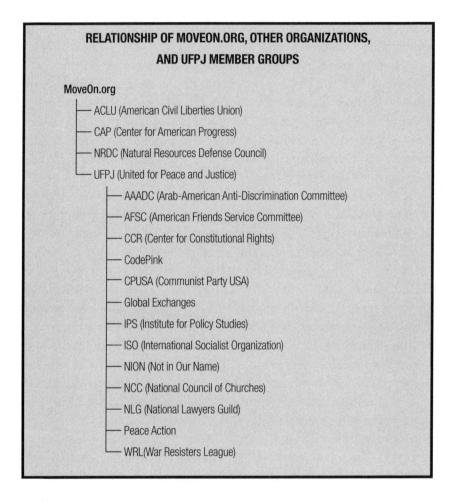

RELATIONSHIP OF MOVEON.ORG, OTHER ORGANIZATIONS, AND UFPJ MEMBER GROUPS

MoveOn.org
- ACLU (American Civil Liberties Union)
- CAP (Center for American Progress)
- NRDC (Natural Resources Defense Council)
- UFPJ (United for Peace and Justice)
    - AAADC (Arab-American Anti-Discrimination Committee)
    - AFSC (American Friends Service Committee)
    - CCR (Center for Constitutional Rights)
    - CodePink
    - CPUSA (Communist Party USA)
    - Global Exchanges
    - IPS (Institute for Policy Studies)
    - ISO (International Socialist Organization)
    - NION (Not in Our Name)
    - NCC (National Council of Churches)
    - NLG (National Lawyers Guild)
    - Peace Action
    - WRL(War Resisters League)

with the Howard Dean campaign in 2004. Also joining MoveOn is John Hlinko, the senior consultant and political director. Hlinko is an online guerrilla marketing and PR specialist who is known to be a supporter of Bill Maher (infamous for the crack that the 9/11 terrorists had "courage"). Both Exley and Hlinko are well known in the Hard-Left activist circles.[89]

One of the best-known officials is Eli Pariser, the group's campaign director. In the days following 9/11, Pariser launched an online petition calling for a "restrained and multi-lateral response" to the terrorist attacks. In early 2005, Pariser stated (about the Democrats), "Now it's our Party: we bought it, we own it, and we're going to take it back." This revealed that MoveOn has attached itself to the party like a leech—whether Democrats like it or not.

The most noteworthy political figures known to be members include Donna Brazile, James Carville, and Al Gore. There is also a sprinkling of actors, musicians, and comics (remember Al Franken?). Film directors are especially noteworthy members, and include Richard Linklater, Michael Mann, arch-distorter Michael Moore, Errol Morris, John Sayles, and Gus Van Sant.[90]

Nearly all of the group's statements bear close scrutiny, for MoveOn notoriously bends the truth. Take, for example, the statement, "Questions are swirling around whether the election was conducted honestly or not."[91] This statement seeks to delegitimize the 2004 election of President Bush, lumping it in the same category as the so-called stolen election of 2000—even though Bush's margin of victory was greater in 2004. The assertion is designed to create doubt or confusion in the minds of many who voted in 2004. Also consider the group's claim that one of its "victories" is "to repudiate the torture of prisoners of war."[92] This statement implies that torture is a systematic policy of U.S. authorities who hold terrorists, radical Islamic militants, or insurgents in captivity, and it further suggests that all of them are to be considered POWs. This statement by itself is a double-barreled insult to the intelligence of most people. It was fashionably in use when MoveOn strongly opposed the confirmation of Alberto Gonzales as attorney general, since he was alleged to be "notorious for opening the door to torture" at the Abu Ghraib and Guantanamo Bay prisons.

Additional scare tactics have been brought out in MoveOn's effort to derail President Bush's plans to reform the Social Security system. The group claims that he has made a priority of "phasing out Social Security as we know it." In one commercial entitled "WMD," the group states, "Now George Bush is misleading us about Social Security." Its commercial entitled "Working Retirement" suggests that many people's retirement plans are in peril in the face of Social Security reforms. Moreover, the group claims, "Privatization means benefit cuts of up to 46%."[93]

MoveOn can reach a large audience. It appears to be a vehicle primarily for reaching those who already share its leftist views, but it can also reach out to untold number of undecideds as well. There is no doubt that MoveOn can influence a wide circle of people with its approach that features sowing doubt and confusion, insulting one's intelligence, fear-mongering, and distortion. The MoveOn Web site claims that founders Joan Blades and Wes Boyd "shared deep frustration with the partisan warfare in Washington DC," yet—isn't it odd?—they and their colleagues have done much to accelerate and sharpen partisan warfare in recent years.

7

GROUPS, LEADERS, AND THEIR LINKAGES
2000–PRESENT

SEVERAL NEW GROUPS HAVE emerged during the so-called Age of Bush. All of them have made sustained efforts to distort, denigrate, and demonize U.S. policy during this period. A close look at these various organizations reveals a confluence of ideology as well as varying levels of coordination between them. The mainstream media have largely ignored the interaction between the modern-day groups and their ties to predecessor organizations.

INTERNATIONAL ANSWER (2001)

International ANSWER stands for Act Now to Stop War and End Racism (the name is shorted to ANSWER hereafter). The organization formed just days after the terrorist attacks on Washington and New York in late September 2001. As indicated earlier, ANSWER owes its existence to the Workers World Party (WWP) and the International Action Center (IAC).[1] Conclusive proof of its orientation is found in its directorship. Remember the troika of the IAC? Ramsey Clark is director of ANSWER, Brian Becker is on its steering committee, and Larry Holmes is a major spokesman of the organization.

Further examination reveals that ANSWER's national office in New York City is the same as the national office of the IAC. The same identical-address situation is also true for offices in Washington DC as well as Los Angeles. Moreover, the contact numbers for ANSWER in several East Coast cities are the same as the contact numbers for IAC. In other cities, the contact numbers for ANSWER are the same as those for the WWP in those cities. In other words, "When a person calls AN-SWER, he is in effect calling the International Action Center and the Workers World Party."[2]

Significantly, ANSWER has been the driving force in each of the major demonstrations in Washington DC since 2002. It organized one on October 26, 2002, was the main organizer of International Mobilization Day on April 12, 2003, sponsored the one on January 18, 2003, and chaired one on January 20, 2005. During the October 26, 2002, demonstration, each member of the IAC troika spoke. Becker and Holmes were credited with organizing and orchestrating the January 18, 2003, demonstration, and Ramsey Clark addressed that gathering. Becker and Clark addressed the January 20, 2005, demonstration, and local ANSWER officials Peta Lindsey and Eugene Puryear were the local ANSWER organizers.[3]

At these demonstrations, "which the media usually portrays as a gathering of mainstream Americans," speaker after speaker condemns the United States with traditional Communist rhetoric. Terms such as *struggle, oppressed peoples, imperialism, revolution,* and *liberation* are bandied about. One speaker once addressed her fellow protesters as *comrades.*[4] As Byron York puts it, "More than a decade after the fall of the Soviet Union, and long after most Americans stopped worrying about the Red Menace, a significant part of the movement that has risen up in opposition to war in Iraq is, in essence, a Communist front."[5] This reflects the fact that some Islamic groups and their supporters have been working with various Communist-oriented groups over the past thirty years, as they share a common enemy—the United States.

At the same time there is widespread acceptance of the role of the WWP and IAC. One reason is the organizational skills they bring. These groups are able to outhustle and outorganize others in the practical work of getting parade permits, organizing big events, and providing logistics. One authority notes, "It causes division among the non-authoritarian

Left groups. They say, 'Do we march at a rally organized by a group like this? I don't feel comfortable with this, but it's the only game in town.'"[6]

These rallies are all conducted in the same way. There are information and merchandise tables put out by a variety of left-wing and Communist organizations, those that have "paid ANSWER a fee for permission to distribute literature or merchandise." There is an elevated stage with a massive sound system. After a musical prelude, the speeches begin—usually more than a dozen. The speakers may include celebrities, politicians (such as those from the Democratic Progressive

NOTEWORTHY FIGURES AT WASHINGTON DEMONSTRATIONS ORGANIZED OR SPONSORED BY ANSWER

October 26, 2002

Brian Becker (WWP, IAC, ANSWER)	Jesse Jackson
Medea Benjamin (GE)	C. Clark Kissinger (RCP, R&R! NION)
Ramsey Clark (IAC, ANSWER)	Cynthia McKinney (D-GA)
Leslie Feinberg (WWP)	Al Sharpton
Sara Flounders (WWP)	Lynne Stewart (IAC)
Larry Holmes (WWP, IAC, ANSWER)	

January 18, 2003

Brian Becker (WWP, IAC, ANSWER)	Sara Flounders (WWP)
Medea Benjamin (GE)	Larry Holmes (WWP, IAC, ANSWER)
Ramsey Clark (IAC, ANSWER)	Jesse Jackson
John Conyers (D-MI)	Jennifer Wager (Cuban Five)

January 20, 2005

Brian Becker (WWP, IAC, ANSWER)	Tom Hayden
Medea Benjamin (GE)	Nathalie Hrizi (Cuban Five)
Phyllis Bennis (IPS)	Jesse Jackson
Leslie Cagan (UFPJ)	Dennis Kucinich
Ramsey Clark (IAC, ANSWER)	Peta Lindsey (event co-chairman)
David Cobb (Green Party)	Eugene Puryear (event co-chairman)
Jodie Evans (CodePink)	Brenda Stokley
Kim Gandy (NOW)	Zack Wolfe
Amy Goodman (Democracy Now!)	James Zogby (Arab-American Institute)
Graylan Hagler (Plymouth Cong. Church)	

Caucus), or various activists. The speeches are often exercises in shrill demonization of the United States and its policies. After the speeches, "the attendees march along the route to the location of the final rally," where they find more literature and merchandise. At various stages, the ANSWER volunteers move through the crowd with large buckets for cash donations.[7]

Many of these groups are drawn together—and overlook the pedigree of ANSWER—because of their hatred for George Bush. The signs they carried at one event "seethed with rage and condescension." Typical of those found in January 2003 were: "He Is A Moron . . . And A Bully," or "Bush, Cheney, Rumsfeld: The Real Axis of Evil." By now you get the picture.

NOT IN OUR NAME (2002)

Not in Our Name (NION) is a Hard-Leftist group founded in March 2002 to resist the U.S. government's course of action after the terrorist attacks of September 11, 2001. The beginnings of NION track right along with the founding of ANSWER. Members of the Workers World Party (WWP) founded the latter group on the eve of the U.S. military campaign against Afghanistan. NION was founded six months later mostly by "members of the Revolutionary Communist Party USA (RCP USA), which continues to be prominent among its leadership."[8] C. Clark Kissinger is a spokesman for NION, and Mary Lou Greenberg is a director of the group.

One difference between the groups is that NION is believed to be "less specifically a front group." Compared with ANSWER, NION has a broader set of endorsers and is generally seen as a "cooperative participant in the broader antiwar movement." Moreover, the RCP USA does not impose its specific positions on NION to the degree that the International Action Center (IAC) does on ANSWER, according to writers Michael Albert and Stephen Shalom. In addition, NION—unlike ANSWER—is itself a member of United for Peace and Justice (UFPJ).[9]

NION's statement of conscience, drafted in early 2002, lists a series of criticisms of the Bush administration and the U.S. Congress and calls on the people of the United States "to resist the politics and overall political direction" that have emerged since 9/11, which pose "grave dangers to the peoples of the world." The statement deplores the U.S. "spirit of revenge" and "simplistic script of good vs. evil," and refers to the USA PATRIOT Act as symbolizing repression. The statement concludes, "We will resist the machinery of war and rally others to do everything possible to stop it."[10]

Various signers of the statement collectively made up a who's who of the Far Left. Among others, they include Medea Benjamin, Noam Chomsky, Ramsey Clark, Angela Davis, Carl Dix, Bernardine Dohrn, Daniel Ellsberg, Jane Fonda, Tom Hayden, Rev. Jesse Jackson, Spike Lee, Rep. Jim McDermott (D-WA), Rep. Cynthia McKinney (D-GA), Rev. Al Sharpton, Martin Sheen, Gloria Steinem, Oliver Stone, Kurt Vonnegut, Howard Zinn, and some fifty-three Maryknoll priests and brothers.[11]

At the time of the second inauguration of George Bush in 2004, NION could not resist making another public statement. First, the group noted that George Bush does not speak for or represent the NION signers and does not act in their name. This statement adds, "No election, whether fair or fraudulent, can legitimize criminal wars on foreign countries, torture, the wholesale violation of human rights, and the end of science and reason." By reading the latest statement, you would discover that our government is sending our youth "to destroy entire cities" and has "carried out torture and detentions without trial around the world." (Hmm, in all 192 countries?) The groups also states, "Not in our name will we allow further crimes to be committed against nations or individuals deemed to stand in the way of the goal of unquestioned world supremacy." This statement was paired with a reference to Syria, Iran, and North Korea—a tacit admission that NION would give a free pass to any of those countries and their policies. The Bush regime, after all, is "nothing but a nightmare for humanity," according to the recent statement.[12]

This statement was yet another sentimental gathering of lefties. The signers this time included Ed Asner, Michael Avery (president of the National Lawyers Guild), Medea Benjamin, Phyllis Bennis (Institute for Policy Studies), Leslie Cagan (United for Peace and Justice), Noam Chomsky, Ramsey Clark, Angela Davis, Daniel Ellsberg, C. Clark Kissinger (Revolutionary Communist Party and Refuse and Resist!), Rep. James McDermott (D-WA), Michael Ratner (Center for Constitutional Studies), Roberta Segal-Sklar (National Gay and Lesbian Task Force), "Starhawk" (a woman who claims to be a witch), and Howard Zinn.[13] If anything, this gathering likely was more color-ful than the one in 2002.

But NION does more than issue signed statements. In August 2004 the group planned a confrontational demonstration in New York City on the night President Bush was to accept the nomination of the Republican Party. NION hoped to "disrupt the convention" by having its march leaders follow a route different from the one that had been submitted in advance to the police. This was a "planned provocation" that had a good chance of ending in violence. Mary Lou Greenberg, a director of NION and a Revolutionary Communist Party USA (RCP USA) member, devel-oped the idea of the march, along with Joe Urgo (also an RCP USA mem-ber). This event pointed out that NION believed—as do other antiwar groups—"that Republicans are more of a threat" than al-Qaeda or the Baathists," according to Michael P. Tremoglie. He notes, "Peace is not even a tertiary consideration for them—destabilizing the United States is. NION, and the other 'peace' groups" are linked to Communist, Is-lamist, and anti-capitalist groups."[14]

Some who have worked with NION have become disillusioned. One individual stated, "I have worked with all three major groups, AN-SWER, UFPJ, and NION, and know how they work together." He was fed up with NION because it is a "vanguard group" whose real objective is to lead people to their ideology and "not do anything for peace." He was particularly upset with the "Communists who run the show."[15] The same person also noted that the leaders of UFPJ, ANSWER, and NION ensured that violence would take place at the Republican National Con-vention in New York City.

PROGRESSIVE DONOR NETWORK (2002)

The Progressive Donor Network (PDN) was formed in April 2002. It re-mains a little-known group but has the potential to be a key asset for liberal causes. According to *Business Week* and SourceWatch, former Clinton White House staffer Mike Lux (a co-founder of the PDN) "had begun meeting with some 150 liberal groups." This so-called Progres-sive Donor Network had hoped to become a "one-stop account" for lib-eral givers who once wrote large checks to the Democratic National Committee (DNC).

Early on this group was aligned with the most powerful of the Democratic Party's special-interest groups. These included People for the American Way (PFAW), NARAL (formerly the National Abortion and Reproductive Rights Action League), the National Association for the Advancement of Colored People (NAACP), the League of Conservation Voters (LCV), and labor groups.[16]

During the time of the group's opening conference in Washington DC, it received public support from selected members of Congress: former Senate majority leader Tom Daschle (D-SD), Senators Barbara Boxer (D-CA) and John Edwards (D-NC), House minority leader Richard Gephardt (D-MO), and former Democratic National Committee (DNC) chairman Terry McAuliffe. Boxer has stated that the group will be "vital for liberal candidates."

Former Clinton administration officials attending the conference included James Carville, Paul Begala, Joe Lockhart, and Gore 2000 campaign manager Donna Brazile.[17]

PDN documents suggest that the group will raise and spend money on targeted television and radio markets and by phone and mail solicitation "using a network of allied organizations," according to SourceWatch.

The group's goals also include forming what are called "rapid response teams" to plant news stories critical of Republicans and the Bush administration. One example from 2004 was the series of negative news stories about the collapse of Enron, which had ties to the White House.[18]

Some opponents of this group have called its formation hypocritical. Roberta Combs, president of the Christian Coalition, stated, "Just weeks after campaign finance reform was signed into law, Democrats are trying to circumvent it. The Democratic Party is now trying to ensure that their own special interests gain even more power." Rep. Bob Barr (R-GA) stated that he was not surprised: "It's sort of the ultimate Washington hypocrisy that you work to support reform publicly but undermine it privately."[19]

UNITED FOR PEACE AND JUSTICE (2002)

One of the most influential groups to emerge in recent years is United for Peace and Justice (UFPJ). The group describes itself as a "coalition of more than 800 local and national groups throughout the United

States who have joined together to oppose our government's policy of permanent warfare and empire building."[20] According to its Web site, since its founding in October 2002, it has spurred "hundreds of protests and rallies" around the United States and organized "the two largest demonstrations against the Iraq War."

At an initial meeting in Washington DC, more than seventy peace and justice organizations agreed to form UFPJ and coordinate their efforts to oppose the war in Iraq. The UFPJ Web site claims that in February 2003 it organized a rally at the UN headquarters in New York City that drew more than five hundred thousand participants. It further claims that in March 2003 it "mobilized more than three hundred thousand people for a protest march down Broadway in New York City."[21]

The highlight for 2004 was its march in March on the one-year anniversary of the start of the Iraq War. UFPJ claimed that "more than two million people worldwide took to the streets" in more than sixty countries. By contrast, in March 2005, various sources reported that antiwar marches in major U.S. cities drew "hundreds" on the second anniversary of the start of the Iraq War.

The organization jelled in June 2003 when many representatives from diverse groups gathered in Chicago at its first strategy and planning conference. The gathering was aimed to help stop the Bush administration's program of "permanent war" as well as to solidify UFPJ's organizational structure.[22]

The guiding force and elected leadership body is the steering committee, which has authority over all financial instruments and media (Web sites, Listservs, and e-mail accounts). Some thirty-five people were elected in 2003 to serve on the group's national steering committee. Among them were Andrea Buffa of Global Exchange, Jen Geiger of the Women's International League for Peace and Freedom (WILPF), Judith LeBlanc of the Communist Party, Kevin Martin of Peace Action, Ignacio Meneses of the National Network on Cuba, Gael Murphy of CodePink, Baltazar Pinguel of the American Friends Service Committee (AFSC), and Amy Quinn of the Institute for Policy Studies (IPS).[23]

A look at the group's criteria for selecting the steering committee's structure tells something about its mind-set. "To ensure that the Steering Committee of UFPJ represents the diversity of the peace and justice constituencies in the United States," it adopted the following criteria: at least 50 percent of the steering committee must be women, at least 50 percent must be "people of color," at least 20 percent must be youth and students (under age twenty-five), and at least 15 percent must be "Lesbian/Gay/Bi/Transgender-identified persons."[24]

Even the choice of the words *steering committee* and *peace and justice* is suggestive, indicating that some terms never go out of style. The former Vietnam Veterans Against the War also had a steering committee. Moreover, there was an earlier group called the People's Coalition for Peace and Justice (PCPJ), a militant antiwar group with clear-cut Communist ties.

As of August 2004 there were noteworthy groups within the organization.[25] These included:

- Arab-American Anti-Discrimination Committee (AAADC)
- American Friends Service Committee (AFSC)
- Center for Constitutional Rights
- CodePink
- Communist Party USA (CPUSA)
- Global Exchange
- Institute for Policy Studies (IPS)

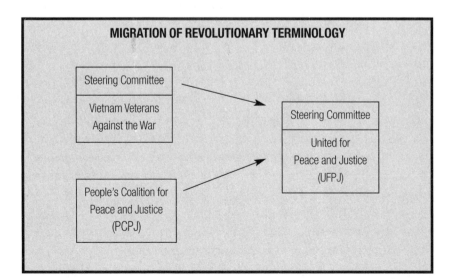

- International Socialist Organization (ISO)
- MoveOn
- Not in Our Name (NION)
- National Council of Churches (NCC)
- National Lawyers Guild (NLG)
- National Organization for Women (NOW)
- Peace Action
- Rainbow/Push Coalition
- Refuse & Resist!
- War Resisters League

Seen in this way, UFPJ is a unique commingling of antiwar groups, social justice militants, declared Communists, those fronting for Communist countries and movements, and apologists and supporters of radical Islamic movements. Thus it is not surprising that UFPJ argues, "The war on Iraq was the leading edge of a relentless drive for a U.S. empire," and that the U.S. government seeks to "impose right-wing policies at home under the cover of fighting terrorism."[26]

The origins of UFPJ are worth noting. According to Ben Johnson, People for the American Way (PFAW) created UFPJ and also chose Leslie Cagan as its leader.[27] PFAW reportedly was in search of a group other than ANSWER to sponsor peace rallies when the radical nature of ANSWER became known. This information is not reflected in the Web sites of either PFAW or UFPJ.

UFPJ founder and thus-far only leader Cagan is clearly one of the most dedicated, militant, and hard-line activists of all those opposed to current U.S. policies. Cagan has remained a Communist even after the fall of the Berlin Wall. She was earlier in Cuba with the Venceremos Brigades (a volunteer group of young people who elected to help with the sugar harvests). She had earlier worked for Sidney Peck and Terry Provance in the Mobilization for Survival. Peck and Provance are two seasoned and veteran pro-Communists who are passionately opposed to U.S. policies. Cagan is also described as a "lifelong devotee of Fidel Castro and the Socialist Party, USA."[28] Along with Medea Benjamin, Cagan is described as a "hard-core Communist," and she and Benjamin are "longtime comrades" (they both have deep ties with Cuba, among other things).

Significantly, UFPJ has joined with a host of other radical groups in

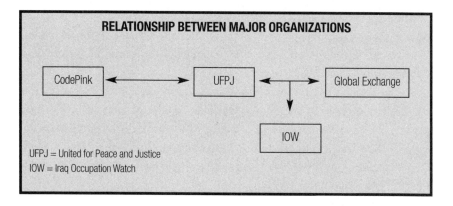

recent years. It has teamed up with Global Exchange (Medea Benjamin), one noteworthy result of which was the creation of a group called Iraq Occupation Watch (IOW, see below). IOW has Cagan, Benjamin, and Phyllis Bennis of the IPS on its current board. IOW operates a group called the International Occupation Watch Center (IOWC) in Iraq, which is led by Gael Murphy. In addition, UFPJ works closely with CodePink. UFPJ collaborates with MoveOn, and MoveOn is a member group of the UFPJ coalition.

UFPJ states that it is not a single-issue organization. It issued a blanket statement describing itself as a "movement-building coalition" that coordinates and supports the work of existing groups and builds linkages and solidarity where none exist. "We will link the wars abroad with the assaults at home, and U.S. militarism to the corporate economic interests it serves."[29] The code words here are *solidarity* and *corporate economic interests*, which say everything about its orientation. The group had prepared a No Stolen Elections campaign and was prepared to take up widespread protest and civil disobedience in the event of significant fraud in the 2004 election.[30] But no such fraud was detected.

CODEPINK (2002)

Four individuals formed CodePink in November 2002: Jodie Evans, Medea Benjamin, Diane Wilson, and "radical Wiccan activist" Starhawk. They and about one hundred other women quickly became a presence on the streets of Washington DC and established a four-month vigil in front of the White House. The group is self-described as a "woman-initiated grass-roots peace and social justice movement that seeks positive social change through proactive, creative protest and nonviolent direct action."[31]

Evans made headlines at the Republican National Convention in 2004 when she was ejected from Madison Square Garden after disrupting the prime-time addresses of speakers at the podium. Earlier in the week Benjamin was dragged out of the convention for the same reason. Evans also sits on the board of directors of the Rain Forest Action Network (RAN), "a coalition of anti-capitalist, anti-corporate environmentalist groups." The co-founder of RAN, Michael Roselle, "also founded the Earth Liberation Front (ELF), which the FBI ranks alongside the Animal Liberation Front (ALF)" as the primary domestic terrorism threats in the United States.[32]

CodePink describes itself as an outrageous group: "We call on women around the world to rise up and oppose the war in Iraq. We call on grandmothers, sisters and daughters, students, teachers, healers, artists, singers, poets, and every ordinary outraged woman willing to be outrageous for peace." CodePink calls for "all outraged women to join us in taking a stand now" and engages in "outrageous acts of dissent."[33]

One of the groups' most outrageous acts was the joint effort with Global Exchange to deliver some $600,000 in money and medicine to the hard-core insurgent center of Fallujah. (See Global Exchange above.) CodePink and Global Exchange thus teamed up to provide substantial aid and comfort to America's enemies. This brought back memories of those unofficial U.S. delegations to North Vietnam that were so fashionable in the late 1960s and early 1970s. Never feeling a shortage of self-importance, those who participated in this effort of December 2004–January 2005 noted the "historic nature" of the delegation and were thrilled that Aljazeera, Dubai television, and Iranian television followed the group "assiduously" from the moment they arrived in Amman, Jordan. If anything, this smacks of pandering to hostile media abroad. Possibly the most ludicrous statement to emerge from that trip was the comparison between the tsunami in Southeast Asia of December 26, 2004, which killed well over 270,000 persons, and a "man-made disaster of similar proportions: the invasion and occupation of Iraq."[34]

This statement is doubly insulting to anyone's intelligence, as it trivializes the deaths of the tsunami victims as well as extraordinary efforts by the U.S. military to limit collateral damage beyond immediate combat areas.

Another outrageous act is the group's propensity to send peace delegations to other hot spots. Its Web site notes that it generates such delegations to "Israel-Palestine" as well as to both North and South Korea.[35] It remains uncertain what—if any—good has come from CodePink's interjecting itself into the delicate balance of powers that are trying to work out a cease-fire and ultimate resolution to the Israel-Palestine issue. It is equally difficult to imagine what leverage it could have on the tyrannical regime of Kim Jong-il in North Korea. Perhaps the peace delegates might tell him to be resolute in standing up to the "U.S. imperialists."

According to John Perazzo, "in addition to scorning America's military action in Iraq, CodePink members also condemn the racism, sexism, poverty, corporate corruption, and environmental degradation they claim are rampant" in the United States. "In this respect, CodePink is like other prominent peace movements in our country—portraying America as a moral cesspool and an imperialist aggressor, while remaining mute about whatever barbarities occur anywhere else on earth. Not even the pre-war atrocities of Saddam Hussein drew a scintilla of condemnation from CodePink."[36]

A system of interlocking leadership positions has emerged in recent years. Medea Benjamin, for example, is a founder of United for Peace and Justice (UFPJ), the head of Global Exchange, a founder of Code-Pink, and a member of the board of directors of Iraq Occupation Watch. Leslie Cagan is a founder and a steering committee member of UFPJ. Andrea Buffa is on the steering committee of UFPJ, a member of Global Exchange, and also serves with CodePink. Finally, Gael Murphy is on the steering committee of UFPJ, on the executive committee of Code-Pink, and on the board of Iraq Occupation Watch. This type of meshing guarantees a level of coordination. It is inevitable that these individuals see eye to eye on most issues, united in their venomous contempt for U.S. policies, the Bush administration, and just about everything this country attempts abroad. (See this example of matrix analysis in chapter 4.)

IRAQ OCCUPATION WATCH (2002)

An organization called Iraq Occupation Watch (IOW), believed to have been formed in 2002, operates the International Occupation Watch Center, or IOWC, which is based in Baghdad. The center is designed to "monitor both the U.S. and the British occupation forces in Iraq as well as the American corporations that have been tasked by the Bush administration "to rebuild and profit" from repairing the infrastructure of Iraq."[37] IOW is dedicated to "exposing the impact of military and economic occupation of Iraq," according to its Web site. Gael Murphy is head of the center in Baghdad.

IOW is closely tied to Global Exchange—formed much earlier—as both have an overseas orientation. IOW (sometimes called Occupation Watch or OW) grew out of a collaborative effort between Leslie Cagan's United for Peace and Justice (UFPJ) and Medea Benjamin's Global Exchange. The members of the board of directors of IOW include Cagan, Benjamin, and Phyllis Bennis of the Institute for Policy Studies (IPS).

This group evidently relies on selected Iraqi sources for much of the "news" it provides. Working with a few aspiring Iraqi journalists, it has arranged to provide views of the occupation through articles "giving voice to those Iraqis who are frequently not heard." The Iraqi journalists write in English, and the group's editorial staff edits their articles, "checking with the Iraqi correspondents to ensure the accuracy of the editing." The names of their correspondents and the people they interview are pseudonyms, and the Iraqi correspondents are "quite enthused" about "having an outlet for what they consider are important stories about the occupation."[38] All of this verbiage suggests controlled, packaged, or directed information from hard-core insurgent sources, perhaps direct from the heart of the Sunni Triangle, which has violently fought against U.S. and allied occupation forces.

Even before the January 30, 2005, election in Iraq had run its course, IOW was questioning its purpose and utility. One headline in its Web site read, "The Iraqi Elections: Is This Really 'A Grand Moment in Iraqi History'?" On the day after, February 1, 2005, there were articles entitled "Train Wreck of an Election," and "What They're Not Telling You About the Election."[39] It took no prompting for this group to mock and belittle millions of brave Iraqi men and women who turned out to vote—in defiance of numerous death threats—and proudly wave their purple index fingers.

This is the election that sent shock waves throughout the Middle East, shock waves that continue to be felt in Egypt, Lebanon, and beyond. This very effort to denigrate the Iraqi election displays the bankruptcy and ultimate irrelevance of the ideas of such radical groups.

MEDIA MATTERS FOR AMERICA (2003)

Media Matters for America (MMA) is a nonprofit organization founded by David Brock to refute or otherwise analyze conservative influence on the media. Its Web site was launched in October 2003. MMA is described as a "Web-based, not-for-profit progressive research and information center dedicated to comprehensively monitoring, analyzing, and correcting conservative misinformation in the U.S. media."[40]

According to the *New York Times*, the group has received "more than $2 million in donations from wealthy liberals," and "was developed with help from the newly formed Center for American Progress."[41]

MMA has attracted some unfavorable comments from conservatives. One of its targets is Rush Limbaugh, who has called it "a clearing house for lib propaganda." Another of its targets is Bill O'Reilly, whose terminology for MMA includes "far-left bomb thrower Web site," "deceitful" and "disgusting," and "character assassins."[42]

Founder David Brock was a conservative journalist in the 1990s but converted to liberalism in 1998 and is now trying to take apart the conservative "machine" that he once served. He had once written for *American Spectator* magazine and had attacked Anita Hill (the accuser of Clarence Thomas) as well as then–Arkansas governor Bill Clinton (accusations that bred Troopergate and had the first printed reference to Paula Jones). In 1997 he published a confessional piece in *Esquire* magazine titled "I Was a Conservative Hit Man," in which he recanted much of what he had said in his two *American Spectator* pieces. Brock's main book is entitled *Blinded by the Right: The Conscience of an Ex-Conservative*. His 2004 book is entitled *The Republican Noise Machine*. This book attempts to detail a "massive, interconnected, concerted effort to raise the profile of conservative opinions in the press through allegedly false accusations" of liberal media bias.[43] Brock's effort underlines one of the most ambitious of the big-lie projects of the Hard Left: making a case that conservatives essentially dominate the news media.

A number of commentators have questioned Brock's veracity since his "transformation," and many have concluded that he is "unable to tell the truth regardless of what his professed political motivations are at any particular time."[44]

IN STEP WITH
OTHER INSTITUTIONS

THUS FAR I HAVE examined twenty-nine organizations, but that is only part of the story. To draw a more complete picture, we need to see how these groups relate to other institutions, and we need to see which issues the members of the Far Left have in common. Accordingly, this chapter will examine the role of opinion makers and policy makers. Let's first review the political leanings of the entertainment industry and selected Hollywood figures, the feminist movement, the black movement, the gay movement, the education establishment, and the legal establishment. Let's then take a hard look at the media and then finally at our own Congress.

ENTERTAINMENT INDUSTRY AND SELECTED HOLLYWOOD FIGURES

With few exceptions, "Hollywood producers, directors, writers, studio executives, and actors are decidedly liberal," especially "when compared with the general public." When asked to self-identify as liberal or conservative, the Hollywood liberals hold a four-to-one ratio over conservatives. Democrats in Hollywood outnumber Republicans by a greater margin—five to one. In general, Hollywood elites are far out of step with mainstream America in that few describe themselves as religious or anti-Communist and most support gay rights. There is no gay conspiracy, but there is a definite gay influence. In 1991 executives from four television networks and eight of the largest studios threw their support to the National Gay and Lesbian Task Force (NGLTF).[1]

According to Michael Medved, the predominant themes in U.S. films today include antipathy to the military, evil industrialists, corrupt cops, "America on trial," poisoning the past (such as the film *JFK* in 1991), and "vicious vets and pristine protesters" (as in *The Big Chill* of 1983). Other current themes include promiscuity, the decline of marriage, the urge to offend, foul language, hostility to heroes, and U.S.-bashing.

Hollywood has no shortage of hate-America and blame-America figures. Many actors and actresses have joined the anti-Bush jihad, and many have taken on some kind of organizational role in the Far-Left movements.

There are so many radical figures populating Hollywood that we can only look at a few of the high-profile individuals. These would include filmmakers Michael Moore and Oliver Stone as well as actors Danny Glover and Sean Penn.

Moore is, of course, well known as a major spokesman for the hate-America and blame-America school of thought. Many Americans view Moore as the head vulgarian at the gate. He has cast George Bush as less trustworthy than Saddam Hussein, and he has demonized Bush to the point of trying to influence the 2004 election through his film *Fahrenheit 9/11.*

As Trevor Bothwell points out, Moore "bears no shortage of responsibility for fomenting the hatred that encourages our enemies to attack and kill American troops." He notes that when the Democrats made Moore the poster boy for the party by giving him a seat next to

---

SELECTED HOLLYWOOD LEFTIST CELEBRITIES

Robert Altman	Jane Fonda	Vanessa Redgrave
Ed Asner	Richard Gere	Julia Roberts
Alec Baldwin	Danny Glover	Susan Sarandon
Harry Belafonte	Woody Harrelson	Martin Sheen
Chevy Chase	Jessica Lange	Oliver Stone
Tom Cruise	Michael Moore	
Mike Farrell	Sean Penn	

Jimmy Carter at their convention, "They neatly framed for all ordinary Americans a snapshot of everything that is wrong with the Democratic Party: the fusion of today's current vulgarity and contempt for American traditions and values, and yesterday's misery and despair personified by timidity in the face of foreign threats." According to Bothwell, Democrats "obviously can't understand that it's Moore's arrogance, vitriol and incessant dishonesty that Americans consequently associate with their party."[2]

Oliver Stone joined many in the arts who signed the pubic statement of conscience drafted by Not in Our Name (NION), in which the signatories promised to resist the U.S. policies "which pose grave dangers to the people of the world" and pledged alliance to those who come under U.S. attack. Stone has also accused the U.S. government of purposefully allowing Osama bin Laden "to escape unharmed while pretending to be hot on his trail." Stone claims that Bin Laden "was completely protected by the oil companies in this country who told [President] Bush not to go after him because it would piss off the Saudis."[3]

Antipathy to the U.S. military is most evident in a revealing remark by director Stone. In September 1987 he said, "I think American boys have to die again. Let the mothers weep and mourn. I think America has to bleed." That very year Stone received an award from the American Civil Liberties Union (ACLU).[4]

Actor Danny Glover has taken up the anti-American cause as well. While attending a film festival in Cuba, he condemned U.S. sanctions and threats of war against Iraq: "Our government has declared itself an uncontested empire." At a New York peace rally, he had nothing bad to say about Saddam Hussein but condemned President Bush and his "administration of liars and murderers."[5]

Sean Penn visited Saddam Hussein's Iraq twice. His first visit was in late 2002, set up by Norman Solomon of the left-wing Institute for Public Accuracy (IPA). His second visit in late 2003 was orchestrated with the help of both Solomon and Medea Benjamin, head of Global Exchange. In this type of trip, Global Exchange leads credulous American leftists "through staged scenes meant to demonstrate the progress of regimes it favors" and the devastation done by the American intervention it opposes.[6]

FEMINIST MOVEMENT AND THE NATIONAL
ORGANIZATION FOR WOMEN (NOW)

The National Organization for Women (NOW) is the largest group of feminist activists in the United States. It has more than 600,000 contributing members and 450 chapters. Since its founding in 1966, its goal has been to bring about equality of all women. NOW describes itself as a "multi-issue, multi-strategy organization." Its current priorities include a constitutional equality amendment, reproductive rights (NOW supports abortion), fighting racism (NOW is committed to ethnic diversity), lesbian rights (NOW seeks to "combat the adverse effects of homophobia"), and economic justice.

Going far beyond its original charter, NOW has joined the ranks of those groups that stand against the war in Iraq as well as the USA PATRIOT Act. Perhaps the best indication is a statement by NOW president Kim Gandy in March 2003: "We must keep raising our voices for peace—and the harder that becomes, the more necessary it is."[7] Gandy is a former senior assistant district attorney in New Orleans and was active in groups such as the Association of Democratic Women and the Lesbian and Gay Political Action Committee (LAGPAC).

NOW seeks to expose the Bush administration's "exploitation" of 9/11 "to advance a right-wing political agenda." It also seeks to end the "U.S. campaign of militarism and corporate profit that has contributed to anti-American sentiment around the world." Moreover, NOW calls for an end to U.S. foreign policy in the Middle East "that exacerbates the plight of women and children in these countries, including U.S. military aggression."[8]

When NOW issued a proclamation denouncing the liberation of Iraq, it included a line that condemned "the draconian homeland defense policies promoted by the Bush administration, and already enacted by Congress in the form of the Patriot Act." Accordingly, NOW called on its members to "expose the stifling of political dissent" by the Bush administration.[9]

NOW had earlier strongly opposed the nomination to the Supreme Court of Clarence Thomas. One source notes that NOW was part of the "lynch mob that conducted the most disgraceful campaign of character assassination in American history" during the Thomas hearings.[10] NOW teamed up with People for the American Way (PFAW) and other groups that spared no effort to discredit Thomas.

Seen in this way, NOW has taken an irrevocable hard left turn. Accordingly, there should be little surprise that NOW works coherently with many of the other groups noted earlier in this book.

BLACK MOVEMENT AND THE NATIONAL ASSOCIATION FOR THE ADVANCEMENT OF COLORED PEOPLE (NAACP)

The National Association for the Advancement of Colored People (NAACP) describes itself as America's "oldest and largest civil rights organization." The group's roots reach back to 1905, with the Niagara Movement founded by W. E. B. DuBois. In 1909 the American Negro Committee was formed, which was soon renamed the NAACP. During the 1960s the group "was seen by millions as a bipartisan beacon of hope for equality" of the races, and its membership bridged the political spectrum from left to right.

"But the NAACP grew from left-bent roots, and those roots have in recent years killed the moderate branches that were briefly grafted to this twisted tree," according to Lowell Ponte.[11] DuBois himself was a socialist who traveled to the USSR twice and praised the "racial attitudes of the Communists." In 1938 the NAACP was represented at the Soviet-controlled World Youth Congress, and during the 1940s it was affiliated with the Soviet-front World Federation of Democratic Youth (WFDY). In 1946 it supported the establishment of the Communist-influenced Progressive Party, which ran Henry Wallace for president in 1948.[12]

Since the glory days of the 1960s, the NAACP has taken a hard left turn. Recently the group has been in the hands of Julian Bond (chairman of its board of directors) and its current president and CEO Bruce S. Gordon. During 2001 Bond told one audience that President Bush's nominees to various positions in the judiciary and his administration were from the "Taliban wing of the GOP." Bond further stated, "We knew that he was in the oil business. We didn't know it was snake oil."[13]

The NAACP is opposed to school vouchers, which is a strange turn of events. In forty years it has gone from opposing segregated schools to opposing school vouchers for inner-city children in failing and bankrupt schools. In this effort it has teamed up with the National Education Association (NEA). To many black parents this is unfortunate, because blacks as a group are very fervent supporters of vouchers.

Today the NAACP functions as nothing more than a "left-wing auxiliary of the Democratic Party," according to one account.[14] The NAACP Foundation in 2000 ran a notorious political television ad showing a chain being dragged behind a pickup truck and claiming that George Bush, as Texas governor, had not signed "hate crimes" legislation to punish the racists who dragged a black man behind their truck and murdered him. The NAACP did not mention that the killers had already received the maximum penalty permitted under Texas law and that this "hate crimes" legislation would add nothing to their punishment. This was an "utterly dishonest, deceitful emotional appeal to frighten, anger, and activate voters."[15]

The NAACP seems to be incapable of a reasonable and respectful exchange of ideas on race, and many African Americans note that it has done nothing for the poor communities in the United States. Ward Connerly has asked whether anyone other than the NAACP can really take this organization seriously anymore. The group has become "largely irrelevant" in the ongoing dialogue about race, and some, according to Connerly, even see it as a "tragic farce." "How can a group like this survive? Or, more importantly, why should a group like this survive?"[16]

The percentage of NAACP members who also participate in Far-Left movements has not been determined. It is clear, however, that some Far-Left groups make special efforts to include black members when they can. For example, the United for Peace and Justice (UFPJ) steering committee must have at least 50 percent of its membership composed of "people of color." Some African Americans who currently sit on the UFPJ steering committee include Ajanu Dillahunt of Black Solidarity Against the War, Danu Smith of Black Voices for Peace, and Graylan Hagler of the Plymouth Congregational United Church of Christ of Washington DC.

Far more significant is the dual membership of some radical members of Congress in both the Congressional Black Caucus (CBC) and the Progressive Caucus (discussed below). Also significant is that prominent black political leaders have occasionally had some "coaching" from radical groups. For example, in 1984 Robert L. Borosage of the Institute for Policy Studies (IPS) was the foreign affairs adviser for Jesse Jackson's presidential bid.

GAY MOVEMENT AND THE NATIONAL GAY AND LESBIAN TASK FORCE (NGLTF)

Founded in 1973, the National Gay and Lesbian Task Force (NGLTF) is the principal organization that represents lesbian, gay, bisexual, and transgender (LGBT) individuals. It was also the first such organization in the country. The NGLTF organizes broad-based campaigns to defeat anti-LGBT initiatives and advance pro-LGBT issues. The organization's research institute provides analysis "to support the struggle for complete equality." The NGLTF sees itself as "part of a broader social justice movement" and the "unwavering and uncompromising national voice within the LGBT movement."[17]

The gay vote is heavily Democratic. In the 2000 presidential and congressional elections, more than 67 percent of gay, lesbian, and bisexual voters "cast their votes for Democratic candidates." The Web site of the NGLTF urged its members to vote for John Kerry in November 2004. The support for Democrats among gay, lesbian, and bisexual voters has been quite consistent over time. In 2002 "Democrats received 71 percent of the gay vote." Overall, the gay vote accounts for 4 to 5 percent of the voting electorate.[18]

The gay movement in the United States is very well organized and sharply focused on building political power. The NGLTF uses four primary strategies to build political power for the LGBT community, among which are:

- Strengthening state and local grassroots activists' power by building their capacity to organize and to initiate and respond appropriately and effectively to a range of political struggles.
- Acting as the movement's primary convener and coalition builder, including working with non-LGBT allies.

Gay activists charge that the Bush administration is resolutely anti-gay. The typical view from the gay Left sees the Bush administration and some members of Congress signaling that they will advance legislation that could override existing state and local laws that ban discrimination based on sexual orientation and gender identity. As one NGLTF spokesman put it, "The Bush administration now thinks it has carte blanche to run roughshod over the LGBT community and others."[19]

Seen in this light, it is no surprise that gay groups tend to gravitate toward the left of the political spectrum and make alliances with some of the groups depicted in earlier chapters. For example, Roberta Segal-Sklar, the communications director of NGLTF, signed the Not in Our Name (NION) statement in late 2004. As a senior officer, she committed the NGLTF to support NION and its goals.

Other radical groups make special amends to include groups such as the NGLTF. For example, according to its bylaws, United for Peace and Justice (UFPJ) maintains that at least 15 percent of the membership of its steering committee must be LGBT-identified persons.

EDUCATION ESTABLISHMENT AND THE NATIONAL EDUCATION ASSOCIATION (NEA)

The National Education Association (NEA) began in 1850 and adopted its present name in 1857. From the beginning it was devoted to promoting government-owned public schools, and it permitted no private school teachers to join. The NEA is the premier group that represents American teachers. With some 2.7 million dues-paying members, it "brings in at least $300 million a year to the national union and perhaps $1.25 billion" annually through its state and local unions. The NEA is believed to expend up to one-third of its enormous income every year on politics. It has "a permanent staff of at least eighteen hundred United Service (UniServ) employees who function as political operatives. This means that NEA on a continuous basis has more full-time paid professional political shock troops than the Republican and Democratic Parties combined."[20]

One observer characterizes the NEA as part labor union, part insurance conglomerate, part self-perpetuating staff oligarchy, and part political party.[21] After Jimmy Carter created the Department of Education, one NEA executive boasted that this was the only union "with its own cabinet department." At recent Democratic conventions, up to one-quarter of delegates have been members of teachers' unions. Other unions include the American Federation of Teachers (AFT) and the American Association of University Professors (AAUP). The NEA and the AFT claim to represent more than 90 percent of unionized faculty and professional staff employed in U.S. colleges and universities.

The NEA "has not been modest about imposing on students its own left-eyed values agenda," according to Lowell Ponte. The NEA promotes the discounting of religion (except for Wiccan paganism and Islam); sex education and social equality for homosexuals; "multiculturalism that praises every minority while teaching that white America has always been racist, sexist, homophobic, imperialistic, and unworthy of respect and teaching even less about patriotism."

As the first anniversary of 9/11 neared, the NEA posted guidelines on its national Web site suggesting that teachers should not "suggest any group is responsible" for the terrorist attacks but should have students "discuss historical instances of American intolerance."[22]

Given the sorry state of U.S. public education, the NEA seeks to banish competition and test-score keeping—the kinds of things that it fears and works to stifle. The NEA and the AFT also announced a joint lobbying effort to combat a provision in the Higher Education Reauthorization Act that would promote greater intellectual diversity in U.S. colleges and universities and combat discrimination against students for their political, religious, or ideological beliefs. This was a preemptive move against the Academic Bill of Rights, which sought to check the pervasive, far-reaching influence of leftist professors in academia.

Between 1990 and 2002, NEA was the second-largest special-interest group to contribute money to federal candidates and political parties. During that time it donated more than $21 million, of which 95 percent went to Democrats and most of the rest went to the most liberal Republicans running in primaries. Only the American Federation of State, County and Municipal Employees (AFSCME) donated more money as a single-interest group—and 98 percent of its money went to Democrats.[23]

LEGAL ESTABLISHMENT AND THE ASSOCIATION OF TRIAL LAWYERS OF AMERICA (ATLA)

There is no shortage of lawyers on the leftist, liberal side of the spectrum. Lawyers, in fact, head some of the most significant organizations

LEFTIST LAWYERS

Joan Blades (MoveOn)	Robert Drinan (NLG)	Michael Ratner (CCR)
Robert L. Borosage (IPS)	Kim Gandy (NOW)	Anthony Romero (ACLU)
Elaine Cassel (CLW)	Harold Ickes	Lynne Stewart (IAC)
Ramsey Clark	Mark Lane	Nadine Strossen (ACLU)
Stanley Cohen (CCR)	Ralph Neas (PFAW)	Leonard Weinglass (NLG)
Bernardine Dohrn (ACLU)	John Podesta (CAP)	

Note: List only shows selected individuals with law degree or who have been practicing lawyers. Group association is the most prominent associated with those persons, and not necessarily their current group.

described earlier. Political groups such as MoveOn and PFAW are headed by lawyers, and lawyers are numbered among the most notorious, vociferous, and self-important of all the Far-Left radicals: Ramsey Clark, Mark Lane, and Lynne Stewart, to name a few.

In 1946 a group of plaintiffs' lawyers "involved in workers' compensation litigation founded the National Association of Claimants' Compensation Attorneys (NACCA)." They were devoted to "securing strong representation for victims of industrial accidents, and the group soon attracted admiralty, railroad, and personal-injury lawyers." The organization soon added lawyers from all facets of trial advocacy. This group was renamed the Association of Trial Lawyers of America (ATLA) in 1972. With its current headquarters in Washington, ATLA describes itself as a "broad-based international coalition of attorneys, law professors, paralegals, and law students."[24] ATLA is the world's largest trial bar, with more than fifty-six thousand members worldwide. It has a network of American and Canadian affiliates involved in diverse areas of trial advocacy.

ATLA is heavily Democratic. To illustrate its stance, in 2004 the Kerry-Edwards campaign put in place six thousand lawyers—most of whom were from ATLA—"to tap every legal gimmick and Democrat-appointed judge" in the United States "to challenge and attempt to overturn" the election if President Bush won reelection.[25] In the days before the November 2, 2004, voting, it was feared that 2004 would be a repeat of the 2000 election, which dragged on for five weeks before George Bush was formally declared the winner.

Significantly, ATLA is a major donor to Hard-Left candidates in the

U.S. Congress. In recent years, ATLA has emerged as one of the leading contributors to the campaigns of Cynthia McKinney (D-GA) and Diane Watson (D-CA), and it has also contributed money to the campaign of Maxine Waters (D-CA). These three are all members of the radical Progressive Caucus, and all three have undertaken outrageous activities in recent years.

MEDIA

A thorough discussion of the media must include the print media, the broadcast media, and the "other" media. Print media include newspapers, magazines, book publishers, direct mail and newsletters, and wire services. Broadcast media include both television and radio. "Other" media are defined here as the Internet and the film industry. This section will focus largely on the print media.

In general, liberals have captured most of the media, and liberal influence is especially apparent in many newspapers and in network television news. There are three major exceptions, however. Radio appears to be split between liberals and conservatives, as is the Internet and direct mail and newsletters.

The instances of misdeeds in the media are well known and well documented by now. One media institution after another has come under heavy fire, from the *New York Times* to CBS News to *Newsweek*. The media's problems include a seemingly endless series of scandals involving plagiarism, nonexistent or unreliable sources, phony memos, sensationalized stories, inflated circulation figures, and other misdeeds. Many believe that CBS tried to influence the 2004 presidential election by its coverage of President Bush's National Guard record, and the most recent retraction by *Newsweek* of its story of U.S. soldiers "desecrating the Koran" was another body blow to the credibility of the print media.

More than ever before, the press is seen as less professional, less moral, less accurate, and "less caring about the interests of the country," according to the Project for Excellence in Journalism, which has tracked the media's steep decline in credibility. Between 1985 and 2002 the percentage of Americans who believed news organizations are politically biased rose from 45 to 59 percent.[26]

At the same time, there is ample evidence of a strong liberal bias in most corners of the print media. According to Bernard Goldberg, "just about every editorial writer and columnist" for the *New York Times, Los Angeles Times, Washington Post,* and *Boston Globe* is a liberal.[27] Moreover, there are ample statistical data that demonstrate the liberal bias of the press:

- In a 1985 survey by the *Los Angeles Times* of three thousand journalists, 55 percent self-identified as liberal (vs. 23 percent of the entire population), 30 percent favored Ronald Reagan (vs. 56 percent of the population), and 81 percent favored affirmative action (vs. 56 percent of the population).[28]
- In a 1996 survey of 139 Washington bureau chiefs and congressional correspondents, 89 percent voted for Bill Clinton in 1992, 7 percent voted for George H. W. Bush, and 2 percent voted for Ross Perot, according to the Freedom Forum and the Roper Center. In the very same survey, 50 percent of this group self-identified as Democrats and 4 percent self-identified as Republicans. Moreover, 61 percent self-identified as liberal or moderate to liberal, while only 9 percent self-identified as conservative or moderate to conservative.[29]
- In a 2000 poll by *Brill's Content,* 74 percent of Republicans believe most journalists are more liberal than they are, and a significant 47 percent of Democrats believed that most journalists are more liberal than they are.[30]

SELECTED CAREER PATTERNS

Closer examination reveals quite a number of individuals with radical links who have served with one or another major newspaper. Here are a few:

- Todd Gitlin is a former Students for a Democratic Society (SDS) president who later become a university professor (New York University, Berkeley, and Columbia, among others), and since then has been a frequent columnist in the *New York Times.*
- Roger Wilkins was a member of the editorial staff of the *Washing-*

ton Post from 1972 to 1974 and a member of the editorial staff of the *New York Times* from 1974 to 1979. He worked at the Institute for Policy Studies (IPS) as a senior fellow from 1982 to 1992 and later became a professor at George Mason University.

- Saul Landau was associated with the IPS starting in 1972 and has been with the Transnational Institute since 1974. He was a columnist with the *San Francisco Chronicle* from 1988 to 1992. He is also an author and filmmaker. Since then he has taken a position at California State Polytechnic University in Pomona.

- William Arkin has been a military affairs columnist with the *Los Angeles Times* and has also served at the IPS. He also serves as a commentator on MSNBC. He is a purveyor of classified information with contacts in the media and policy-making world.

FLEETING PARTNERSHIPS

There is also the issue of fleeting partnerships between journalists and radical sources. These often may result in a series of stories or a book. Sometimes the story can complicate or alter U.S. policy or damage U.S. relations with allies. A few examples:

- Robert Kaiser of the *Washington Post* was assigned to look at El Salvador, specifically to rebut a State Department white paper on Communist interference there—after an Institute for Policy Studies (IPS) official urged the *Post* to challenge the report. The central part of Kaiser's investigation of the report relied on information from Philip Agee (former CIA officer and traitor). After the State Department responded with a telling refutation of Kaiser's story, the *Post* reluctantly and belatedly apologized for the Kaiser-Agee story—but editors relegated the apology to the back of the paper. Kaiser also participated in IPS's alternative arms-control talks in May 1983 and in September 1985, events that brought together many in the U.S. peace movement as well as Soviet intelligence officials.[31]

- In his 1986 book about the shooting down of a Korean airliner in 1983, *The Target Is Destroyed,* Seymour Hersh credits William Arkin and others (with whom "he worked closely . . . in shaping

. . . requests for documents under the Freedom of Information Act"). "Hersh exposed new information about U.S. technical intelligence collection," and CIA director William Casey stated that Hersh was "perilously close to prosecution" for revealing so much about intelligence secrets. Hersh did not mention that Arkin was working on a project at that time for the IPS. By way of background, Hersh had been influenced by I. F. Stone early in his career and is a friend of Daniel Schorr, who himself was involved in a major leak of CIA information in 1976.[32]

- William Arkin also teamed up with Leslie Gelb in a major disclosure of classified information. Gelb has worked with the *New York Times* as a columnist, national security correspondent, and op-ed page editor from 1981 to 1993. Before that he had served at the Defense Department and State Department. Arkin (then with the IPS) leaked classified information to Gelb, who published a story in February 1985 entitled "U.S. Tries to Fight Allied Resistance to Nuclear Arms." Gelb revealed that the United States had contingency plans to deploy nuclear depth charges in many countries abroad. This story "severely damaged U.S. relations with its NATO allies."[33] Gelb's earlier career may be tracked back to at least 1970, when he participated in an IPS conference with Daniel Ellsberg and Morton Halperin.

- When Harrison Salisbury of the *New York Times* was finally admitted to North Vietnam, Wilfred Burchett (a notorious agent of influence) "was at his side to guide his tour and to serve as liaison" when Salisbury's North Vietnamese hosts offered him material. When Salisbury's stories appeared in the front page of the *New York Times*, their perspective was replete with Burchett's interpretation of events: the United States was "purposefully bombing civilian targets."[34] Throughout his reporting Salisbury was manipulated by the North Vietnamese as he played up the David-and-Goliath theme of the war.

NEWSMAGAZINES AND WIRE SERVICES

Those newsmagazines with the greatest circulation are largely liberal in outlook. They include *Time*, with a circulation of more than 4 million, as well as *Newsweek*, with a circulation of more than 3 million. *U.S. News and World Report*, with a circulation of more than 2 million is more middle-of-the-road. Meanwhile, those with less circulation are liberal as well; they include *Atlantic Monthly* (circulation about 460,000) as well as *Harper's* (circulation about 213,000). Some very liberal journals include *Mother Jones* (circulation about 151,000) and *New Republic* (circulation about 96,000).

The upshot here is that these newsmagazines generally do not bother to dig deep into the roots and connections of Far-Left organizations. Most of them are likely to give benign or positive coverage to these groups in one way or another.

PUBLISHING INDUSTRY

Another media branch that receives little attention is the publishing industry. It is no secret that most publishers in Manhattan are liberal to one shade or another. There is also no question that conservative authors always have a hard time getting their books published by the mainstream publishing houses. Michael Medved has stated, "New York book publishing is actually the last bastion of one-party rule in the world . . . even after Albania became a two-party state." One source

---

BUSH-BASHING BOOKS BY THE BUSHEL

Wave 1: 2003

Jim Hightower. *Thieves in High Places: They've Stolen Our Country—And It's Time to Take It Back.* New York: Viking, 2003.

Al Franken. *Lies and the Lying Lars Who Tell Them: A Fair and Balanced Look at the Right.* New York: Dutton Books, 2003.

Molly Ivins and Lou Dubose. *Bushwhacked: Life in George W. Bush's America.* New York: Random House, 2003.

David Corn. *The Lies of George W. Bush: Mastering the Politics of Deception.* New York: Crown, 2003.

Michael Moore. *Dude, Where's My Country?* New York: Warner Books, 2003.

Jack Huberman. *The Bush-Haters Handbook: A Guide to the Most Appalling Presidency of the Past 100 Years.* New York: Nation Books, 2003.

BUSH-BASHING BOOKS BY THE BUSHEL (CONTINUED)

Wave 2: Pre-election Titles in 2004

Kevin Phillips. *American Dynasty: Aristocracy, Fortune, and the Politics of Deceit in the House of Bush.* New York: Viking, 2004.

Ron Suskind. *The Price of Loyalty: George W. Bush, the White House, and the Education of Paul O'Neill.* New York: Simon & Schuster, 2004.

John Dean. *Worse than Watergate: The Secret Presidency of George W. Bush.* New York: Little, Brown, 2004.

Michael John Dobbins. *Stop Bush in 2004: How Every Citizen Can Help.* Lincoln, NE: iUniverse, 2004.

Bill Press. *Bush Must Go: The Top Ten Reasons Why George Bush Doesn't Deserve a Second Term.* New York: Dutton Books, 2004.

Ben Fritz, Bryan Keefer, and Brendan Nyhan. *All the President's Spin: George W. Bush, the Media, and the Truth.* New York: Simon and Schuster, 2004.

Maureen Dowd. *Bushworld: Enter at Your Own Risk.* New York: Putnam, 2004.

Paul Krugman. *The Great Unraveling: Losing Our Way in the New Century.* New York: Norton, 2004.

Seymour Hersh. *Chain of Command: The Road from 9/11 to Abu Ghraib.* New York: HarperCollins, 2004.

Kitty Kelly. *The Family: The Real Story of the Bush Dynasty.* New York: Doubleday, 2004.

Note: The last five books appeared in August and September, within three months of the 2004 election.

---

claimed in a blog on "Free Republic" that the "first thing to remember is that most publishers are liberal whores, controlled by liberal whores or intimidated into conformity by liberal whores."[35]

The fact that most publishing houses are decidedly liberal was most apparent during 2003 and 2004 and especially in the months before the November 2004 election. Bush bashing was in full force then, with an unprecedented host of anti-Bush titles by a variety of authors.

CONGRESS

Radicals from the Far Left have infiltrated all U.S. institutions to one degree or another, but the influence of radical groups is most telling in the

U.S. Congress. It is there where our laws are passed, and it is there where lawmakers set the tone for the rest of the country. Accordingly, it is in the halls of Congress that the most decisive political collisions and struggles take place.

During an earlier era there were radical members of the House of Representatives. Several were swept in during the aftermath of the Vietnam War. Ron Dellums (D-CA) was perhaps the greatest champion of radical groups to appear in Congress during the last half of the twentieth century. He endorsed the Black Panthers, addressed the World Peace Council meeting in 1970, and supported the Institute for Policy Studies (IPS) in a number of ways. Dellums served from 1971 to 1999. Father Robert Drinan (D-MA) was involved in a host of radical causes and served from 1971 to 1981. Bella Abzug (D-NY) was a founder of the Women's Strike for Peace (WSP), a Communist-infiltrated organization, and was a strident voice for liberal and radical causes. She served from 1971 to 1977.

During this era there was also a group in the Senate called the Members of Congress for Peace Through Law (MCPL). Among others, they included Senators George McGovern (D-SD), Ted Kennedy (D-MA), Walter Mondale (D-MN), and Philip Hart (D-MI).

It is also illuminating to see which congressmen have been backers of the IPS over the years. In the 1970s and 1980s its staunchest supporters in the House were George Miller (D-CA), Don Edwards (D-CA), Ted Weiss (D-NY), and the ever-present John Conyers. On the Senate side, Senators Tom Harkin (D-IA), Mark Hatfield (D-OR), and John Kerry (D-MA) were dedicated partisans of the IPS.[36]

Some members of Congress have kept very questionable company. To cite an example from the House, Michael Harrington (D-MA) was a contact of Orlando Letelier, a notorious agent of influence. Harrington demanded classified testimony from CIA director William Colby, and then leaked this material to Seymour Hersh of the *New York Times*. This resulted in a sensational story about U.S. involvement in Chile in September 1974, a story that set the stage for the "time of troubles" for CIA and the intelligence community during the various investigations from 1975 to 1978.[37]

The Senate has its own issues as well. For example, Senator Walter Mondale served on the Senate Intelligence Committee headed by

Senator Frank Church (D-ID) in the 1970s. One of Mondale's aides, David Aaron of the Center for International Policy, employed Rick Inderfurth and Gregory Treverton—both of whom are also contacts of Orlando Letelier (the former Chilean ambassador to the United States and IPS executive who was assassinated in Washington DC on September 21, 1976).

On top of that, Senator Church himself was influenced by a report on U.S. intelligence prepared by the Center for National Security Studies (CNSS), a report that had the benefit of direct input from an agent of influence, Wilfred Burchett, and traitor Philip Agee.[38]

It is not always easy to tell where party loyalties fall. One example is that several members of Congress are also members of the Democratic Socialists of America (DSA). These include Major Owens (D-NY), Bernie Sanders (I-VT), and Danny Davis (D-IL, who has been rumored to be a DSA member). Former Congressman Ron Dellums is also a DSA member. In any event, nearly all of the Democrats named below belong to the socialist wing of the Democratic Party. A key question is to what extent this wing has spread its influence and values to the rest of the Democratic Party.

HOW FAR TO THE LEFT?

The *Progressive Caucus* is made up of the most Far-Left members of Congress and best represents the socialist wing of the Democratic Party. This group shares a common belief in the "principles of social and economic justice, non-discrimination, and tolerance in America and in our relationships with other countries." Specifically this group supports curbs on defense spending; it seeks a more progressive tax system that soaks the rich; and it is for social programs that are designed "to extend help to low and middle-income Americans in need." The Progressive Caucus has long been allied with the Democratic Socialists of America.[39] As of 2003, there were some fifty-four members, of whom eight were officers. The current heads are Dennis Kucinich and Barbara Lee. (There is no recent data for the 109th Congress, which meets from 2005 to 2006.)

The *Congressional Black Caucus (CBC)* dates back to 1969, when thirteen black members of the House joined together to strengthen their efforts to address the concerns of black and minority citizens. In the

109th Congress, there are forty-three members. This group is committed to back legislation designed "to meet the needs of millions of neglected citizens." It also pushes for a national commitment to fair treatment for middle- and low-income wage earners, the economic disadvantaged, and a "new world order."[40] Many of these members of Congress come from artificially drawn districts produced by racial gerrymandering, and some of these individuals slant so far to the Left it is easy to detect their radical orientation. Of fourteen selected members of Congress considered the most liberal, some ten have dual membership in both the Progressive Caucus and the CBC.

Some CBC members have long associated with Far-Left elements, and they often do not hesitate to associate publicly with groups that other progressive congressmen shun. In mid-1983 a demonstration

RADICALS IN THE HOUSE OF REPRESENTATIVES			
	PC	CBC	HR104
John Conyers (D-MI, 14th)	X	X	N
Danny Davis (D-IL, 7th)	X	X	?
Jesse Jackson Jr. (D-IL, 2nd)	X	X	P
Sheila Jackson-Lee (D-TX, 18th)	X	X	P
Barbara Lee (D-CA, 9th)	X	X	N
Jim McDermott (D-WA, 7th)	X	0	N
Cynthia McKinney (D-GA, 4th)	X	X	N/A
Major Owens (D-NY, 11th)	X	X	P
Nancy Pelosi (D-CA, 8th)	X	0	Y
Charles Rangel (D-NY, 15th)	0	X	N
Stephanie Tubbs-Jones (D-OH, 11th)	X	X	N
Maxine Waters (D-CA, 35th)	X	X	N
Henry Waxman (D-CA, 30th)	X	0	?
Diane Watson (D-CA, 33rd)	X	X	N

Key:
Number = Congressional district; PC = Progressive Caucus; CBC = Congressional Black Caucus; HR 104 = bill supporting military members; X = member; 0 = not a member; Y = yes; N = no; P = present; ? = do not know; N/A = out of office

opposing President Reagan's Central American policy was held in Washington DC. It featured the People's Anti-War Mobilization, which was dominated by members of the Workers World Party. Five members of the Congressional Black Caucus endorsed the movement: George Crockett, Ronald Dellums, Mickey Leland, Parren Mitchell, and John Conyers. At this very function, a Communist Party member addressed the crowd and stated that the United States is not going to El Salvador to kill Communists, "but to kill women and children."[41]

House Resolution (HR) 104 was conceived with the goal of "expressing the support and appreciation of the nation for the President and the members of the armed forces who are participating in Operation Iraqi Freedom." It was intended as a "nonpartisan declaration of solidarity with U.S. military forces" engaged in combat there. It was not an endorsement of the war, but was merely meant to "provide symbolic support for the troops in the field."

This nonbinding House resolution passed easily (392–11 in the House and 99–0 in the Senate). But 11 members of Congress voted against this resolution. All were Democrats, and most were members of the CBC. Another 21 Democrats voted "present" for the resolution, a nonvote of "political cowardice," in which they were unwilling to decide whether they stood behind American troops risking their lives in Iraq.[42]

INDIVIDUAL PERFORMANCES

John Conyers represents the Fourteenth District of Michigan. First elected to that office in 1964, he is the second-longest-serving member of the House of Representatives. He is a leading figure in the Democratic Party and the House Judiciary Committee, and in 1971 he was one of the original members of President Nixon's "enemies list." He is one of the most radical members of Congress, and even appeared in Michael Moore's *Fahrenheit 9/11*, discussing the aftermath of the 9/11 attacks. During all his years in Washington, Conyers has been a consistent champion of radical causes, including the Institute for Policy Studies (IPS). In 1981 Conyers co-hosted a delegation from the Soviet front World Peace Council, giving that group a forum in Congress.[43] Conyers endorsed a Communist-led antiwar demonstration in Washington in 1983, and he also spoke at another Washington demonstration led by

ANSWER in 2003. In between those events, he has spent great efforts to rail against American policy. He is a founding member of the Congressional Black Caucus and a member of the Progressive Caucus.

Barbara Lee represents Berkeley and all it stands for. She cast the lone vote against authorizing President Bush to fight al-Qaeda. Speaking just three days after 9/11, she stated that the president really wanted to "embark on an open-ended war with neither an exit strategy nor a focused target." She had "previously cast the lone vote against a resolution expressing support of the troops already fighting in Serbia." She "served for nine years on the staff of her predecessor, Rep. Ron Dellums," rising to become his chief of staff. In 1983 Lee conducted a "fact-finding" mission to the pro-Soviet regime of Grenada and later submitted a propaganda "report" to Congress "that was doctored" by Grenadian dictator Maurice Bishop himself, thereby operating as a de facto agent of influence. Elected to Congress herself in 1998, she led a delegation to Cuba, reflecting her own admiration for Castro. Barbara Lee has been described as "an anti-American Communist who supports America's enemies and has actively collaborated with them in their war against America."[44] Lee was recently the co-chairman of the Progressive Caucus as well as the whip of the Congressional Black Caucus, highly significant in her holding influential positions within both groups.

Maxine Waters is also one of the most radical members of Congress. Once a social worker, she now represents the Thirty-fifth District of California (south-central Los Angeles). In 1984 she was co-chairman of Jesse Jackson's presidential campaign. She once referred to President George H. W. Bush as a "racist" and routinely refers to the Republican Party as "the enemy." Waters has publicly blamed the epidemic of crack-cocaine use among blacks on the U.S. government. She steadfastly maintained that the CIA sold the deadly drug to black communities in a deliberate campaign of decimation. Regardless of the sensational and baseless nature of these charges, she has never recanted them, even after 9/11. She has also publicly supported racist violence. She called the 1992 Los Angeles riots a "revolution," defending the anti-white and anti-Asian violence, and paid a personal visit to the home of one of the most notorious rioters. She saw the riots as a "spontaneous reaction to a lot of injustice." Waters once claimed that she never saw LA police officers abuse "little white boys" and has also stated, "I don't have time to be polite."[45] Waters has also "traveled several times to Cuba," heaped praise on Castro, and has called for an end to the U.S. embargo against his government. President Bill Clinton appointed Waters's second husband, a former car salesman, to be the U.S. ambassador to the Bahamas. Organized labor is by far Waters's biggest campaign contributor, and she also benefits from contributions from the Association of Trial Lawyers of America (ATLA) and Viacom, which owns CBS.[46] She is a member of both the Progressive Caucus and the Congressional Black Caucus, and she headed the latter group from 1997 to 1998.

Cynthia McKinney represents the Fourth District of Georgia. She has accused President Bush of being responsible for the 9/11 attacks and of having personally profited by them. When her outrageous remarks were published, she later "apologized," saying, "I am not aware of any evidence showing that President Bush . . . personally profited from the attacks . . . [but] a complete investigation might reveal that to be the case."[47] Fellow Georgia Democrat Senator Zell Miller described McKinney's conspiracy theory as "loony" and "dangerous and irresponsible," and the *Atlanta Journal-Constitution* derided her as "the most prominent nut" among conspiracy-peddling nuts. As such, McKinney has elevated to the level of fine art the "anyone who stands to gain must be responsible" school of thought.[48] McKinney was voted out of office in 2002, after which time her father and campaign manager blamed the Jews for her defeat, but she was voted back into office in 2004. When out of office, she held a position of visiting professor at Cornell University. At that time, one professor emeritus stated that she is a racist and anti-Semite of the first rank, and, "If she were white and male, she would be David Duke."[49] McKinney has taken a very high profile against the Iraq War, speaking at demonstrations organized by Act Now to Stop War and End Racism (ANSWER) in October 2002 and in January 2005. She has also provided propaganda for anti-government guerrillas in Colombia, has voted against school vouchers for black parents in Washington DC, and voted against ending racial preferences in college admissions. She has voted repeatedly to cut U.S. aid to Israel and enjoys strong support from the Arab and Muslim interest groups, who see her as a strong backer of a Palestinian state. One of McKinney's biggest contributors is the Association of Trial Lawyers of America (ATLA), because she has voted against legislation that would limit their profits. She is strongly supported by organized labor as well, since a very large proportion of her contributions originate from outside the state and especially from California.[50] She belongs to the Congressional Black Caucus.

Diane Watson represents the "carefully gerrymandered" Thirty-third District in Southern California. Watson is a former teacher and school psychologist who was named as ambassador to Micronesia by President Clinton in 1999 and who was sent to Congress in a special election of June 2001. She is quick to play the race card. She claimed, "America is a racist state" to a UN-sponsored symposium in Durban, South Africa, in 2001. At that time she and six other congressional Democrats attended and lent their prestige to what was an anti-Jewish, anti-America hatefest.[51] She has voted against the use of force in Iraq. Her biggest campaign contributors are labor unions and the Association of Trial Lawyers of America (ATLA). She is a member of both the Progressive Caucus and the Congressional Black Caucus.

Jim McDermott represents the Seventh District of Washington. He set off for Iraq with fellow Congressmen David Bonior (D-MI) and Mike Thompson (D-CA) and "concluded that President Bush was a liar." He stated, "I think that the president would mislead the American people," and he charged Bush with trying to provoke Iraq into a war. He also stated, "I think you have to take the Iraqis at face value," and claimed that the Iraqi officials "said they would allow us to go look anywhere we wanted." This performance was in the best tradition of the discredited U.S. ambassador to the USSR in the 1930s, Joseph Davies, and earned McDermott and his fellow travelers the titles of "spokespeople for the Iraqi government" and "the three stooges of Baghdad." They distinguished themselves as they did the bidding of Saddam Hussein and his corrupt and tyrannical regime in the halls of Congress.[52] McDermott is a member of the Progressive Caucus.

CONGRESSIONAL AIDES AND STAFF

There are only 100 senators and 435 members of the House of Representatives. Yet the population of Capitol Hill is about 25,000 persons. According to data from 1993, a typical House member had 22 personal assistants, and a typical senator had 42. Currently some senators have a staff of 70 or more. This presents unlimited opportunities for ambitious people to be close to lawmakers, to help with their workload, and to influence them in a number of ways.

There have been agents of influence on Capitol Hill in earlier years, and they continue to work the Hill today. The best case in recent years concerns congressional aide Susan Lindauer. She is a very public antiwar activist, from the bumper stickers on her aging Mazda to her signature on a published antiwar petition. She fits in well with her leftist home suburb of Takoma Park, Maryland. In March 2004 Lindauer was arrested and "charged with conspiracy, acting as an unregistered agent of a foreign government, and taking money from a government that supports terrorism." Lindauer engaged in "prohibited dealings with several members" of the Iraqi Intelligence Service (IIS) in visits to the Iraqi Mission to the United Nations in New York. In early 2002 she traveled to Baghdad and "received about $10,000 for her services." In mid-2003 she met twice in Baltimore with an undercover FBI agent who was posing as a Libyan intelligence officer "seeking to support resistance groups fighting U.S. forces in postwar Iraq." Lindauer communicated clandestinely, as she filled two dead drops in Takoma Park, Maryland.[53]

Significantly, "Lindauer worked in the offices of four prominent Democratic lawmakers." In May 1993 she was hired by Congressman Peter DeFazio (D-OR), "whose political views matched her own." DeFazio has been not just a member but also an officer of the Progressive Caucus, one of the group's key decision makers and drivers. DeFazio's ADA (Americans for Democratic Action) rating was 90 in 2000 and 95 in 2002. ADA ratings are percentages that indicate the frequency of voting to support issues backed by the Left. In January 1994 Congressman Ron Wyden (D-OR) hired Lindauer. Wyden is another denizen of the Far Left, winning ADA ratings of 90 in 2000 and 85 in 2002. In January 1996 Lindauer was hired as press secretary to Senator Carol Moseley Braun (D-IL), but worked for her only until September 1996. Moseley Braun's lifetime ADA rating is 88. In 2002 Lindauer was hired by Congresswoman Zoe Lofgren (D-CA), and worked with her office for only two months. Lofgren's ADA rating in 2000 was 85, and her rating in 2002 was a perfect 100.[54]

According to the mainstream media, Lindauer's jobs on the staffs of four prominent Democratic lawmakers were "buried many paragraphs" into any stories about their work, if they were reported at all. The fact that these were four of the most hard-line Left members of Congress did not warrant mention at all.[55] Given the atmosphere of Capitol Hill, these leftist Democrats likely knew one another's staffs, and Lindauer's first three jobs transitioned smoothly from DeFazio to Wyden to Moseley Braun.

Lindauer's statement after her arrest says plenty about her and how she saw her role: "I'm an antiwar activist and I'm innocent. I did more to stop terrorism in this country than anybody else. I have done good things for this country."[56] Some of the press coverage about the case says a lot about the media as well. This headline appeared in the *Seattle Post-Intelligencer*: "Accused Spy Is Cousin of Bush Staffer." That headline helps you understand why the media are held in such low regard by the public, with public acceptance ratings that usually come in "somewhere between Nigerian e-mail scammers and serial pedophiles."[57]

WHAT THEY SAY AND CARRY

I'T'S QUITE DIFFICULT TO fully understand what many on the Far Left say. Their opinions reflect a blend of acute liberal guilt for U.S. sins and undiluted admiration for the world's tyrants, all of which is held together with the spit of raging anti-Bush hatred. At the same time, they display a breathtaking, even stupefying degree of naïveté about the world around them and especially about our country's adversaries.

THE SPOKEN WORD

CARPING ABOUT AN INAUGURATION

Elaine Cassel is a law professor and practicing lawyer in the Washington DC area, a legal commentator who contributes to *Counterpunch,* and the author of *The War on Civil Liberties: How Bush and Ashcroft Have Dismantled the Bill of Rights.* Cassel exercised no restraint in her observations about the January 2005 inauguration festivities. On her Web site, called Civil Liberties Watch, she authored "Questions While Watching an Insipid Inaugural."[1] The following are quoted from this Web page:

- "Was Laura Bush squinting because of the dazzling white of her cashmere suit that she appeared to be poured into, like a sausage?"

- "Speaking of sausages, what's up with Jeb Bush? If Bill Parcells is Tuna, Jebbie is the Whale."
- "What was Cheney's lesbian daughter doing holding the Bible? Was that some kind of in-your-face to the Christian right?"
- "Will George ever learn to speak his 's's' without hissing? Could someone give him an elocution lesson?"
- "Those twins. Could they get a fashion consultant or something? Fat Jenna in her pants and too-tight top. Barbara in her mismatched coat, dress, and belt. What a rag-tag team they are."
- "Did Laura and George honestly think they were dancing? Standing stiffly and swaying side to side for 30 seconds?"
- "Is that tasteless, tepid show the best that $40 million can buy?"
- "Finally, did the world that Bush ordered to get on the freedom train—or else—get a good glimpse of freedom? Missile launchers, jet fighters, swat teams, cops with assault weapons, dogs, barbed wire, barricades, surveillance cameras—that's what they have to look forward to?"

What Cassel churned up was a collection of condescending, sour-grapes, hate-filled speech. She had something nasty to say about the Bush family's dress as well as the security precautions. This set of opinions is quite popular with the Georgetown set and with much of the entrenched legal establishment in Washington. Evidently most in the Bush family did not measure up to Cassel's extraordinarily high standards of fashion or speech. This was a ready reminder of just how petty, carping, small-minded, and downright vicious many elements of the Far Left can be.

HOLLYWOOD HOWLERS

Hollywood director Robert Altman stated, "If George W. Bush is elected president, I'm leaving for France," and also, "It will be a catastrophe for the world if George Bush is elected."[2]

Susan Sarandon appeared at a French film festival and spouted, "We stand a chance of getting a president who has probably killed more people before he gets into office than any president in the history of the United States."[3]

Michael Moore says of Americans, "They are possibly the dumbest people on the planet . . . in thrall to conniving, thieving, smug pricks."[4]

Left-wing activist and "comedienne" Janeane Garofalo stated, "This was about oil. . . . It wasn't about human rights. . . . Team Bush is more radically corrupt than Richard Nixon ever tried to be. . . . It is, in fact, a conspiracy of the 43rd Reich." At the time she was appearing on CNN's *Crossfire* program as a guest co-host.[5]

Jessica Lange spoke out at the San Sebastian film festival in Madrid: "Today it makes me feel ashamed to come from the United States—it is humiliating. . . . The atmosphere in my country is poisonous, intolerable for those of us who are not right-wing, so thank you for inviting me to this festival and allowing me to get out for a few days." This was after her statements, "I hate Bush," and, "Bush stole the elections and since then we have all been suffering the consequences."[6]

Not to be outdone, Ozzy Osbourne opened one of his concerts with the song "War Pigs," featuring a video portrait that compared President Bush to Hitler. The video featured the two on the same screen with the caption: "Same sh—t different a—hole." The footage added images of "bombs dropping and Hitler marching as Ozzy screamed and guitars screeched." Bush was also pictured with a clown nose and the caption "The White House Circus."[7]

WASHINGTON WHOPPERS

Bill Moyers says that Republicans are planning "the deliberate, intentional destruction of the United States of America."[8]

Julian Bond says about Republicans that their idea of equal rights "is an American flag and Confederate swastika flying side by side."[9]

Senator Patty Murray (D-WA), a former teacher, says that Osama bin Laden has "been out in these countries for decades, building schools, building roads, building infrastructure, building day-care facilities, building health-care facilities, and these people are extremely grateful. We haven't done that."[10]

Howard Dean told his fellow Democrats to "remember that George Bush is the enemy" during a debate and in the middle of a war against a foreign enemy.[11]

Dennis Kucinich stated, "I have a holistic view of the world . . . I see the world as interconnected and interdependent and that leaves no room for war."[12]

PESSIMISM FROM THE PRESS ON IRAQ

Chris Hedges of the *New York Times* tells us, "We have forfeited the goodwill, the empathy the world felt for us after 9/11, we have folded in on ourselves. . . . We are far less secure today than we were before we bumbled into Iraq."[13]

James Carroll of the *Boston Globe* saw nothing useful in Saddam's capture. "That he was caught in a hole, obviously unrelated to the guerrilla resistance, is a turning point in nothing that matters now; not in restoring order to Iraq, not in rebuilding structures of international law, not in thwarting terrorism, not in stemming the proliferation of weapons of mass destruction, not in reconciling the West and the world of Islam."[14]

Eric Alterman noted that the capture of Saddam Hussein "does little to justify what remains a dishonest, self-destructive, hubristic adventure that continues to undermine our security and the stability of the region with each passing day."[15]

Joe Sobran stated, "So Saddam Hussein, who hasn't broken any American laws, will stand trial under the supervision of President Bush, who has pretty much shelved the U.S. Constitution."[16]

THE PRESS TOUTS THE BIG LIE . . . AGAIN

Former *Washington Post* and *New York Times* reporter E. J. Dionne stated in 2002, "It took conservatives a lot of hard and steady work to push the media rightward . . . What it adds up to is a media heavily biased toward conservative politics and conservative politicians."[17]

Howell Raines, the discredited former executive editor of the *New York Times,* stated, "We must be aware of the energetic effort that is now underway to convince our readers that we are ideologues. It is an exercise in disinformation of alarming proportions, this attempt to convince the audience of the world's most ideology-free newspapers that they're being subjected to agenda-driven news reflecting a liberal bias." Raines was fired in the wake of the Jayson Blair scandal of 2003.[18]

NUTTY PROFESSORS

The recently promoted chairman of the sociology department of Brooklyn College, Timothy Shortell, had a few comments about the current administration: "This is certainly the most fanatically ideological administration in U.S. history." He notes, "Just as in any fascist state, the megalomania of the ruling elite is paid for in working class blood." In the same breath, Shortell refers to President Bush as the "war-criminal-in-chief" and states that Karl Rove "owes a lot to Joseph Goebbels."[19]

Professor Shortell has plenty of company in academia.

- Nicholas De Genova of Columbia reminds us that the "true heroes" are the ones who defeat the U.S. military.
- H. Bruce Franklin of Rutgers supported victory for North Vietnam and has long been an apologist for Joseph Stalin.
- Ward Churchill of Colorado made himself infamous with his crack about the "little Eichmanns" who perished in the collapse of the World Trade Center on 9/11.
- Robert Jensen of Texas reminds us that America is the "world's greatest terrorist state."
- Noam Chomsky of MIT has more outrageous quotes than are possible to mention in the span of one chapter.

MEN OF LETTERS?

Gore Vidal has very little use for U.S. political institutions or traditions. "How we dare even prate about democracy is beyond me. One form of democracy is bribery, on the highest scale. It's far worse than anything that occurred in the Roman Empire, until the Praetorian Guard started to sell the principate. We're not a democracy, and we have absolutely nothing to give the world in the way of political ideas or political arrangements. God knows, the mention of justice is like a clove of garlic to Count Dracula."[20]

Kurt Vonnegut has towering contempt for U.S. conservatives, whom he calls "bullies" and "crazy as bedbugs." "What are the conservatives doing with all the money and power that used to belong to all of us? They are telling us to be absolutely terrified, and to run around in circles like chickens with their heads cut off. But they will save us." He had previously blamed conservatives for "having stolen a major fraction of our private savings, have ruined investors and employees by means of fraud and outright piracy." In a lecture at Hartford, Connecticut, he also brought up past U.S. sins of the Mexican War (annexing western states and "butchering Mexican soldiers who were only defending their homeland against invaders") and the insurgency in the Philippines ("the slaughter of 600 Moro men, women and children").[21]

The late Hunter Thompson evidently tried to outdo both Vidal and Vonnegut. In February 2002 he stated, "This blizzard of mind-warping war propaganda out of Washington is building up steam. . . . If we believed all the brutal, frat-boy threats coming out of the White House, we would be dead before Sunday. It is pure and savage terrorism reminiscent of Nazi Germany." In July 2003 he stated, "This goofy child president we have on our hands now. He is demonstrably a fool and a failure, and this is only the summer of '03. The American nation is in the worst condition I can remember in my lifetime, and our prospects for the immediate future are even worse." About that time he noted, "The utter collapse of this profoundly criminal Bush conspiracy will come none too soon for people like me." By the fall of 2003, Thompson referred to the "monumentally failed backwoods politician" and "our embattled child President."

In April 2004 Thompson said, "The 2004 presidential election will be a matter of life and death for the whole nation. We are sick today, and we will be even sicker tomorrow if this wretched half-bright swine of a president gets reelected in November." This may have been a premonition, for even before Bush's reelection later that year, Thompson stated in May 2004 that he was "really ashamed to carry an American passport."[22]

IT JUST GETS BETTER AND BETTER

Jill Nelson said on MSNBC in 2003: "I do not feel safer now than I did six, or 12, or 24 months ago. In fact, I feel far more vulnerable and frightened than I ever have in my 50 years on the planet. It is the United States government that I am afraid of. In less than two years the Bush administration has used the attacks of 9/11 to manipulate our fear of terrorism and desire for revenge into a blank check to blatantly pursue imperialist objectives internationally and to begin the rollback of the Constitution, the Bill of Rights, and most of the advances of the 20th century."[23]

A look at the British press can be both horrifying and revealing. Margaret Drabble, writing in the *Daily Telegraph* in 2003, reached a state of hysteria: "My anti-Americanism has become almost uncontrollable. It has possessed me, like a disease. It rises up in my throat like acid reflux, that fashionable American sickness. I now loathe the United States and what it has done to Iraq and the rest of the helpless world."[24]

John Pilger stated in the *Daily Mirror* in 2003, "Unelected in 2000, the Washington regime of George W. Bush is now totalitarian, captured by a clique whose fanaticism and ambitions of 'endless war' and 'full spectrum dominance' are a matter of record. Bush's State of the Union speech last night was reminiscent of that other great moment in 1938 when Hitler called his generals together and told them: 'I must have war.' He then had it."[25]

THE WRITTEN WORD

The same carping, hate-filled, and occasionally hysterical thoughts have been much in evidence at some of the major demonstrations against the war in Iraq during the period between 2003 and 2005. A thorough review of Web sites reveals a few common themes in what these people carry at demonstrations. The wording of the signs is accurately depicted, including spelling and capitalization, but some graphic language has been edited.[26]

The year 2003 got things off to a roaring start:

- "End the Colonial Occupation of Iraq"
- "Bush Strategy: Endangering America, Enraging the World"

The following signs were observed at a march in New York City in 2004:

- "I am tired of being ashamed by my government's arrogance"
- "Bush: Stop Me Before I Stupid Again"
- "No More Bush—t"

- "NY Hates Bush More Than Ever"
- "No One Likes You Dubya"
- "F—k Bush"
- "Bush, Cheney, Rumsfeld: The Real Axis of Evil"
- "The Difference Between Bush and Saddam Is That Saddam Was Elected"
- "He Is A Moron . . . And a Bully"
- "Free the Cuban Five" (referring to the convicted Cuban spies)
- "Axis of Evil My A—. Iranian-Americans against Occupation"
- "Dignity, Sovereignty, and True Freedom" (referring to Hugo Chavez in Venezuela)

These were seen in another New York City march in 2004:

- "No War For Empire"
- "Bush Lies. Who Dies?"
- "Darn Good Liar" (Bush picture)
- "Vote Out this Immoral Administration"
- "Jesus was a Socialist"
- "My Bush Smells Like Sh—t"

By 2005 things had heated up even more:

- "Wake Up and Smell the Fascism"
- "Since 1945 the U.S. has bombed 25 countries"
- "Solidarity with Iraqi Sisters"
- "Support the Global Struggle Against U.S. Imperialism"
- "Bush Lied!"
- "How Many Lives Per Gallon?"
- "World War IV! Wiping out the Many So the Few Can Inherit the Earth. Compliments of your friendly corporate election system."
- "Evil Rules in the Land of Fools"

These have been seen here and there at different times:

- "U.S. Government is a Traitor to the American People"
- "World's #1 Terrorist" (Bush picture)

- "Bush Ur a Jacka—"
- "Defend Iraq from U.S. Imperialist Attack!"
- "No Sanctions! No Bombs! No More Blood for Oil! International Socialist Organization"
- "Workers of the World Unite! Smash All Borders"
- "Poland 1939 Iraq 2003"
- "Many More Defeats for U.S. Imperialism"
- "Stomp Out Mad Cowboy Disease"
- "George Bush Voodoo Dolls $5"
- "Called by God. Controlled by Satan!" (Bush picture)
- "From Fallujah to San Fran We Are All Iraqi"

MAYBE A QUIET WORD WOULD HELP

The following are unassailable facts. Perhaps it would be good to convey them to the legions of the Far Left that have been ranting about the current administration and U.S. policies.

Fact 1. While in college, George Bush scored a 556 on his verbal Scholastic Aptitude Test (SAT) and a 640 on his math SAT. The combined score of 1,206 put him in the 91st percentile. If the same score were to be added up today (the SAT scoring system has changed since then), he would have scored a 632 and a 648, for a combined 1,280.[27] Bush graduated from Yale University as a history major in 1968 and took an MBA from Harvard Business School in 1975, the latter one of the preeminent business colleges in the United States. Bush learned to fly the F-102 jet interceptor while in the Texas Air National Guard. He also served as owner of the Texas Rangers baseball team. He was elected twice as governor of Texas for two consecutive four-year teams (re-elected in 1998), the first Texas governor to have done so. Is this what some call "stupid"?

Fact 2. U.S. authorities have provided a number of things to make camp life in Guantanamo Bay suitable for Islamic detainees. "Each detainee's cell has a sink installed low to the ground" to make it easier for him to wash his feet before Muslim prayer. Each detainee is fed two *halal* (religiously correct) meals a day in addition to an MRE (meal ready to eat). Every detainee receives a prayer mat, a cap, and a Koran. "Every cell has a stenciled arrow pointing toward Mecca." Moreover, the camp's library is stocked with jihadi and Muslim-oriented books. Meanwhile, U.S. MPs have endured plenty of abuse from manipulative, hate-mongering enemy combatants. "Detainees have spit on and hurled water, urine, and feces on the MPs" and have taken pleasure in causing disturbances.[28] Is this what some call the "gulag"?

Fact 3. The U.S. military has no interest in making Iraq some distant addition to a "colonial empire." There is a total lack of interest among GIs and Defense Department civilians in occupying that country. Nobody has any desire to add Iraq as any kind of U.S. possession. Even the old Ottoman Empire had little regard for Iraq, considering it a backwater of three remote provinces during the days when the Turks ruled it. Is this what some call "imperialism"?

Fact 4. The United States is committed to fielding the most advanced array of precision-guided munitions possible. These high-technology weapons have the effect of: (a) sharply reducing collateral (unintended) damage to nontargeted structures; (b) minimizing the hits against innocent noncombatants; and (c) reducing the risk to U.S. fighting men by minimizing the danger of "friendly fire." Those used during the most recent campaigns in both Afghanistan and Iraq included aerial weapons employing GPS (Global Positioning System), laser-guided bombs, and terrain-following cruise missiles. Roughly two-thirds of all U.S. weapons used in Operation Iraqi Freedom were precision weapons. At the same time, U.S. military planners in recent years have prepared strict rules of engagement to prevent unnecessary damage to nontarget structures, and put many humanitarian and cultural facilities on the "do not strike" list. Is this what some call "wanton terror bombing"?

LOSING THE COMPASS
EPISODES FROM
JOHN KERRY'S CAREER

THE COMPASS HERE REFERS to a politician's inner sense of right and wrong. It is an internal guide to what is worth supporting and what should be opposed. You can learn a lot about politicians when you find out who gives aid and comfort to whom. So it's revealing when you examine who has received the benefit of aid and comfort from John Kerry and who has not. These episodes taken together make a sobering account of how a major politician can lose his compass.

DANIEL ORTEGA AND NICARAGUA

Daniel Ortega was president of Nicaragua from 1985 to 1990, the time of the Sandinista government. He was one of several guerrilla leaders who took power in 1979. Under his leadership the Sandinistas "became undisputed heads of the new government and undertook a radical program" for economic transformation. Parts of their program were inspired by Castro's socialist system in Cuba. The Sandinistas actively suppressed dissent and violated human rights, and the "Nicaraguan constitution was suspended and freedom of the press was curtailed." Ortega was defeated in a fair election in 1990; he stood for election again in 1996 and 2001 but lost on those occasions as well.[1]

In April 1985 Ortega was on the receiving side of Kerry's help. Kerry joined Senator Tom Harkin (D-IA) on a fact-finding tour to Nicaragua, which was organized by Peter Kornbluth of the Institute for Policy Studies (IPS). Evidently the objective was to block congressional support for the Contras (the Nicaraguan opposition) by portraying the Sandinistas in a positive light. Just forty-eight hours before a crucial vote in the Senate on aid to the Contras, Harkin and Kerry flew to Nicaragua. Their celebrated meetings with Sandinista leaders captured headlines and helped to sway the opinion of Congress. Kerry returned to the United States waving a "promise" from Ortega that the Communist leader would moderate his policies. Kerry reported to his colleagues that Ortega was a "misunderstood democrat rather than a Marxist autocrat."[2] Secretary of State George Schultz denounced Kerry publicly for "dealing with the Communists" and letting himself be used by Ortega. Within a week, Ortega flew to Moscow where he secured "$200 million in Soviet aid." Shocked and embarrassed, Congress reversed its decision to deny aid to the Contras and "granted $27 million in humanitarian aid" to them.[3]

Kerry was a champion of the Sandinista regime during that time. In early 1985 the IPS brought together its Latin American players and compiled one of its "reports" entitled *In Contempt of Congress*, which was designed to compile "the Reagan record of deceit and illegality on Central America." Its main intention apparently was to sow distrust of the Reagan administration. This got wide circulation in Congress, and Kerry called it "essential reading for every American who remembers Vietnam and Watergate." Not only was the IPS on very good terms with Kerry but also with Daniel Ortega and other Sandinista officials, lauding them with honors.[4]

JEAN-BERTRAND ARISTIDE AND HAITI

Jean-Bertrand Aristide is a former Catholic priest who was president of Haiti in 1991, 1994–96, and 2001–4. Supporters lauded him as a friend of the poor, but he "became dictatorial and corrupt once in power and was twice overthrown." The first time was in a military coup (1991) and subsequently in a rebellion in which former soldiers participated (2004). By 2003 he was ruling by decree and using violence to attack his political opponents. He maintained close ties to the police as well as to street gangs such as the so-called Cannibal Army. Aristide remains in exile in South Africa, where he argues that he is the legitimate president and that U.S. forces kidnapped him.[5]

In 1994 and 2004 Haitian dictator Aristide was on the receiving end of Kerry's help. In 1994 Kerry tried to pass off the deranged Marxist thug—whom he called "Father Aristide"—as a conciliatory priest and played the role of apologist. In early 2004 Kerry wrote about the need to restore the ousted dictator through U.S. military might just as Aristide's corrupt regime was being swamped by a popular rebellion. Kerry's remarks were published on the same day that Aristide's gunmen shot more than twenty-five peaceful demonstrators who were celebrating his departure.

OSWALDO PAYA AND CUBA

Oswaldo Paya is a longtime opponent of the Castro regime and heads the Varela Project, which has circulated a petition to call for a Cuban national plebiscite on basic human rights (including freedoms of association, speech, the press, worship, and elections). The project relies on the provisions in the Cuban constitution, which provides for "citizen initiatives on a petition of ten thousand signatures." Paya's group gathered three times more than the required signatures for a referendum on free elections, but the project was rebuffed by the Cuban government. Paya is a courageous dissident who belongs to a group called the Christian Liberation Movement.[6]

In June 2004 Paya did not receive much aid and comfort from Kerry. Castro's security forces cracked down hard on the movement's supporters, and some were sentenced to twenty-eight years in prison. Paya issued a desperate call for international support. But Kerry told a *Miami Herald* reporter, the Varela Project "has gotten a lot of people in trouble . . . and it brought down the hammer in a way that I think wound up being counterproductive."[7] This opportunity to give heart to a bright light of democracy in Cuba ended with a spineless statement that supported appeasement. Many saw Kerry as dead wrong on his lack of support for the Varela Project, especially when the European Union had embraced it. In police states such as Cuba, the only shred of hope that dissidents have is that some influential persons from free countries will take up their cause or pay respects to the great sacrifices they make.

IYAD ALLAWI AND IRAQ

Iyad Allawi was the interim prime minister of Iraq. A prominent exile political activist, he is a politically secular Shi'a Muslim who became a member of the Iraq Interim Governing Council that was established after the 2003 Iraq War. In June 2004 he became Iraq's "first head of government since Saddam Hussein." Allawi's term as prime minister ended in April 2005, after the selection of Ibrahim al-Jaafari by the newly elected transitional Iraqi National Assembly. Allawi continues to lead the Iraqi National Accord Party in the new assembly. His wife and children still live in the United Kingdom "for their security," and Allawi "survived an assassination attempt" on April 20, 2005.[8]

Allawi did not fare any better with Kerry. In late 2004 Kerry stated that Allawi was sent before the U.S. Congress to put the best face on the Bush administration's Iraq policy, which Kerry claimed contradicted the reality on the ground. So instead of supporting a courageous leader in a very tight spot with a price on his head, Kerry condescendingly gave him the back of his hand.

Kerry's words were matched—actually outdone—by one of his senior advisers, Joe Lockhart. Lockhart said, "The last thing you want to be seen as is a puppet of the United States [referring to Allawi], and you can almost see the hand underneath the shirt today moving the lips." If possible, this comment was even more bizarre, stupid, and condescending than Kerry's, and—naturally—there was no effort by Kerry to discipline Lockhart or to object to the remark.[9]

Just after the Iraqi election of January 2005, Kerry claimed that it was no big deal. "No one in the United States should try to overhype this election," he told NBC's *Meet the Press*. He also questioned the legitimacy of the election: "It's hard to say that something is legitimate when a whole portion of the country can't vote and doesn't vote."

When he was asked whether he believed that Iraq was now less of a terrorist threat, he stated, "No, it's more. And, in fact, I believe the world is less safe today than it was two and a half years ago."[10]

By running down this historic election, Kerry joined a chorus of other naysayers on the Left. Many of them took every opportunity to diminish the achievements of courageous people who participated in the "purple-finger revolution." The naysaying began quite a while ago. In July 2003 Howard Dean stated, "We don't know whether in the long run the Iraqi people are better off."[11]

RAMSEY CLARK AND KERRY'S OTHER COMRADES

But it was reassuring to see that John Kerry himself received aid and comfort from none other than Ramsey Clark. In February 2004 the disgraced former attorney general stated that he would be voting for Kerry because he would take U.S. foreign policy in a new direction. "I think John Kerry is a great human being," Clark said, calling Kerry "deeply concerned for peace and the well-being of other people." The Clark-Kerry ties date back from their time together with Vietnam Veterans Against the War (VVAW). Kerry's fellow GIs received no aid and comfort from him, as Kerry leveled charges of "war crimes" and "genocide." But the North Vietnamese jailers of American POWs got plenty of aid and comfort from Clark, who falsely declared that the POWs were in good health and their conditions "could not be better."

Seen in this light, these particular actions by Kerry cannot be explained away, nor can they be ducked. They are far more revealing and relevant than what he did or did not do in the Mekong Delta during his few months there in the navy.

Kerry's stances are not surprising considering those who influenced him at an early stage of his political career. His sister Peggy was an antiwar activist, often associated with the Vietnam Moratorium Committee (VMC). She brought Kerry into supporting that group in 1969, when Kerry was still on active duty. The VMC was formed by associates of the American Friends Service Committee (AFSC) and National Committee for a Sane Nuclear Policy (SANE). Kerry also chaired the congressional campaign of Father Robert Drinan, a left-wing priest and lawyer who was also an officer in the National Lawyers Guild (NLG). Drinan's background was a maze of Communist connections, and Kerry continued his relationship with him after that campaign. Kerry interacted with Al Hubbard, who appointed him to the National Executive Committee of VVAW. Kerry was elevated to this job because of his speaking ability and his contacts with the Democratic National Committee and with Senator Ted Kennedy (D-MA). The VVAW formed alliances with other antiwar groups, and its leadership interlocked with the Communist-front People's Coalition for Peace and Justice (PCPJ). Finally, Kerry was influenced by Adam Walinsky, a key leader of the New York office of the VMC. Earlier Walinsky was a legal and speech writing assistant to Robert F. Kennedy.[12] In addition, during the 1980s, Kerry was deriving much of his foreign policy advice from the Institute for Policy Studies (IPS) and its cadre.

11

THE ROAD AHEAD

SOME CAUTIONARY NOTES

WARNING #1: WE COULD ALL GROW UP TO BE GREENS

Perhaps you have always wanted to live in a "more democratic, cooperative, cleaner, safer world where we the people, not the corporations,
make the decisions that affect our lives." And perhaps you believe in
"grass-roots political and economic democracy, nonviolence, social justice, and ecological sustainability."[1] If that is the case, you have found a
home in the Greens/Green Party USA, the official name for today's Green
Party.

Want to know more? For the Greens, the fights against racism, sexism, class exploitation, bureaucratic domination, war, and "other forms
of social domination and violence" are central to the movement for an
ecologically sustainable society. In order to harmonize society with nature, "we must first harmonize human with human."[2]

Even a passing glance at the Greens' platform is alarming. Some
people actually believe this way! And—what's more—there are a
number of groups described earlier here that would like to push us in
this direction. So this is the way that we could end up: the subjects of a
nanny state, infested with lawyers, quota-obsessed, egalitarian, and

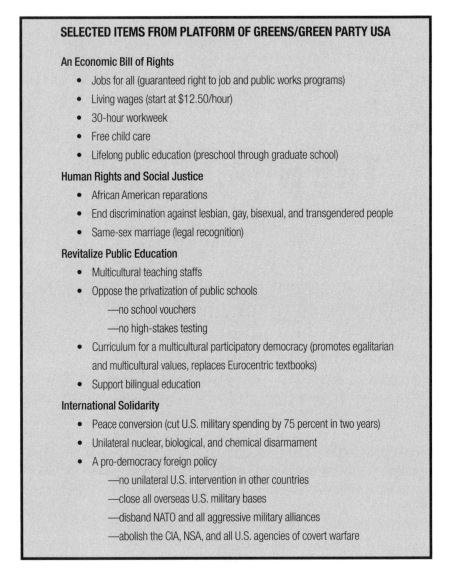

SELECTED ITEMS FROM PLATFORM OF GREENS/GREEN PARTY USA

An Economic Bill of Rights

- Jobs for all (guaranteed right to job and public works programs)
- Living wages (start at $12.50/hour)
- 30-hour workweek
- Free child care
- Lifelong public education (preschool through graduate school)

Human Rights and Social Justice

- African American reparations
- End discrimination against lesbian, gay, bisexual, and transgendered people
- Same-sex marriage (legal recognition)

Revitalize Public Education

- Multicultural teaching staffs
- Oppose the privatization of public schools
    - —no school vouchers
    - —no high-stakes testing
- Curriculum for a multicultural participatory democracy (promotes egalitarian and multicultural values, replaces Eurocentric textbooks)
- Support bilingual education

International Solidarity

- Peace conversion (cut U.S. military spending by 75 percent in two years)
- Unilateral nuclear, biological, and chemical disarmament
- A pro-democracy foreign policy
    - —no unilateral U.S. intervention in other countries
    - —close all overseas U.S. military bases
    - —disband NATO and all aggressive military alliances
    - —abolish the CIA, NSA, and all U.S. agencies of covert warfare

toothless in both foreign policy and national defense. It's called social-ism American style.

WARNING #2: EVERYBODY IS CONNING SOMEBODY ELSE

In politics there is a great deal of deception at work every day. Hard-core Left groups try to portray themselves as "mainstream." Radical lawyers try to portray themselves as "social justice" advocates. De facto agents of influence try to portray themselves as "concerned citizens." Or radical or liberal opinion makers in the media try to portray themselves as "honest reporters." Communists and socialists in the organized Far Left do not admit that they have taken over many of the antiwar movements. Political candidates themselves deny that they are beholden to special interests.

Let's look once more at People for the American Way (PFAW). That group portrays itself as promoting tolerance, equality, and other liberties. According to its stated objectives, PFAW seeks to advance "pluralism, individuality, freedom of thought, expression and religion, a sense of community, and tolerance and compassion for others."[3] Unfortunately, those nice-sounding words have been hijacked, for PFAW practices the opposite of those, as made clear by its strident fight against prior nominees to the Supreme Court and its current campaigns against the nominees of 2005 and 2006.

This realization that everyone is conning someone else must be coupled with an awareness that the media have poisoned public opinion to a great degree. As events of the past year have proved, the media can exert tremendous influence through the frequency, the timing, and the subject matter of stories, as well as the vocabulary used. Certainly what the media choose and choose not to publish or broadcast is critical. We already know that the media have shown themselves to be irresponsible in a number of ways: obsession with scandal, appetite for fights, propensity for character assassination, urge to create news rather than report it, and overall lack of accountability.[4] The media can make it easy for a political figure to misrepresent himself, giving him a free pass or overlooking things that many ordinary citizens should know.

WARNING #3: MANY ARE LOSING FAITH IN CONGRESS

The general level of contempt for Congress is worrisome. In the previous decade we witnessed the following:

- In the mid-1990s, more than 140 former members of Congress were lobbying their former colleagues.
- Two senior members of the House resigned their seats in midsession to run major lobbies.

- A member of Congress was cohabiting with a prostitute of the same sex (Barney Frank, D-MA).
- A member of Congress had seduced a page (Gerry Studds, D-MA).
- There was suspicious book-deal profiteering (David Durenberger, R-MN).
- A congressman steered contracts of the Department of Housing and Urban Development (HUD) to friends (Al D'Amato, R-NY).[5]

In November 2005 Representative Randy "Duke" Cunningham (R-CA) resigned his office after admitting to taking some $2.4 million in bribes. Among his top "prizes" were a yacht and a Rolls-Royce. He faces imprisonment for tax evasion and conspiracy.

At the same time, Congress has been subject to the bullies of special-interest groups while regularly engaging in pork-barrel politics. Bipartisanship has often immobilized Congress from taking any effective action—and especially now, it seems. Congress itself has contributed to governmental bloat, given its inflated staff and extraordinary spread of committees and subcommittees on Capitol Hill.

We are now seeing unmistakable signs that Congress is unable to step up to the critical issues of the day. These issues include illegal immigration to the United States as well as a national long-term energy policy, to name just two. Nor is there any movement in Congress (as of early 2006) about the crisis in public education or the massive shortfalls in pension funding in many major U.S. firms. Instead, Congress has fixated itself on issues that are beyond the purview of U.S. government policy, such as the sad case of Terri Schiavo in the spring of 2005. And then there are the charges of obstructionism—especially with the entrenched opposition to President Bush's nominees to judgeships. All of these factors have combined to give Congress a bad reputation in the minds of many Americans—even before many become aware of the extent of the radicalism of the Progressive Caucus and the Congressional Black Caucus.

Some opinion polls about the performance of Congress serve as proof of the malaise. In a May 2005 NBC/*Wall Street Journal* poll, respondents indicated by a margin of 65 to 17 percent that Congress did not share their priorities. A poll by CBS showed the approval ratings for Congress at a feeble 29 percent, the lowest in almost a decade.[6]

WARNING #4: IT CAN HAPPEN HERE

Some Western countries have had agents of influence in high positions, whether as policy makers, chief assistants to policy makers, or opinion makers. It can happen anywhere, even in the United States. Many of the groups described earlier have craved access to high places in Washington, so it should be no surprise that they place their own people close to the top policy-making levels. Below are just a few examples of high-level agents in high places:

George Galloway, a Scottish Member of Parliament from the Labour Party, received money from Saddam Hussein's regime, taking a slice of oil earnings worth about $550,000 annually, according to Iraqi intelligence documents found in Baghdad. A confidential memo sent to Hussein by his spy chief stated that Galloway had even asked an Iraqi intelligence agent for a greater cut of Iraq's exports under the UN Oil for Food program. These payments went on for some ten years. Galloway was expelled from the Labour Party in October 2003 as a result of his stance on the Iraq War. He was called "a mouthpiece to the Iraqi regime over many years," and Labour chairman Ian McCartney said that Galloway's comments "incited foreign forces to rise up against British troops."[7]

Arne Treholt was a former Norwegian "diplomat and deputy minister convicted of spying for the USSR and Iraq." He provided the Soviets with details of meetings between Norwegian political leaders and visiting foreign dignitaries and had access to cabinet documents. In the late 1960s he became a strong opponent of U.S. foreign policy. The KGB recruited Treholt in 1968, and his espionage career ended with his arrest in 1984. He was described as "one of the Soviets' best" penetration agents in the West, but he also functioned as an agent of influence due to his involvement in negotiations with the USSR over territorial and fishing rights.[8]

Guenther Guillaume was a personal assistant to West German chancellor Willy Brandt. Originally from East Germany, he was already a spy when he began working as Brandt's secretary in 1970 and "became Brandt's personal assistant in 1973." Guillaume was arrested in 1974, and the spy scandal caused Brandt's resignation. "Guillaume was considered East Germany's best penetration agent into the West German political system." There is no other espionage case in the public realm of such a close associate to a European head of state.[9]

Winston Burdett admitted that, in the early part of his career, he had been a Soviet espionage agent. In the 1950s longtime CBS correspondent Burdett admitted taking Soviet espionage assignments as a newspaper reporter in the 1940s.[10] Details are lacking, but one search reveals that Burdett had accumulated some 969 pages of files in the FBI, according to its Freedom of Information Act (FOIA) Reading Room Index.[11] Burdett was the CBS chief European correspondent from 1956 to 1978 and had reported on dozens of governments. He lived in Rome before his death in 1993.

THEIR ANTICIPATED ACTIONS IN THE FUTURE: FOREIGN ISSUES

In the foreign arena, the United States is certain to have tensions over the more worrisome nations that possess weapons of mass destruction (WMD). As of 2006, two nations that evoke special concern are Iran and North Korea. In addition, the United States will also have foreign terrorist groups at the top of its intelligence priorities for as far as anyone can envision.

It is inevitable that some Far-Left individuals and groups will make great efforts to take the side of Iran and North Korea. They will try to explain away these countries' pursuits of WMD as well as their repressive regimes, and the far-leftists will spare no effort to hinder or obstruct the United States from taking resolute actions. For example, Ramsey Clark has already acted on behalf of Iran's Islamic dictatorship, at the "Crimes of America" forum at Tehran in mid-1980. In addition, one of the stated objectives of the ANSWER demonstration of March 19, 2005, was to include demands to "stop the threats against Iran and Cuba." Brian Becker of the Workers World Party and International Action Center visited North Korea in 2000 and pledged his solidarity with the Pyongyang regime. Should the United States ratchet up the pressure against either Iran or North Korea, it is inevitable that other denizens of the Far Left will take the side of Tehran or Pyongyang. In addition, these very same Far-Left individuals and groups will be the first to advocate limits on the ability of the United States to seek out and pursue foreign terrorists.

The CIA is mandated to report to Congress each year about other countries' acquisitions of technology relating to weapons of mass destruction and advanced conventional weapons (ACW). The unclassified annex to this report gives a good account of the progress that major adversaries have made in attaining such weapons. It is necessary to offer evidence of the very real threats posed by adversary countries and foreign terrorist groups. If nothing else, this material shows that there are sound reasons why we have such sustained efforts to penetrate the regimes of major adversary states and terrorist groups—all of which rank as the most difficult intelligence targets in recent history. The material also underscores the rationale for domestic security measures such as the USA PATRIOT Act.

The following passages are only portions of the unclassified report but are taken verbatim from this document that covers the period of July 1 to December 31, 2003.[12]

IRAN

Iran continued to vigorously pursue indigenous programs to produce nuclear, chemical, and biological weapons. Iran is also working to improve delivery systems as well as ACW [advanced conventional weapons]. To this end, Iran continued to seek foreign materials, training, equipment, and know-how.

Nuclear. The United States remains convinced that Tehran has been pursuing a clandestine nuclear weapons program, in contradiction to its obligations as a party to the Nuclear Non-proliferation Treaty (NPT). During 2003, Iraq continued to pursue an indigenous nuclear fuel cycle ostensibly for civilian purposes but with clear weapons potential.

Ballistic Missile. Iran's ballistic missile inventory is among the largest in the Middle East and includes some 1,300-km range Shahab-3 medium-range ballistic missiles (MRBMs) and a few hundred short-range ballistic missiles (SRBMs)—including the Shahab-1 (Scud-B), Shahab-2 (Scud-C), and Tondar (CSS-8)—as well as a variety of large unguided rockets. Iran is also pursuing longer-range ballistic missiles.

Chemical. Iran may have already stockpiled blister, blood, choking, and possible nerve agents—and the bombs and artillery shells to deliver them—which it previously had manufactured.

Biological. Iran probably has the capability to produce at least small quantities of BW [biological warfare] agents.[13]

NORTH KOREA

Nuclear. After announcing in early 2003 its withdrawal from the Treaty on Non-Proliferation of Nuclear Weapons (NPT) and its intention to resume operation of nuclear facilities at Yongbyon, which had been frozen under the terms of the 1994 U.S.–North Korea Agreed Framework, North Korea announced in early October 2003 that at the end of June it had completed reprocessing all of the 8,000 spent fuel rods previously under IAEA (International Atomic Energy Agency) safeguards.

In late April 2003 during the Six Party Talks in Beijing, North Korea privately threatened to "transfer" or "demonstrate" its nuclear weapons. North Korea repeated these threats at the Six Party Talks in August 2003. In December 2003, North Korea proposed freezing its nuclear activities, including not exporting nuclear weapons, in exchange for rewards. We continued to monitor and assess North Korea's nuclear weapons efforts amidst diplomatic efforts to arrange a second round of Six Party Talks.

Ballistic Missile. North Korea is nearly self-sufficient in developing and producing ballistic missiles and continued to procure needed raw materials and components from various foreign sources. In the second half of 2003, North Korea continued to abide by its voluntary moratorium on flight tests adopted in 1998 but announced it may reconsider its September 2002 offer to continue the moratorium beyond 2003. The multiple-stage Taepo Dong-2—potentially capable of reaching parts of the United States with a nuclear-weapon-sized payload—may be ready for flight-testing.

Chemical. North Korea's CW [chemical warfare] capabilities included the ability to produce bulk quantities of nerve, blister, choking, and blood agent, using its sizable, although aging, chemical industry. North Korea may possess a stockpile of unknown size of these agents and weapons, which it could employ in a variety of delivery means.

Biological. North Korea has acceded to the Biological and Toxin Weapons convention but nevertheless has pursued BW [biological warfare] capabilities since the 1960s. Pyongyang acquired dual-use biotechnical equipment, supplies, and reagents that could be used to support North Korea's BW program. North Korea is believed to possess a munitions production infrastructure that would have allowed it to weaponize BW agents and may have some such weapons available for use.[14]

CHEMICAL, BIOLOGICAL, RADIOLOGICAL, AND NUCLEAR TERRORISM

The threat of terrorists using chemical, biological, radiological and nuclear (CBRN) materials remained high. Many of the thirty-three designated foreign terrorist organizations and other nonstate actors worldwide have expressed interest in using CBRN; however, most attacks probably will be small-scale, incorporating improvised delivery means and easily produced or obtained chemicals, toxins, or radiological substances. Although terrorist groups probably will continue to favor long-proven conventional tactics, such as bombings and shootings, the arrest of ricin plotters in London indicated that international Mujahideen terrorists were actively plotting to conduct chemical and biological attacks.

One of the biggest concerns is al-Qaeda's stated readiness to attempt unconventional attacks. As early as 1998 Osama bin Laden publicly declared that acquiring unconventional weapons was "a religious duty." In 2003 an extremist cleric who supports al-Qaeda issued a fatwa that purports to provide a religious justification for the use of WMD against the United States.

Documents and equipment recovered from al-Qaeda facilities in Afghanistan show that al-Qaeda had conducted research on biological agents. Many believe that al-Qaeda's biological warfare program is primarily focused on anthrax for mass casualty attacks, although the group most likely will also pursue opportunities to produce and use other biological agents in smaller-scale attacks.

Information from 2003 details the construction of a terrorist cyanide-based chemical weapon that can be made with easily available items, requiring little or no training to assemble and deploy. The plans are widely available to any terrorist. Such a device could produce a lethal concentration of poisonous gasses in an enclosed area.[15]

IRAN, NORTH KOREA, AND TERRORISM

The United States remains concerned about the terrorist ties and leanings of Iran and North Korea. Their activities are summarized by the U.S. State Department in its annual report on terrorism.

Iran remained the most active state sponsor of terrorism in 2004. Its

Islamic Revolutionary Guard Corps and Ministry of Intelligence and Security were involved in the planning and support of terrorist acts and continued to exhort a variety of groups to use terrorism. Iran has continued to encourage anti-Israeli terrorist activity, both rhetorically and operationally. The Iranians have provided Lebanese Hezbollah and Palestinian terrorist groups with funding, safe havens, training, and weapons. In addition, some officials of the Iraqi interim government (IIG) have expressed concern that Iran is interfering in Iraq, and some reports show Iran providing funding, safe transit, and arms to Iraqi insurgent elements.

North Korea is not known to have sponsored any terrorist acts since the bombing of a Korean Airlines flight in 1987. Yet the State Department notes that although North Korea is a party to six international conventions and protocols relating to terrorism, the North Koreans have not taken any substantial steps to cooperate in efforts to combat international terrorism.

The al-Qaeda network remains a deadly threat to the United States and its citizens. It is dedicated to attacking the U.S. homeland as well as U.S. interests overseas. That organization has been weakened and degraded operationally, but it remains a moral force in inspiring local terrorist groups in the Middle East and elsewhere.

Al-Qaeda is perhaps the most difficult intelligence adversary the United States has even faced. Network members demonstrate extraordinary loyalty to their cause, arising from either ideological faith or possibly intimidation. Some speculate that the families of network members may be hostages so that terrorist agents will act without question. The fact that there have been no defections by any network members in recent years may be an indication of such control. Moreover, in view of the hundreds or thousands of people needed to support the network's affairs, there were no leaks or shreds of information coming out to the network until the roundup of prisoners from Afghanistan in 2001. The network is so efficiently organized and compartmentalized that no one person— with the exception of bin Laden himself—knows the big picture. In late 2001 and early 2002, the bin Laden network showed itself adept at outflanking U.S. technological intelligence collection, and the most deadly terrorist groups make the greatest use of the new Web-based technology, which invariably includes encryption of messages.[16]

OTHER FOREIGN CHALLENGES

One of the few certain things about the next decade is that the United States will encounter some radical changes abroad, some of them expected and some not. Should the United States head into a crisis with any of the countries noted below, there will be a predictable collection of the "usual suspects" who will inevitably take the other side and point out how very wrong our policies are.

There are several very large, very sick, and very corrupt countries with Islamic populations or large majorities that pose potential troubles. Problems in these countries could well become unmanageable, spill over their borders, and affect U.S. interests. Such countries include Indonesia, Pakistan, and Nigeria—with populations of 230 million, 150 million, and 130 million, respectively. All may plausibly become "failed states," in which basic institutions stop functioning and chaos and radicalism flourish.[17]

A European Union may well rise up as the principal global competitor of the United States. Even after the stinging defeats (in France and the Netherlands) of the proposed Europe-wide constitution in May and June 2005, Europe is still likely to solidify its current security partnerships, and it may well unite against the United States and vie for preeminence with the United States. Some experts suggest that an ascendant EU will eventually test its muscle against America, especially if the unilateralist bent in U.S. foreign policy continues. A once-united West may well separate into competing halves.[18] Even now, some European political leaders are calling for a more integrated Europe to offset U.S. hegemony, a superpower—with some 457 million citizens in mid-2005—to stand equal to the United States and to act as a counterweight to U.S. world domination. Given the current enlarged state of the EU (twenty-five nations since May 2004), it is more difficult to manage internally but has far more economic power potential than ever before.

Closer to home, Venezuela has emerged as a major concern. According to Mortimer Zuckerman of *U.S. News and World Report,* Venezuela, long one of Latin America's strongest democracies, is now under siege by its president, Hugo Chavez. "Chavez has rewritten Venezuela's Constitution to enhance his powers, purged critics in the military, set up legislation to pack the Supreme Court, intimidated the media by threatening the expropriation of the licenses of private television stations that supported the opposition, and given succor to thousands of Castro's military and intelligence officers, along with many social and medical workers, while tens of thousands of young Venezuelans have been sent to Cuba for indoctrination."[19] In addition, "Chavez provides Castro with some eighty thousand barrels" of essential oil each day while allowing the Cubans to run his intelligence services and train his military. Chavez has also made an "alliance with the worst criminal organizations in Latin America, especially the narco-terrorists in Columbia." Secretary of State Condoleezza Rice has remarked that Chavez is a danger not just to Venezuela but also to much of Latin America.[20]

THEIR ANTICIPATED ACTIONS IN THE FUTURE—DOMESTIC ISSUES

DOMESTIC SECURITY

Nearly all of the Far-Left groups profiled earlier here have had some comments or positions about U.S. domestic-security practices. Many of these groups have taken particular aim at the USA PATRIOT Act.

The USA PATRIOT Act passed 98–1 in the Senate and 357–66 in the House and was signed into law on October 26, 2001. The act was intended to enhance the authority of U.S. law-enforcement bodies to investigate and preempt potential terrorism, and it allows for more effective practices than before. The act extends the use of pen registers and trap-and-trace devices (that determine the destinations and origins of telephone calls, respectively). It authorizes roving, multipoint wiretaps, a response to the ongoing "communications revolution" afoot today. And the act amends the existing Foreign Intelligence Surveillance Act (FISA, 1978), easing requirements for technical surveillance—which is the most contentious part of the USA PATRIOT Act.

This act grew out of earlier legislation, namely FISA (which was primarily concerned with espionage and terrorism) and the USA Act that passed the Congress in early October 2001. The newer USA PATRIOT Act also provides for features such as a foreign-student-monitoring program, machine-readable passports, and a clearer definition of "electronic surveillance."[21]

There are continued misunderstandings about this act, and there are some deliberately crafted falsehoods about it as well. The act was designed to pursue and catch terrorists, not to undermine the Bill of Rights. Up to mid-November 2004, this act had been used to charge 372 suspected terrorists and to convict 194 of them.[22] There has been no use of this act to punish anyone for expressing dissenting opinions about U.S. policy or the Bush administration.

Much of the liberal, radical backlash against the act has been directed at the provisions for "sneak-and-peek searches." The act's detractors "make a general claim that the government may search anyone's home or gain access to a person's library, finance, or work records without a warrant." This is blatantly false. In fact, a sneak-and-peek search requires a warrant. In special cases covered by the FISA, the warrant may come from the Foreign Intelligence Surveillance Court (FISC), in which case it is not a public record and not required to be released; other warrants must be released, especially to the person under investigation.

In August 2004 the American Civil Liberties Union (ACLU) ran an expensive ($1.5 million) ad campaign against this act. The ad claimed, "So the government can search your house . . . My house . . . Our house . . . Without notifying us. Treating us like suspects. It's part of the PATRIOT Act." Some critics noted that the phrase "without notifying us" implied that one would never be notified of a search.[23] There is a provision in the act that allows for delayed notification of warrants in "special cases," but the ACLU's implication was far off the mark and deliberately so.

Several of the surveillance portions of the USA PATRIOT Act were to expire on December 31, 2005, under the so-called sunset provision unless Congress renewed them. These provisions pertain to authority to intercept communications, roving surveillance authority, seizure of voice-mail messages, interception of "computer trespasser communications," and search warrants for electronic evidence. Any effort to renew them will trigger another eruption from the usual suspects of the Far Left. The primary groups expected to speak up will include lawyer-heavy organizations such as the American Civil Liberties Union, the National Lawyers Guild, the Center for Constitutional Rights, People for the American Way, MoveOn, United for Peace and Justice, and their allies.

Far-Left groups are likely to take advantage of the fact that the public is wary but ignorant about the act. In January 2002 some "47 percent of Americans wanted their government to stop terrorism even if it reduced civil liberties. By November 2003 this number had dropped to 31 percent." By 2005 the U.S. public was about evenly divided for and against the USA PATRIOT Act. At the same time, in mid-April 2005, pollsters asked the question, "What do you know about the USA PATRIOT Act?" Only 13 percent responded "a lot," while 28 percent answered "some," 28 percent answered "not much," and 29 percent answered "nothing."[24]

THE SUPREME COURT

Until late 2005, the composition of the Supreme Court had stayed unchanged since 1994. This has been the second-longest period without a membership change in the history of the Court, the longest having been from 1812 to 1823.[25] As a result, the Court is in the midst of a significant change. Some current justices are now at an age where they are thinking of retirement or facing health problems that may compel them to retire. Some justices will be seventy years old or approaching that age.

This change will not be limited to the vacancies created by the recent death of Chief Justice William Rehnquist and the announced retirement of Associate Justice Sandra Day O'Connor. Justices who are likely to leave the bench in the next few years include:

- John Paul Stevens, born in 1920 and on the Court since 1975, is by far the oldest member of the Court.
- Ruth Bader Ginsburg, born in 1933 and on the Court since 1993, has had health issues (colon cancer) but has since recovered.

Two justices are less likely to leave soon, but they will soon be seventy. They include:

- Antonin Scalia, born in 1936 and on the Court since 1986.
- Anthony M. Kennedy, born in 1936 and on the Court since 1988.

Three "spring chickens" are less likely to retire soon:

- Stephen G. Breyer, born in 1938 and on the Court since 1994.
- David H. Souter, born in 1939 and on the Court since 1990.
- Clarence Thomas, born in 1948 and on the Court since 1991.

There can be no doubt about the importance of the Supreme Court. It is the umpire of the U.S. federal system, interpreting the Constitution in an endless number of ways. Legal scholars note that Supreme Court nominations are among the most significant that a president can make, "for no other choices have longer (or, possibly, larger) impact on the workings of government, and the law of the land."[26]

Of course, the Supreme Court has been especially controversial in recent years. This is largely due to its crucial role in the 2000 presidential election.

President Bush has stated that he would pick "strict constructionists," that is, justices who would interpret the Constitution and not try to make laws from the bench. He is in the process of nominating conservative jurists to fill the emerging vacancies. Both the White House and major liberal interest groups had been preparing for many months in the face of these developments on the Court. Groups on both the Left and the Right have spent this time "picking through potential nominees' old opinions and law review articles. Both sides are e-mailing backgrounders to their members and circulating memos to Senate staffers. There are blogs and focus groups, polls and message points."[27] The White House had been reviewing a number of candidates and their views.

Meanwhile, groups such as People for the American Way (PFAW)—the likely leader of the coalition opposed to any conservative judge—had been getting ready. PFAW's war room at its M Street headquarters in Washington DC sprang into full combat mode once President Bush named his first nominee in the summer of 2005.[28] PFAW continued to be active throughout late 2005 as well.

- On July 19 the president nominated John G. Roberts for associate justice, but after Chief Justice Rehnquist's death, he amended the Roberts nomination on September 5 to name him as Rehnquist's successor. In late August PFAW issued a fifty-page report on Roberts's record and stated that he had demonstrated "hostility" to the fundamental rights and liberties of all Americans.

After the Senate confirmed Roberts as the seventeenth chief justice, PFAW predictably issued a statement noting that it was "deeply disappointed" that Roberts had been confirmed to that lifetime position.

- On October 31, the president nominated Samuel A. Alito to succeed Associate Justice O'Connor. Shortly after that PFAW issued a statement declaring Alito's judicial philosophy to be "far to the right" and noted that his confirmation would "seriously jeopardize" the rights of Americans. In December 2005, speaking about Alito's record, PFAW president Ralph Neas noted a "disturbing lack of credibility" beginning to emerge across a range of key issues.

Under Neas's leadership, PFAW influences a broad array of groups, and this time around it has the capability to mobilize up to one thousand organizations if nominees do not meet liberal standards. One of these groups is the Alliance for Justice, led by Nan Aron, a group that helped to block the nomination of Robert Bork to the Supreme Court in the late 1980s. Aron stated, "I think it will be a fight that will shape our lives for decades."

EFFECTIVE COUNTERMEASURES FOR THE REST OF US

There is hope for us yet. A search of Internet sites reveals good evidence that some of us are speaking up and hitting back. Consider the titles of these blogs that appeared in 2003:

- "ANSWER's Steering Committee: Traitors, and Commies, and Jew-haters—Oh my!"
- "Useful Idiots and Useless Arguments: The Depressing Iraq War Debate"
- "Marxist Groups in the Anti-War Movement"
- "Who's Paying for It All?"
- "Anti-War protesters Are Warmongers for Our enemies"
- "America Bashing Is the Only Permissible Kind of Hate Speech"
- "Never Have So Many Been So Wrong About So Much"
- "Willful Ignorance: The antiwar Left just doesn't get reality"
- "The liberal left is the enemy within our borders"

Some Americans are urging that our lawmakers and judges take a hard look at 501(c)(3) groups. Such groups are supposed to acquire most of their funds through charitable contributions. Many such groups (noted earlier in this work) are stepping over the line, and some wonder whether anything can be done about it.

Some other Americans are starting to urge that the Democrats reclaim their party. Perhaps we need to ask some of those party stalwarts the following questions:

- Who invited Michael Moore and George Soros and MoveOn to attach themselves to your party and take it over?
- Do you know, care about, or intend to buy the line of the socialist wing of the Democratic Party, as typified by the Progressive Caucus?

SOME EXAMPLES

You can fight back against tyrannical leftist professors. For the first time, leftist professors are on the run—at least in some places. There are now some 150 chapters of Students for Academic Freedom, formed by David Horowitz in late 2003 after repeated episodes in which conservative thinkers were belittled or shut out of classroom discussions, graduate programs, and even denied tenure. The group's motto is, "You can't get a good education if they are only telling you half the story."[29] As such, liberal professors across the nation are now being accused of abusing their conservative students by humiliating them in class, lowering their grades, and forcing them to listen to radical leftist views. Naturally this group has encountered fierce opposition from faculty and college administrators, but Horowitz presses the issue. Legislators in fifteen states are considering an "academic bill of rights" or "student bill of rights," efforts to offset the very lopsided leftist tilt in major universities.[30]

You can fight back against old antagonists. In a letter to his fans in April 2004, Michael Moore claimed that the so-called resisters in Fallujah, Iraq, are not terrorists nor the enemy, but are "Minutemen" and revolutionaries, and that their numbers will grow—"and they will win."[31]

You may well ask: Which aspects of this so-called resistance does Michael Moore prefer? Would it be the hostage taking, the beheadings, the car-bomb factories, the use of human shields, or the terrorizing of innocent Iraqi citizens who do not accept terrorism? Or maybe you prefer those resisters in Fallujah who killed, mutilated, burned, and then dangled on a bridge the bodies of four U.S. contract workers?

Moore wants you to believe that our troops are the oppressive, colonial enemy of the freedom-fighting Iraqis. This is exactly the kind of remark one expects from him. And a number of observers and critics have exposed his dishonest, hypocritical character. Moore is considered one of the most manipulative individuals in the U.S. film industry. He is bullying, polarizing, shrill, and his works are replete with distortions. His most noteworthy film in recent years, *Fahrenheit 9/11*—which many reviews note is "not a documentary"—reveals a complete lack of anything resembling journalistic integrity.

You can also fight back against new and emerging antagonists. In late May 2005, Irene Khan, the secretary general of Amnesty International, accused the United States of a range of abuses of detainees in Guantanamo Bay. She stated, "The detention facility at Guantanamo Bay has become the gulag of our time."[32]

In mid-2005 there were 540 prisoners from some 40 countries held at the detention facility there. These are individuals who have taken up arms against the United States or who have violated international law. More than 200 others have already been released. In fact, all detainees have been treated humanely, and the U.S. government is investigating all claims of abuse. So what kind of gulag is this anyway?

You may well ask Khan if she knows anything about a *real* gulag? The actual gulag, as practiced by the former USSR, is characterized this way: innocent people are arrested; kangaroo courts sentence them under trumped-up charges based on Article 58 of the Soviet Constitution (- "anti-Soviet activities"); the convicted are deported in railroad cars; "class enemies" are singled out for arrest (such as Baltic citizens or wealthy landowners); prisoners are starved; regular summary executions take place; prisoners are worked to death; prisoners are given inadequate clothing in subzero weather; cells have no sanitation; and inmates terrorize one another (political prisoners at the mercy of hardened criminals). Just in terms of scale, some three million citizens were slaughtered in the Kolyma region of the far northeastern USSR from 1936 to 1953—Soviet citizens were shot, stabbed, thrown into pits, or starved. This was just in one corner of the vast labor camp system in the former Soviet Union. Let it not be forgotten that there was a gigantic network of camps that stretched across the northern USSR—from Vorkuta to Norilsk to Magadan. (Note: In Russian, *gulag* is an abbreviation of *Glavnoe upravlenie ispravitel'no-trudovykh lagerei*, which translates "Main administration for Camps.") During the height of the purges in the late 1930s, the crematory at the Donskoi Monastery in Moscow was incinerating the bodies of one thousand persons each day.[33]

Of course, it's unlikely that Irene Khan would know anything about the real gulag. She has no experience dealing with the USSR or Russia, instead having worked in the UN since 1980. Most of her career she has been with the United Nations High Commissioner for Refugees (UNHCR), with duties at UN headquarters in New York and in selected third world countries such as Sudan, Burundi, and Pakistan, Her study of law at the University of Manchester and Harvard Law School evidently did not prepare her to come to grips with a real gulag. In this case, her remark about the gulag is not only a towering insult to the United States, but even more so to the memory of the millions of innocent Soviet citizens who perished or suffered for many decades in the vast network of concentration camps in the former USSR.

BASIC GUIDELINES FOR STRIKING BACK

Make their strategy come apart. This is time-honored advice from ancient Chinese strategists such as Sun Tzu. It pays to discover what factions make up a group and what groups make up a coalition. For these groups to be outfought, they must be thoroughly understood and then outthought. A good awareness of these organizations and their operational style is essential.

Separate those that pose a significant political threat from those who do not. A group's net influence is related to its organizing skill, its financial management, its longevity, and its ability to mobilize large numbers of people to its causes. As of 2006, the most significant threats appear to emanate from those organizations that appear to be the best-organized. They include United for Peace and Justice (UFPJ), People for the American Way (PFAW), MoveOn, Institute for Policy Studies (IPS), and Act Now to Stop War and End Racism (ANSWER). Of some of the Washington-based groups, their nerve centers are listed below.

Institute for Policy Studies
733 15th Street NW, Suite 1020
Washington DC 20005
(202) 234–9382

ANSWER and International Action Center (IAC)
1247 E Street SE
Washington DC 20003
(202) 544–3389

People for the American Way
2000 M Street NW, Suite 400
Washington DC 20036
(202) 467–4999

Use their own tools against them. The Far Left should not enjoy a monopoly on the campus tactics of guerrilla theater or "truth squads" that follow controversial speakers around. Ridicule is a powerful weapon, for example, and especially when you can use their very own words against them. It is easy to tell those within these groups who are self-appointed, self-important, self-absorbed, self-serving, and self-righteous.

THIS WE'LL DEFEND . . . A WORD OF HOPE

This work has explored one side of America. But there is a very different side as well. Each night the U.S. Constitution, the Bill of Rights, and the Declaration of Independence are carefully lowered into a secure bombproof vault beneath the floor of the National Archives. These precious documents are enclosed in helium-filled cases day and night to protect them. To many of us, these documents remain our most treasured national assets.

Each sunrise greets the sentries at the Tomb of the Unknown Soldiers. They stand on perpetual guard over those who gave their lives in campaigns of sacrifice for noble ideals. We can never give thanks enough to the unknown soldiers and their brothers who lie at rest at Arlington Cemetery.

Each day many thousands of U.S. and foreign visitors flock to the many buildings that make up the Smithsonian Institution. This is sometimes called "the nation's attic," but a better description is a vast storehouse of more than two centuries of miracles. These miracles are the result of American ingenuity, inventiveness, and persistence: the yield of a free and confident society.

CONCLUSION

WE HAVE JOURNEYED DOWN Alice in Wonderland's rabbit hole into a world where black is white, right is wrong, and wet is dry. It is a strange and perplexing political world where nothing is quite the way it seems.

In the preceding pages, we have seen the various weapons of mass distortion our adversaries used during the cold war, some of which are used today. We have seen that some Americans chose to side with our country's enemies as early as the 1920s. We have shed light on those groups that go back to World War I and those that were formed after 2000, all the while trying to capture their connections as well as their beliefs and operating philosophies. We have seen that larger enterprises (elements of the feminist, black, and gay movements or the mass media and even the U.S. Congress) are in step with many of these Far-Left groups. We have looked at how people in these groups choose to express themselves. And we have explored what such groups are likely to do in the future.

Some key findings emerged along the way. These groups have recurring patterns of operations and tactics. They continue to look for new ways to undermine our country's ability to defend itself at home and abroad. A de facto alliance has emerged between some radical Islamic elements, those with a traditional pro-Communist background, and those who seek to apologize for and protect both groups. Some radical groups give aid and comfort to U.S. enemies while liberal groups give aid and comfort to the radical groups. We now know that the money flow really matters but is little understood, and also we know that there is a paramount need to check one's sources of information. There is probably greater interaction between Far-Left groups and foreign officials than is apparent. And finally, it appears that the best way to counteract the influence of these groups is to use the time-honored tools of exposure and awareness.

To maintain perspective, I will now reintroduce you into the outside world and point out where the world of the Far Left fits into the larger picture.

A SENSE OF PERSPECTIVE

Of our population of about three hundred million, those who inhabit these Far-Left groups comprise a small percentage. Yet they are loud, persistent, and often—but not always—well organized. They exert influence far out of proportion to their overall membership numbers. They distort issues to achieve political ends. And they will not go away.

These various groups fit into the larger picture simply because they are a permanent presence on the American political scene. They will be active in antiwar demonstrations, in Supreme Court confirmation hearings, on television and radio talk shows, in the op-ed pages of major newspapers, and in a host of everyday political activities.

They will play a role in the political collisions of each election year in the near and distant future. In addition to these electoral collisions there will also be collisions—or at least major scrapes—over issues such as immigration, energy, homeland security, abortion, and public prayer. But what will be the outcome of such collisions? Which leaders of the Far Left and which groups are most likely to emerge at those times? How likely are they to get what they want?

One cannot speak of facts about the future, but there are some constants that will not change. One will be the ongoing battle for the hearts and minds of young people. Their opinions are especially malleable in the age of instant messaging, instant gratification, and instant "answers" to the world's problems.

RUMORS, OPINIONS, DISTORTION

Why emphasize the mass media and the techniques of propaganda, opinion shaping, perception management, and linguistic distortion? Look back at how people were so easily misled in the days after Hurricane Katrina struck New Orleans. Rumors spread rapidly, including:

- a monster crocodile was fished out of New Orleans floodwaters

- sharks were swimming through the submerged streets
- babies were being raped
- rat-gnawed corpses were floating in the streets
- police officers were being shot point-blank in the head
- snipers were firing at rescue helicopters

   In *Henry IV,* Shakespeare observed, "Rumor is a pipe blown by sur-mises, jealousies, conjectures." Factor in the frenzied nature of the New Orleans atmosphere, the lack of adequate communications, and the pervasiveness and the embellishment of these stories in cyberspace. All were ideal conditions for rumors to flourish, as Anne Applebaum of the *Washington Post* has noted. Unfortunately, race and social status emerged as issues as well, for many politicians quickly played those cards and claimed that the Bush administration neglected the hurricane victims because they were black or poor. And many people were eager to accept rumors, half truths, or other urban legends if such falsehoods served to vilify the present administration.

LIBERALS AND RADICALS

Do not confuse mainline liberals who seek peace and social justice with the Far-Left figures in this book. I have focused on the latter—those who give material aid and comfort to our enemies, those who work to weaken us from within, those who apologize for and encourage foreign tyrants, and those who seek to impose a smothering socialist nanny state.

   Many liberal causes are proud traditions in American history. One is the civil rights movement of the 1950s and 1960s. It permanently changed the nature of this country. Another is the environmentalist movement that took shape in the 1970s and 1980s. Those environmen-tal protections put in place have done much to protect our air, drinking water, forests, wetlands, and coral reefs. But much legislation that has been issued in the intervening years and the issues of today are not the same as those of fifty years ago—which have been addressed by civil rights laws and environmental regulations that are now on the books. Significantly, there is a vast difference between these original causes and the distorting and divisive twists that radicals later added to them. Note, for example, those civil rights and environmental pioneers of earlier times and the radicals of today who have tried to hijack those movements—those pushing for black "reparations" or the ecoterrorists of the Earth Liberation Front (ELF).

DEMONOLOGY

We do not need any more demonology. Let us not forget that Americans have a long history of working together. They can be political adversaries and not enemies. They can have different interpretations of issues without drawing battle lines and lobbing media grenades. For example, traditional adversaries such as President Lyndon Johnson and Senator Everett Dirksen (R-IL) could reflect at the end of the day over a drink.

Wouldn't it be nice if we could stop the demonizing, ranting, smearing, screaming, and hyperventilating? Sometimes it is easy to forget that we are all Americans, born under the same flag, carrying the same passports, using the same currency. Many are wishing to reintroduce civility, courtesy, mutual respect, and acceptance of democratic political outcomes.

However, such a truce—an Appomattox moment—is unlikely to come anytime soon, that time when both sides of the cultural civil war call for an end to hostilities. Ramsey Clark (who accused President Bush of high crimes and impeachable offenses) is unlikely to extend his hand first. Nor is Danny Glover (he calls the Bush administration liars and murderers). Nor is Howard Dean ("I hate the Republicans and everything they stand for"). More likely, some of the most radical will extend their hand to our country's principal adversaries, from Fidel Castro to Kim Jong-Il to whoever else stands against us.

There is no grand reconciliation on the horizon. There is no immediate indication that the lion and the lamb shall lie down together in the U.S. political pasture, nor a realistic prospect of a Red and Blue love-in. Until that time comes, we can take stock of the claims of the Far Left and expose them for what they are, part of an ongoing con job. We can work to isolate those remaining hard-core committed souls who inhabit the never-surrender Far Left. And we can look for ways to outmaneuver them by democratic and not fascist means. There is no excuse for passively accepting what they profess or for sitting on the sidelines, for there is too much at stake.

APPENDIX
NOTES
BIBLIOGRAPHY
INDEX

APPENDIX

OUTRAGEOUS QUOTATIONS

"The broad mass of a nation . . . will more easily fall victim to a big lie than to a small one."

Adolf Hitler

"I hate the Republicans and everything they stand for."

Howard Dean,
U.S. News and World Report, February 2005

[About Democrats] "Now it's our Party: we bought it, we own it, and we're going to take it back."

Eli Pariser,
MoveOn.org, e-mail to followers, early 2005

"We join your nation in your struggle against U.S. terrorism."

and

"I sincerely plead with my own government to cease its hypocritical lies and distortions about Cuba's human rights record—for in fact the United States itself is the worst violator of human rights in this hemisphere."

and

"You are the light of this world. . . . Hold on to your Revolution."

Rev. Lucius Walker Jr.,
Plaza of the Revolution, Havana, May 1, 2003

[About Iraq and WMD issue] "Inspections are war in another form."

> *Sara Flounders,*
> Workers World Party conference, September 2002

"[Compared with tsunami of December 26, 2004] we did learn horrifying details of a man-made disaster of similar proportions: the invasion and occupation of Iraq. . . . We had heard allegations of U.S. atrocities that made Abu Ghraib seem like childish pranks."

> CodePink delegation to Fallujah, Iraq, December
> 27, 2004–January 4, 2005

"Questions are swirling around whether the election was conducted honestly or not."

> MoveOn.Org Web site, January 28, 2005

"[The war against the Taliban and al-Qaeda has been] one of the great crimes and acts of terrorism in modern times."

> *Brian Becker*

"Comrade Fidel Castro asserts that the preservation of socialist values is of decisive importance. We could not agree more. . . . It is crucial that revolutionaries fight tooth and nail for their values, their principles and the revolutionary conceptions put forward by Marxism and Leninism."

> *Brian Becker,* Cuba

"The Korean people are firmly defending socialism despite the continued isolation and suffocation moves of the imperialists."

> *Brian Becker,*
> Pyongyang, North Korea, February 24, 2000

"[NOW calls on feminists to] expose the stifling of political dissent by the Bush administration through such policies as the USA PATRIOT Act."

> NOW Progressive Agenda for Peace

Condemned President Bush and "his administration of liars and murderers."

> *Danny Glover*

"I think you have to take the Iraqis on their face value."

and

"I think the President would mislead the American people."

Rep. James McDermott (D-WA)

"I don't believe in anarchistic violence, but directed violence . . . against the institutions which perpetuate capitalism, racism, and sexism, and the people who are the appointed guardians of those institutions."

Lynne Stewart

"[Abuses against individuals' basic rights] also occur regularly here in the United States, and our money-saturated political system hardly deserves the title 'democracy.'"

Medea Benjamin

"The war against terrorism is overstated."

William Arkin

"The war against terrorism is terrorism. The whole thing is just bulls—t."

Woody Harrelson

"I think Joe Stalin was a guy that was hugely misunderstood."

and

"I feel that George Bush's actions are desecrating the America that I grew up in and believed in. He is making us an imperialist government."

Ed Asner

"We not only want to stop the war; we want to bring the war home where it belongs."

and

"We appreciate that this is an act of solidarity Iraq really needs right now."

Larry Holmes,
Workers World newspaper, October 3, 2002

"No election, whether fair or fraudulent, can legitimize criminal wars on foreign countries, torture, and wholesale violation of human rights, and end of science and reason."

Not in Our Name (NION) statement

"[President Bush's foreign policies are] criminal offenses, they are high crimes, they are indisputable offenses, and they are impeachable offenses."

Ramsey Clark,
October 26, 2002

"I think that the largest single failing that we made during that whole period of time was not sending a contingent to North Vietnam to fight on the North Vietnamese side. For example, to man antiaircraft gun emplacements around Hanoi."

and

"I felt it was significantly important for the movement to take on a more treasonous edge. I wanted to up the ante of the struggle politically."

C. Clark Kissinger
(Tom Wells, *The War Within*)

"I have a confession. I have at times, as the war has unfolded, secretly wished for things to go wrong. Wished for the Iraqis to be more nationalistic, to resist longer. Wished for the Arab world to rise up in rage. Wished for all the things we feared would happen."

Gary Kamiya,
executive editor, *Salon*

"I'm not comparing Bush to Adolf Hitler—because George Bush, for one thing, is not as smart as Adolf Hitler. And secondly, George Bush has much more power than Adolf Hitler ever had."

David Clennon, actor

"I hate Bush. I despise him and his entire administration."

Jessica Lange

"Now we're all Vietcong."

> *Tom Hayden* (attributed),
> after 1967 meeting with North Vietnamese and
> Vietcong officials in Czechoslovakia

"We live in a time where we have a man sending us to war for fictitious reasons. . . . Shame on you, Mr. Bush. Shame on you."

> *Michael Moore*

"When I see an American flag flying, it's a joke."

> *Robert Altman*

"When I see the American flag, I go, 'Oh my God, you're *insulting* me.'"

> *Janeane Garofalo*

"Every government is run by liars, and nothing they say should be believed."

> *I. F. Stone*

AND A FEW PERCEPTIVE ONES

"They are cheerleaders for some of the most sinister regimes and insurgencies on the planet."

> *Michelle Goldberg,*
> Salon.com, November 4, 2002, regarding
> International Action Center and the
> Revolutionary Communist Party USA

"And always the fellow travelers slunk behind, alongside, and sometimes even ahead of the Communists, gifted in deceit, more practiced still in self-deceit, despised even by the Communists who, when they came to power, exterminated such despicable and untrustworthy allies."

> *Henry Fairlie,*
> about Alexander Cockburn, *The New Republic,*
> December 28, 1987

"Democratic society is the first in history to blame itself because another power it trying to destroy it."

Jean-Francois Revel

"The New Left faced difficult tasks after Richard Nixon assumed the presidency and would have had trouble fighting off COINTELPRO's dirty tricks and simultaneous efforts to isolate the radicals from the moderates within a loose antiwar coalition. The difficult was turned into the impossible when the New Left promptly, figuratively, and sometimes literally blew itself to bits. By late 1969, the ideological and organizational coherence of the New Left approximated that of a cauldron into which somebody had thrown an assortment of boa constrictors, rabbits, mice, wolverines, and camels by way of experiment. In other words, it was a howling, thumping, heaving, sad, silly mess."

Kim McQuaid,
The Anxious Years, p. 161

"Lying is universal—we all do it. Therefore the wise thing is for us diligently to train ourselves to lie thoughtfully, judiciously . . . to lie gracefully and graciously, with head erect."

Mark Twain

"They have learnt nothing, and forgotten nothing."

Charles-Maurice de Tallyrand
(about the House of Bourbon)

"War is an ugly thing, but not the ugliest of things; the decayed and degraded state of moral and patriotic feeling which thinks that nothing is worth war is much worse. A man who has nothing for which he is willing to fight; nothing he cares about more than his own personal safety; is a miserable creature who has no chance of being free, unless made and kept so by the exertions of better men than himself."

John Stuart Mill

NOTES

CHAPTER 1: WHAT'S AT STAKE NOW

1. The quotes from the State of the Union speech are taken from the White House Web site: http://www.whitehouse.gov/news/releases/2005/02/20050202–11.html.
2. S. Steven Powell, *Covert Cadre: Inside the Institute for Policy Studies* (Ottawa, IL: Green Hill Publishers, 1987), 63.

CHAPTER 2: LESSONS FROM THE COLD WAR

1. "Interagency Intelligence Study: Active Measures," Exhibit in Hearings before the Permanent Select Committee on Intelligence, House of Representatives, 97th Congress, Second Session, July 13–14, 1982. Washington DC: U.S. Government Printing Office, 1982, 32. (Hereafter referred to as IIS/AM, U.S. Congress.)
2. John Goldsmith, publisher of *L'Express*, NSIC seminar, Washington DC, May 22, 1984.
3. John Lenczowski, Heritage Foundation Seminar, Washington DC, May 16, 1984.
4. IIS/AM, U.S. Congress, 34–35.
5. Roy Godson, Heritage Foundation Seminar, Washington DC, May 16, 1984.
6. Richard Gid Powers, *Not Without Honor: The History of American Anti-Communism* (New York: Free Press, 1995), 397.
7. IIS/AM, U.S. Congress, 44.
8. Ibid., 45.
9. Ibid., 33.
10. Bill Moyers, *The Secret Government: The Constitution in Crisis* (Cabin John, MD: Seven Locks Press, 1988).
11. Accuracy in Media, "AIM Report: Communists Run Anti-War Movement," February 19, 2003, http://www.aim.org/aim_report/A217_0_4_0_C/.

12. Common Dreams News Center, "Peace Correspondent," January 27, 2005, http://www.commondreams.org/headlines03/0310–02.htm.

13. Herbert Romerstein, Heritage Foundation Seminar, Washington DC, March 13, 1985.

14. IIS/AM, U.S. Congress, 42–43.

15. Ibid., 61.

16. Ibid., 69.

17. S. Steven Powell, *Covert Cadre: Inside the Institute for Policy Studies* (Ottawa, IL: Green Hill Publishers, 1987), 211–22. This is a remarkable detailed source on the Institute for Policy Studies (IPS) and has many details on Letelier and his association with the IPS.

18. "The Soviet and Communist Bloc Defamation Campaign," *Congressional Record,* September 28, 1965.

19. Lenczowski, Heritage Foundation Seminar, Washington DC, May 16, 1984.

20. Arnaud de Borchgrave, speech, International Club, Washington DC, October 2, 1985.

21. Ann Coulter, *Treason: Liberal Treachery from the Cold War to the War on Terrorism* (New York: Crown Forum, 2003), 175.

22. Thomas Dorman, "Brainwashing," http://www.mindcontrolforums.com (accessed February 25, 2005).

23. Powers, *Not Without Honor,* 120.

24. Ibid.

25. Ibid.

26. David Horowitz, "Missing Diversity on American Campuses," Discoverthenetwork.org: A Guide to the Political Left, http://www.discoverthenetwork.org/guideDesc.asp?gid=88 (accessed March 12, 2005).

27. Jeff Jacoby, "Academic Thought Police," Front Page Magazine, December 6, 2004, http://www.frontpagemag.com/Articles/Printable.asp?ID=16232 (accessed March 12, 2005).

28. Ibid.

29. Horowitz, "Missing Diversity on American Campuses."

30. Ibid.

31. Ibid.

32. Ibid.

33. Bernard Goldberg, *Arrogance: Rescuing America from the Media Elite* (New York: Warner, 2003), 215.

34. David Horowitz and Eli Lehrer, "Political Bias in the Administrations and Faculties of 32 Elite Colleges and Universities," Front Page Magazine,

http://www.frontpagemag.com/Content/read.asp?ID=55 (accessed March 12, 2005).

35. Ibid.

36. The sentiments of Weiss, Hayden, and Dellinger are found in Powell, *Covert Cadre*, 32, 40. For Murphy, see "Debriefing: Operation Military Shield," in ProtestWarrior.com, October 31, 2004, http://hq.protestwarrior .com/?page=/featured/Miami/military_shield.php (accessed February 2, 2005).

CHAPTER 3: IT HAS ALL HAPPENED BEFORE

1. Robert Edwin Herzstein, *Roosevelt and Hitler: Prelude to War* (New York: Paragon House, 1989), 140.

2. Ibid., 189–90.

3. Ibid., 291.

4. Ibid., 190.

5. Ibid., 166.

6. Ibid., 168–69.

7. Ibid., 169.

8. Ibid., 158, 160.

9. Albert Fried, *FDR and His Enemies* (New York: St. Martin's Press, 1999), 153.

10. Ibid., 155.

11. Ibid., 157.

12. Herzstein, *Roosevelt and Hitler,* 170–71.

13. Ibid., 327. See also Richard Gid Powers, *Not Without Honor: The History of American Anti-Communism* (New York: Free Press, 1995), 170.

14. Herzstein, *Roosevelt and Hitler,* 125.

15. Ibid., 145.

16. Sean Hannity, *Deliver Us from Evil: Defeating Terrorism, Despotism, and Liberalism* (New York: Regan Books/HarperCollins, 2004), 31. The material on the Duke of Windsor is derived from Rob Evans and David Hencke, "Hitler Saw Duke of Windsor as 'no enemy,' US file reveals," *Manchester Guardian,* January 25, 2003. The material on Kennedy is derived from Edward Renehan Jr., "Joseph Kennedy and the Jews," History Network, April 29, 2002, http://hnn.us/articles/697.html.

17. Herzstein, *Roosevelt and Hitler,* 152–53.

18. Fried, *FDR and His Enemies,* 3.

19. Thomas E. Woods Jr., *The Politically Incorrect Guide to American History* (Washington DC: Regnery, 2004), 158–59.

20. Dennis J. Dunn, *Caught Between Roosevelt and Stalin: America's Ambassadors to Moscow* (Lexington: University Press of Kentucky, 1998), 20.
21. Woods, *Politically Incorrect Guide to American History,* 160.
22. Nikolai Tolstoy, *Stalin's Secret War* (London and Sydney: Pan Books, 1981), 343.
23. William R. Corson and Robert T. Crowley, *The New KGB: Engine of Soviet Power* (New York: Morrow, 1985), 310.
24. Kenneth S. Davis, *FDR: The New Deal Years, 1933–1937* (New York: Random House, 1979), 651.
25. Joseph E. Davies, *Mission to Moscow* (New York: Pocket Books, 1943). The original was published by Simon and Schuster in 1941. The page references cited here are from the paperback version by Pocket Books.
26. Davies, *Mission to Moscow,* 319, 299.
27. Ibid., 371.
28. Ibid., 125, 129, 295.
29. Ibid., 325.
30. Tolstoy, *Stalin's Secret War,* 344–45.
31. Dunn, *Caught Between Roosevelt and Stalin,* 68.
32. Ibid., 74.
33. Ibid., 77.
34. Ibid.
35. Ibid., 267.
36. Ibid.
37. Ibid., 81. This is derived from Robert C. Williams, *Russian Art and American Money, 1900–1940* (Cambridge, MA: Harvard University Press, 1980), 253.
38. Dunn, *Caught Between Roosevelt and Stalin,* 268.
39. Davies, *Mission to Moscow,* 451.
40. Ibid., 307–8.
41. Corson and Crowley, *The New KGB,* 213.
42. Ibid., 425. Why did Stalin praise him? He probably wanted to encourage Walter Duranty's bland acceptance of the Stalinist line during the Moscow show trials and likely approved of Duranty's refusal to publish information about the great famine of the early 1930s—despite the fact that Duranty knew of the tragedy and its dimensions.
43. Maxine Block, ed., *Current Biography: Who's News and Why, 1942* (New York: Wilson, 1942), 179.
44. Corson and Crowley, *The New KGB,* 213.
45. Woods, *Politically Incorrect Guide to American History,* 165.
46. Ibid., 165.

47. Ibid.

48. Ibid., 166.

49. Powers, *Not Without Honor,* 484–85.

50. Ibid., 332–33.

51. Michael Parenti Political Archive, http://www.michaelparenti.org (accessed February 28, 2005).

52. Charles DeBenedetti and Charles Chatfield, *An American Ordeal: The Antiwar Movement of the Vietnam Era* (Syracuse, NY: Syracuse University Press, 1990), 192.

53. Tom Wells, *The War Within: America's Battle over Vietnam* (Berkeley and Los Angeles: University of California Press, 1994), 162.

54. Ibid., 526.

55. Ibid., 208.

56. DeBenedetti and Chatfield, *An American Ordeal,* 337.

57. Ibid., 286.

58. Wells, *The War Within,* 551–52.

59. Ibid., 142.

60. Ibid., 141–42.

61. Richard Poe, *Hillary's Secret War: The Clinton Conspiracy to Muzzle Internet Journalists* (Nashville: WND Books, 2004), 197.

62. "John Kerry's Fellow Travellers," a five-part series. This is derived from part 3, posted on October 11, 2004, by an individual known as "Fedora," http://www.freerepublic.com/focus/f-news/1241847/posts (accessed February 18, 2005).

63. Wells, *The War Within,* 65.

64. Ibid., 339.

CHAPTER 4: GET THE RIGHT TOOLS

1. George Soros, *The Bubble of American Supremacy: Correcting the Misuse of American Power* (New York: Public Affairs, 2004). See also Bill Moyers, *The Secret Government: The Constitution in Crisis* (Cabin John, MD: Seven Locks Press, 1988).

2. Richard Viguerie and David Franke, *America's Right Turn: How Conservatives Used New and Alternative Media to Take Power* (Chicago: Bonus Books, 2004). See also two books by Bernard Goldberg: *Bias: A CBS Insider Exposes How the Media Distort the News* (Washington DC: Regnery, 2002), and *Arrogance: Rescuing America from the Media Elite* (New York: Warner Books, 2003).

3. Viguerie and Franke, *America's Right Turn,* 333.

4. Ibid., 277, 283.

5. "John Kerry's Fellow Travellers," a five-part series. This is derived from part 3, posted on October 11, 2004, by an individual known as "Fedora," http://www.freerepublic.com/focus/f-news/1241847/posts (accessed February 18, 2005). See also Christopher Andrew and Vasili Mitrokhin, *The Sword and the Shield: The Mitrokhin Archive and the Secret History of the KGB* (New York: Basic Books, 1999), 228. This book refers to Borovik as a KGB agent. It further refers to Mark Lane's book, *Rush to Judgment.* CPUSA officials who visited Moscow in 1971 stated that this book was "advantageous" and useful to the Communists, adding that Lane's motive was his own "self-aggrandizement."

6. Information on the caravans and the Havana address are on different parts of the Interreligious Foundation for Community Organization/Pastors for Peace Web site. For the caravans shipping materials to Cuba, see http://www.cubasolidarity.net/pastors.html. For information on the address in Havana, see http://ifconews.org/cuprovacations.html (both accessed February 5, 2005).

7. Robert Trigaux, "NY Times boss: We'll adapt, fix mistakes," *St. Petersburg Times,* February 23, 2005).

8. David Horowitz, "Defining the Left," FrontPageMagazine.com, March 2, 2005, http://www.frontpagemag.com/Articles/ReadArticle.asp?ID=17190 (accessed March 12, 2005). This is a sophisticated assessment of the Left by one of the "masters of the game."

CHAPTER 5: GROUPS, LEADERS, AND
THEIR LINKAGES: BEFORE 1960

1. "American Friends Service Committee," in Wikipedia, http://en.wikipedia.org/wiki/American_Friends_Service_Committee (accessed February 4, 2005).

2. "American Friends Service Committee (AFSC)," http://www.discoverthenetwork.org/groupProfile.asp?grpid=6172 (accessed February 22, 2005).

3. Ibid.

4. Ibid.

5. "American Civil Liberties Union," in Wikipedia, http://en.wikipedia.org/wiki/ACLU (accessed January 26, 2005).

6. Ibid.

7. Ibid.

8. "War Resisters League," in Wikipedia, http://en.wikipedia.org/wiki/War_Resisters_League (accessed February 4, 2005).

9. "National Lawyers Guild," Discoverthenetwork.org, http://www.discoverthenetwork.org/groupProfile.asp?grpid=6162 (accessed February 21, 2005).

10. National Lawyers Guild, http://www.nlg.org/about/aboutus.htm (accessed February 5, 2005).

11. Central Intelligence Agency, "Soviet Covert Action and Propaganda," provided to the Oversight Committee, House Permanent Subcommittee on Intelligence, February 6, 1980.

12. Ibid.

13. "National Lawyers Guild," Discoverthenetwork.org.

14. "Workers World Party," in Wikipedia, http://en.wikipedia.org/wiki/Workers_World_Party (accessed March 26, 2005).

15. Ibid.

16. "International Action Center" in Discoverthenetwork.org, http://www.discoverthenetwork.org/groupProfile.asp?grpid=6155 (accessed February 22, 2005). See also "International ANSWER" in Discoverthenetwork.org, http://www.discoverthenetwork.org/groupProfile.asp?grpid=6147 (accessed February 22, 2005). Convincing and substantial documentary evidence of the Workers World Party–International Action Center–Act Now to Stop War and End Racism (ANSWER) connection can be found in many different sources.

17. "Claud Cockburn" in Wikipedia, http://en.wikipedia.org/wiki/Claud_Cockburn (accessed January 27, 2005). Supplementary material on Cockburn can also be found in such reference works as *Contemporary Authors*, vol. 102, 14–115.

18. Henry Fairlie, book review, *The New Republic*, December 28, 1987, 27.

19. "Alexander Cockburn" in Wikipedia, http://en.wikipedia.org/wiki/Alexander_Cockburn (accessed January 27, 2005).

20. See Andrew Cockburn, "Ivan the Terrible Soldier," *Harper's*, March 1983, 50–57. This is a major effort to debunk the "big threat" image of the Soviet army, written when the numerical strength of the Soviet military was very high.

21. "Andrew Cockburn" in Wikipedia, http://en.wikipedia.org/wiki/Andrew_Cockburn (accessed January 27, 2005).

22. Ibid.

23. "Patrick Cockburn," in Wikipedia, http://en.wikipedia.org/wiki/Patrick_Cockburn (accessed January 27, 2005).

24. "Undue Influence: Institute for Policy Studies," http://www.undueinfluence

.com/ips.htm (accessed February 4, 2005). See also S. Steven Powell, *Covert Cadre: Inside the Institute for Policy Studies* (Ottawa, IL: Green Hill Publishers, 1987), 15. This book notes that Rubin was a registered member of the Communist Party.

25. "Undue Influence: Institute for Policy Studies." *Covert Cadre* contains many references to Cora Weiss.

26. "Undue Influence: Institute for Policy Studies." *Covert Cadre* also has many references to Peter Weiss.

27. Susan Braudy, *Family Circle: The Boudins and the Aristocracy of the Left* (New York: Knopf, 2003). A former KGB officer as well as decrypted Soviet message traffic indicate that Stone was an agent. See also Ann Coulter, *Treason: Liberal Treachery from the Cold War to the War on Terrorism* (New York: Crown Forum, 2003), 97.

28. Ibid.

29. "Harold Ickes," in Spartacus, http://www.spartacus.schoolnet.co.uk/USARickes.htm (accessed February 25, 2005).

30. Herzstein, *Roosevelt and Hitler,* 328.

31. Ibid., 340.

32. Coulter, *Treason,* 43.

33. Dennis J. Dunn, *Caught Between Roosevelt and Stalin: America's Ambassadors to Moscow* (Lexington: University Press of Kentucky, 1998), 92.

34. "Harold Ickes," in Discoverthenetwork.org, http://discoverthenetwork.org/individualProfile.asp?indid=1624 (accessed February 21, 2005).

35. Ibid.

36. Ibid.

37. Ibid.

38. Ibid.

39. "Norman Thomas," in Spartacus, http://www.spartacus.schoolnet.co.uk/USAthomas.htm (accessed February 25, 2005).

40. "George Soros," in Wikipedia, http://en.wikipedia.org/wiki/George_Soros (accessed January 26, 2005).

41. Ibid.

42. Byron York, "Soros Funded Stewart Defense," National Review Online, http://www.nationalreview.com/york/york200502170843.asp (accessed March 26, 2005).

43. George Soros, *The Bubble of American Supremacy: Correcting the Misuse of American Power* (New York: Public Affairs, 2004), 74, 26.

44. Ibid., 189–90.

45. David Horowitz and Richard Poe, "The Shadow Party: Part III" in Front-

PageMagazine, October 11, 2004, http://www.frontpagemag.com/articles/
readarticle.asp?ID=15461 (accessed February 22, 2005).

46. Ibid.

47. Richard Gid Powers, *Not Without Honor: The History of American Anti-Communism* (New York: Free Press, 1995), 316–17.

48. Note Moyers's biography in his book *The Secret Government: The Constitution in Crisis* (Cabin John, MD: Seven Locks Press, 1988).

49. "Undue Influence: The Moyers Mafia," http://www.undueinfluence.com/bill_moyers.htm (accessed February 2, 2005).

50. Ibid.

51. Ibid.

52. Biography in Northeastern University Voice, Commencement 1998, http://www.voice.neu.edu/980622/citations/richards.html (accessed February 25, 2005).

53. David Horowitz and Richard Poe, "The Shadow Party: Part II" in Front-PageMagazine, October 7, 2004, http://www.frontpagemag.com/articles/readarticle.asp?ID=15410&p=1 (accessed March 26, 2005).

CHAPTER 6: GROUPS, LEADERS, AND THEIR LINKAGES: 1960–99

1. Eva Allouche, "The Weaponization of Religion," *The Intelligencer: Journal of U.S. Intelligence Studies*, vol. 14, no. 2 (Winter–Spring 2005): 26.

2. Frank J. Rafalko, ed., *A Counterintelligence Reader,* vol. 3: *Post-World War II to Closing the 20th Century* (Washington DC: National Counterintelligence Center, n.d.).

3. Richard Gid Powers, *Not Without Honor: The History of American Anti-Communism* (New York: Free Press, 1995), 307–8.

4. "Institute for Policy Studies," Discoverthenetwork.org, http://www.discoverthenetwork.org/groupProfile.asp?grpid=6991 (accessed February 21, 2005). See also S. Steven Powell, *Covert Cadre: Inside the Institute for Policy Studies* (Ottawa, IL: Green Hill Publishers, 1987), which examines the Institute for Policy Studies (IPS) in great detail. Its conclusions are as valid today as they were in 1987, when the book was published.

5. "Institute for Policy Studies—Marxist Think Tank," http://www.geocities.com/CapitolHill/Senate/1777/ips1.htm (accessed February 7, 2005).

6. "Institute for Policy Studies," Discoverthenetwork.org, http://www.discoverthenetwork.org/groupProfile.asp?grpid=6991 (accessed February 21, 2005).

7. Ibid.

8. "Institute for Policy Studies—Marxist Think Tank."

9. Institute for Policy Studies, http://www.ips-dc.org/projects/newinternat .htm (accessed January 28, 2005).

10. "Building the Enemies of America," http://www.geocities.com/ CapitolHill/Senate/1777/cep.htm?20051 (accessed March 1, 2005).

11. "Center for Constitutional Rights," Wikipedia, http://en.wikipedia.org/ wiki/Center_for_Constitutional_Rights (accessed January 26, 2005).

12. "Building the Enemies of America."

13. Ibid.

14. North American Congress on Latin America (NACLA), http://www.nacla .org (accessed March 1, 2005).

15. Ibid.

16. Alberto Armendariz, "NACLA," *New York Review of Magazines*, Spring 2002, http://www.jrn.columbia.edu/studentwork/nyrm/2002/nacla.asp (accessed March 1, 2005).

17. "Building the Enemies of America."

18. Center for National Security Studies (CNSS), http://www.cnss.org (accessed March 2, 2005).

19. "Morton Halperin and his ultra-radical Center for National Security Studies," http://www.geocities.com/CapitolHill/Senate/1777/halpcnss.htm (accessed February 7, 2005).

20. Ibid.

21. Ibid.

22. Ibid. See also "Morton Halperin," in Wikipedia, http://en.wikipedia.org /wiki/Morton_Halperin (accessed February 5, 2005).

23. "Morton H. Halperin," SourceWatch, http://www.sourcewatch.org/index .php?title=Morton_H._Halperin (accessed January 26, 2005).

24. Center for National Security Studies (CNSS), http://www.cnss.org (accessed March 2, 2005).

25. People for the American Way (PFAW), http://www.pfaw.org/pfaw/general/ default.aspx?oid=2974 (accessed March 2, 2005).

26. "Revolutionary Communist Party, USA," in Wikipedia, http://en.wikipedia .org/wiki/Revolutionary_Communist_Party,_USA (accessed February 4, 2005).

27. Ibid.

28. Ibid.

29. This is treated later in this chapter in the section about Refuse and Resist!

30. "World-wide solidarity," published by WISE Bulletin, May 1978, http://www.antenna.nl/wise/b1/solidarity.html (accessed March 2, 2005).

31. Ibid.

32. Accuracy in Media, "The New Nuke Hysteria," Aim Report, May 1982, http://www.aim.org/publications/aim_report/1982/05a.html (accessed January 29, 2005).

33. Ibid.

34. "World-wide solidarity," WISE Bulletin, http://www.antenna.nl/wise/b1 /solidarity.html (accessed March 2, 2005).

35. "People for the American Way," Capital Research Center, w http://ww.cap-italresearch.org/search/orgdisplay.asp?Org=PAW1000 (accessed March 2, 2005).

36. "People for the American Way," SourceWatch, http://ww.sourcewatch.org /index.php?title=People_for_the_American_Way (accessed March 2, 2005).

37. Ibid.

38. People for the American Way (PFAW), http://www.pfaw.org/pfaw/general/ default.aspx?oid=3686 (accessed February 2, 2005).

39. Kay R. Daly, "Bench Brawl," National Review Online, October 28, 2004.

40. Ibid.

41. Ibid.

42. Evan Gahr, "Sins of the Extremist Left," WorldNetDaily, January 12, 2005, http://worldnetdaily.com/news/article.asp?ARTICLE_ID=42346 (accessed January 27, 2005).

43. "Democratic Socialists of America," Answers.com, http://www.answers .com/topic/democratic-socialists-of-america (accessed March 3, 2005).

44. Ibid.

45. All quotes are from RightNation.US, http://www.rightnation.us/forums/ index.php?act=ST&f=18&t=3902 (accessed February 5, 2005).

46. Ben Johnson, "Hollywood Hate Group Assaults Bush," FrontPageMagazine .com, July 12, 2004, http://www.frontpagemag.com/Articles/ReadArticle .asp?ID=14174 (accessed February 3, 2005).

47. "Fairness and Accuracy in Reporting," Wikipedia, http://en.wikipedia.org/ wiki/Fairness_and_Accuracy_in_Reporting (accessed February 4, 2005).

48. Fairness and Accuracy in Reporting (FAIR), http://www.fair.org/index.php ?page=100 (accessed March 3, 2005).

49. "Fairness and Accuracy in Reporting," Wikipedia, http://en.wikipedia.org/ wiki/Fairness_and_Accuracy_in_Reporting (accessed February 4, 2005).

50. FAIR, http://www.fair.org/index.php?page=100 (accessed March 3, 2005).

51. Refuse and Resist! http://www.refuseandresist.org/altindex.php (accessed March 3, 2005).

52. Ibid.

53. Ibid.

54. Ibid.

55. Tom Wells, *The War Within: America's Battle over Vietnam* (Berkeley and Los Angeles: University of California Press, 1994), 44.

56. "Revolutionary Communist Party: The Battle for the Future Will Be Fought from Here Forward!" on Refuse and Resist! http://www .refuseandresist.org/rnc/art.php?aid=1699 (accessed March 5, 2005).

57. Peace Action, http://www.peace-action.org/abt/timeline.html (accessed March 3, 2005).

58. Ibid.

59. Ibid.

60. Ibid.

61. "Pastors for Peace," SourceWatch, http://www.sourcewatch.org/index .php?title=Pastors_for_Peace (accessed February 18, 2005).

62. Interreligious Foundation for Community Organization–Pastors for Peace, http://www.cubasolidarity.net/pastors.html (accessed February 5, 2005).

63. Ibid.

64. "Reverend Lucius Walker, Jr.," Discoverthenetwork.org, http://www .discoverthenetwork.org/individualProfile.asp?indid=779 (accessed February 21, 2005).

65. Ibid.

66. Ibid.

67. Program Summary, Global Exchange, http://www.globalexchange.org/ about/programSummary.html (accessed March 7, 2005).

68. "Global Exchange," Orion Grassroots Network, http://www.oriononline .org (accessed March 7, 2005).

69. Program Summary, Global Exchange, http://www.globalexchange.org/ about/programSummary.html (accessed March 7, 2005).

70. "Medea Benjamin," Discoverthenetwork.org, http://www .discoverthenetwork.org/individualProfile.asp?indid=626 (accessed February 22, 2005).

71. "Medea Benjamin," Wikipedia, http://en.wikipedia.org/wiki/Medea_ Benjamin (accessed February 2, 2005).

72. John Perazzo, "The Anti-American: Medea Benjamin," FrontPageMagazine, November 15, 2002, http://www.frontpagemag.com/Articles/ReadArticle .asp?ID=4631 (accessed January 27, 2005).

73. "Medea Benjamin," Discoverthenetwork.org, http://www .discoverthenetwork.org/individualProfile.asp?indid=626 (accessed February 22, 2005).

74. Ibid.

75. Ibid.

76. Byron York, "Reds Still," National Review Online, January 23, 2003, re-posted on FreeRepublic, http://www.freerepublic.com/focus/news/828043/posts (accessed February 10, 2005).

77. Larry Holmes, "What will U.S. movement do to stop war?" *Workers World*, October 3, 2002, http://ww.workers.org/ww/2002/larry1003.php (accessed January 28, 2005).

78. This coordination is reported in sources such as Discoverthenetwork.org, FreeRepublic, National Review Online, and FrontPageMagazine. See Sherrie Gossett, "Has anti-war movement been hijacked?" in WorldNetDaily, November 4, 2002, http://wnd.com/news/article.asp?ARTICLE_ID=29524 (accessed January 25, 2005).

79. Peace Action, http://www.peace-action.org/abt/timeline.html (accessed March 3, 2005).

80. Ibid.

81. Ibid.

82. "Political Action Committee of nation's largest peace organization formally calls for the defeat of Bush," in Peace Action, March 29, 2004, http://www.peace-action.org/pub/releases/re1032904.html (accessed March 3, 2005).

83. "Fahrenheit 9/11 Moviegoers Turn Up the Heat," in Peace Action, June 25, 2004, http://www.peace-action.org/pub/releases/re1062404.html (accessed March 3, 2005).

84. "MoveOn," in Wikipedia, http://en.wikipedia.org/wiki/MoveOn.org (accessed February 4, 2005).

85. Ibid.

86. Ibid.

87. Ibid.

88. Ibid.

89. David Ware, "Exposing the Anti-War Movement, Part I: MoveOn.org (You Don't Know Jack!), FreeRepublic, posted on February 28, 2003, http://www.freerepublic.com/focus/news/854062/posts (accessed February 10, 2005).

90. "MoveOn.org," NNDB, http://www.nndb.com/org/674/000051521/ (accessed February 7, 2005).

91. MoveOn, http://www.moveon.org/front/ (accessed January 28, 2005).

92. Ibid.

93. Ibid (accessed March 5, 2005).

CHAPTER 7: GROUPS, LEADERS, AND
THEIR LINKAGES: 2000–PRESENT

1. David Corn, "Behind the Placards," LA Weekly, November 1–7, 2002, http://www.laweekly.com/ink/02/50/news-corn.php (accessed September 24, 2004). See also Sherrie Gossett, "Has anti-war movement been hijacked?" in WorldNetDaily, November 4, 2002, http://wnd.com/news/article.asp?ARTICLE_ID=29524 (accessed January 25, 2005).

2. See "International Action Center," http://www.discoverthenetwork.org/groupProfile.asp?grpid=6155, and "International ANSWER," http://www.discoverthenetwork.org/groupProfile.asp?grpid=6147.

3. ANSWER, which gave names of speakers and officials in charge, http://answer.pephost.org/site/PageServer?pagename=ANS_homepage (accessed 25 January 2005).

4. Byron York, "Reds Still," National Review Online, January 23, 2003, reposted on FreeRepublic, http://www.freerepublic.com/focus/news/828043/posts (accessed February 10, 2005).

5. Ibid.

6. Ibid.

7. "International ANSWER," http://www.discoverthenetwork.org/groupProfile.asp?grpid=6147.

8. "Not in Our Name," Wikipedia, http://en.wikipedia.org/wiki/Not_in_Our_Name (accessed February 4, 2005).

9. Ibid.

10. Ibid.

11. Ibid.

12. Not in Our Name (NION), http://www.nion.us/ (accessed February 3, 2005).

13. Ibid.

14. A revealing look at NION and some of its tactics is found at Michael P. Tremoglie, "A Peace Group's War Plans," FrontPageMagazine, 30 August 2004, http://www.frontpagemagazine.com/Articles/ReadArticle.asp?ID=14856 (accessed February 3, 2005).

15. Ibid.

16. "Progressive Donor Network," SourceWatch, http://www.sourcewatch.org/index.php?title=Progressive_Donor_Network (accessed March 8, 2005).

17. Ibid.

18. Ibid.

19. Ibid.

20. United for Peace and Justice (UFPJ), http://www.unitedforpeace.org/article.php?list=type&type=16 (accessed January 27, 2005).

21. Ibid.
22. Ibid.
23. Ibid.
24. United for Peace and Justice (UFPJ), http://www.unitedforpeace.org/article .php?id=1765 (accessed February 2, 2005).
25. "United for Peace and Justice," Wikipedia, http://en.wikipedia.org/wiki/ United_for_Peace_and_Justice (accessed February 2, 2005).
26. Ibid.
27. Ben Johnson, "'Charitable' Foundations: ATMs for the Left," Front-PageMagazine, March 2, 2004, http://www.frontpagemag.com/Articles/ ReadArticle.asp?ID=12423 (accessed March 24, 2005). This is one of the clearest analytical pieces to penetrate the maze of funding of leftist movements.
28. John Perazzo, "Jodie Evans: Activist in Pink," FrontPageMagazine, December 8, 2003, http://www.frontpagemag.com/Articles/ReadArticle.asp? ID=11186 (accessed January 27, 2005).
29. "United for Peace and Justice," Wikipedia, http://en.wikipedia.org/wiki/ United_for_Peace_and_Justice (accessed February 2, 2005).
30. Ibid.
31. CodePink, http://www.codepinkalert.org/working_for_peace.shtml (accessed February 2, 2005).
32. "Relentless Protest: CodePink Activists Ejected from RNC Three Nights in a Row," Democracy Now! September 3, 2004. This is Amy Goodman's radio program, http://www.democracynow.org/article.pl?sid=04/09/03/ 1457225 (accessed February 2, 2005).
33. CodePink, http://www.codepinkalert.org/working_for_peace.shtml (accessed February 2, 2005).
34. Ibid.
35. Ibid.
36. John Perazzo, "Jodie Evans," http://www.frontpagemag.com/Articles/Read Article.asp?ID=11186 (accessed January 27, 2005).
37. Global Exchange, http://www.globalexchange.org/countries/iraq/links.html (accessed February 2, 2005).
38. Iraq Occupation Watch (IOW), http://www.occupationwatch.org/ (accessed February 2, 2005).
39. Ibid.
40. "Media Matters for America," Wikipedia, http://en.wikipedia.org/wiki/ Media_Matters_for_America (accessed February 4, 2005).
41. Ibid.
42. Ibid.

43. "David Brock," Wikipedia, http://en.wikipedia.org/wiki/David_Brock (accessed January 28, 2005).

44. Ibid.

CHAPTER 8: IN STEP WITH OTHER INSTITUTIONS

1. Quote from Thomas R. Dye, *Politics in America*, 4th ed. (Upper Saddle River, NJ: Prentice-Hall, 2001. For detailed data on political leanings in Hollywood, see David Prindle, "Hollywood Liberalism," *Social Science Quarterly* 74 (March 1993): 121. See also Michael Medved, *Hollywood vs. America: Popular Culture and the War on Traditional Values* (New York: HarperCollins, 1992), 312–13.

2. Trevor Bothwell, "Michael Moore offers encouragement for lefties," *Insight on the News*, March 21, 2005.

3. Ben Johnson and John Perazzo, "The Ten Most Dishonorable Americans," FrontPageMagazine.com, 3 March 2004, http://www.frontpagemag.com/Articles/ReadArticle.asp?ID=6432 (accessed February 3, 2005).

4. Medved, *Hollywood vs. America*, 217.

5. Johnson and Perazzo, "Ten Most Dishonorable Americans."

6. Ben Johnson, "Sean Penn's Baghdad Homecoming," FrontPageMagazine .com, January 21, 2004, http://ww.frontpagemag.com/Articles/ReadArticle .asp?ID=11837 (accessed February 21, 2005).

7. "NOW and the Peace Movement," http://www.now.org/issues/peace/index .html (accessed May 16, 2005).

8. Ibid.

9. Chris Weinkopf, "Anti-Patriot Feminists," FrontPageMagazine.com, July 10, 2003, http://www.frontpagemag.com/Articles/ReadArticle.asp?ID= 8810 (accessed May 16, 2005).

10. David Horowitz, "First Blood: The Battle over Bush's Cabinet," FrontPageMagazine.com, January 8, 2001, http://www.frontpagemag.com/Articles/ReadArticle.asp?ID=1060 (accessed May 16, 2005).

11. Lowell Ponte, "Unholy Trinity," FrontPageMagazine.com, July 16, 2004, http://www.frontpagemag.com/Articles/ReadArticle.asp?ID=14258 (accessed May 16, 2005).

12. Ibid.

13. Ward Connerly, "The NAACP's Decline and Fall," FrontPageMagazine.com, July 17, 2002, http://www.frontpagemag.com /Articles/Printable.asp?ID=1932 (accessed May 16, 2005).

14. Ponte, "Unholy Trinity."

15. Ibid.

16. Connerly, "The NAACP's Decline and Fall," http://www.frontpagemag
    .com/Articles/Printable.asp?ID=1932 (accessed May 16, 2005).

17. "Strategic Direction," http://www.thetaskforce.org/aboutus/direction.cfm
    (accessed May 17, 2005).

18. "Elections," http://www.thetaskforce.org/theissues/issue.cfm?issueID=32
    (accessed May 16, 2005).

19. Stephen H. Miller, "Gay Activists and Religious Conservatives: Through
    the Looking Glass," FrontPageMagazine.com, June 10, 2003, http://www
    .frontpagemag.com/articles/Printable.asp?ID=8275 (accessed on May 17,
    2005).

20. Ponte, "Unholy Trinity."

21. Ibid. This phrase originates from Peter Brimelow, *The Worm in the Apple:
    How the Teacher Unions Are Destroying American Education* (New York:
    HarperCollins, 2003).

22. Ponte, "Unholy Trinity."

23. Lowell Ponte, "The Demo-cash-ic Party," FrontPageMagazine.com, Au-
    gust 10, 2004, http://frontpagemag.com/Articles/ReadArticle.asp?ID=
    14585 (accessed May 16, 2005).

24. "About ATLA," http://www.atla.org/about/index.aspx (accessed May 16,
    2005).

25. Ponte, "The Demo-cash-ic Party."

26. Journalism.org, Overview, http://www.stateofthemedia.org/2005 (accessed
    May 19, 2005).

27. Bernard Goldberg, *Arrogance: Rescuing America from the Media Elite* (New
    York: Warner, 2003), 11–12.

28. Bernard Goldberg, Bias*: A CBS Insider Exposes How the Media Distort the
    News* (Washington DC: Regnery, 2002), 126.

29. Ibid., 123.

30. Ibid., 220–21.

31. S. Steven Powell, *Covert Cadre: Inside the Institute for Policy Studies* (Ot-
    tawa, IL: Green Hill Publishers, 1987), 109–10.

32. Ibid., 115.

33. Ibid., 24, 90.

34. Ibid., 116.

35. For Medved quote, see Marv Essary, "Hot Conservative Authors Celebrate
    New Publishing House," in Chronwatch, June 22, 2003, http://www
    .chronwatch.com/editorial/contentDisplay.asp?aid=3193 (accessed Sep-
    tember 24, 2004). For second quote, see "Vigilanteman" posting to Joseph
    Nemie in blog "Crushed by liberal publishers, I need suggestions. Please!"
    Free Republic, August 28, 2004 (accessed September 24, 2004).

Vigilanteman notes that "crime would drop like a sprung trapdoor if we brought back good old-fashioned hangings."

36. Powell, *Covert Cadre*, 22.

37. Ibid., 59.

38. Ibid., 75.

39. "U.S. Congress Progressive Caucus—Articles of Organization," on Progressive Caucus Web site, http://progressive.house.gov (accessed May 12, 2005). On the issue of the alignment with the Democratic Socialists of America, see Lowell Ponte, "The Face of Treason," FrontPageMagazine .com, March 15, 2004, http://frontpagemag.com/Articles/ReadArticle.asp? ID=12577 (accessed March 30, 2005).

40. Congressional Black Caucus Web site, http://www.congressionalblack caucus.net/ (accessed May 22, 2005).

41. Powell, *Covert Cadre*, 265–66.

42. Brian Maher, "The Dirty (Near) Dozen," FrontPageMagazine.com, April 7, 2003, http://frontpagemag.com/Articles/ReadArticle.asp?ID=7119 (accessed May 12, 2005).

43. "John Conyers," Wikipedia. http://en.wikipedia.org/wiki/John_Conyers (accessed February 5, 2005). See also Powell, *Covert Cadre*, 78.

44. Johnson and Perazzo, "The Ten Most Dishonorable Americans." See also David Horowitz, "Horowitz's Notepad: An Enemy Within," FrontPageMagazine.com, September 19, 2001, http://www.frontpagemag.com /Articles/ReadArticle.asp?ID=4520 (accessed May 12, 2005).

45. Larry Elder, "Rapping with Waters," FrontPageMagazine.com, March 29, 2002, http://frontpagemag.com/Articles/ReadArticle.asp?ID=125 (accessed May 12, 2005). See also "Maxine Waters," Discoverthenetwork.org, http://www.discoverthenetwork.org/individualProfile.asp?indid=1264 (accessed May 14, 2005).

46. "Maxine Waters," http://www.discoverthenetwork.org/individualProfile .asp?indid=1264 (accessed May 14, 2005).

47. William Bacon, "A List of Fanatics," FrontPageMagazine.com, August 7, 2003, http://frontpagemag.com/Articles/ReadArticle.asp?ID=9275 (accessed May 12, 2005).

48. Chris Weinkopf, "Rep. Cynthia McKinney: Not Just Nutty," FrontPageMagazine.com, April 10, 2002, http://www.frontpagemag.com/ Articles/ReadArticle.asp?ID=787 (accessed May 12, 2005).

49. "Cynthia McKinney," Discoverthenetwork.org, http://www .discoverthenetwork.org/individualProfile.asp?indid=1508 (accessed May 14, 2005).

50. Ibid.

51. "Diane Watson," Discoverthenetwork.org, http://www.discoverthenetwork .org/individualProfile.asp?indid=1269 (accessed May 14, 2005).

52. Johnson and Perazzo, "The Ten Most Dishonorable Americans."

53. Centre for Counterintelligence and Security Studies, "Susan Lindauer Case," http://www.cicentre.com/Documents/DOC_Susan_Lindauer _Case.htm (accessed March 30, 2005).

54. Lowell Ponte, "The Face of Treason."

55. Ibid.

56. Centre for Counterintelligence and Security Studies, "Susan Lindauer Case."

57. Thanks to the *Chicago Sun-Times*, March 14, 2004, for this colorful phrase.

CHAPTER 9: WHAT THEY SAY AND CARRY

1. Elaine Cassel, "Questions While Watching an Insipid Inaugural," January 21, 2005, http://blogs.citypages.com/ecassel/2005/01/questions_while.asp (accessed January 26, 2005).

2. Jonah Goldberg, "Hollywood Fools," National Review Online, 18 September 2000, http://www.nationalreview.com/goldberg/goldberg091800.shtml (accessed June 1, 2005).

3. Ibid.

4. "Lazamataz," in "Collecting Crazy, Hatefilled and Lunatic Liberal Quotes," Free Republic, December 28, 2004, http://www.freerepublic.com/focus/ f-news/1047657/posts (accessed June 1, 2005).

5. "Ex-Dem" in ibid.

6. David Cogswell, "Jessica Lange Speaks Out Against Bush," October 1, 2002, http://www.davidcogswell.com/MediaRoulette/LangeSpeaks.html (accessed June 1, 2005).

7. "Ozzy Osbourne," Celiberal: Celebrity Liberal Whine List, http://www .celiberal.com/showCeliberal.php?id=69 (accessed June 1, 2005).

8. "Lazamataz," in "Collecting Crazy, Hatefilled and Lunatic Liberal Quotes."

9. Ibid.

10. Ibid.

11. "KC_Conspirator" in ibid.

12. "CounterCounterCulture," in ibid.

13. "Ex-Dem." in ibid.

14. "Dighton" in ibid.

15. Ibid.

16. Ibid.

17. "Ex-Dem" in ibid.

18. Ibid.
19. Lisa Makson, "CUNY promotes an Anti-Christian Hatemonger," Front-PageMagazine.com, June 1, 2005, http://www.frontpagemag.com/Articles/ReadArticle.asp?ID=18256 (accessed June 1, 2005).
20. "Gore Vidal," Celiberal: Celebrity Liberal Whine List, http://www.celliberal.com/show/Celiberal.php?id=32 (accessed June 1, 2005).
21. Kurt Vonnegut, "Strange Weather Lately," AlterNet, May 19, 2003, http://www.alternet.org/story/15939 (accessed June 1, 2005).
22. Maureen Farrell, "Hunter Thompson, George W. Bush and the Free Republic," Buzz-Flash.com, June 16, 2004, http://www.buzzflash.com/farrell/04/06/far04020.html (accessed March 9, 2005).
23. "Qwinn" in "Collecting Crazy, Hatefilled and Lunatic Liberal Quotes."
24. Ibid.
25. Ibid.
26. One approach is to use a search engine such as Google and set it to "images." Keywords such as *antiwar demonstration* or *anti-Bush demonstration* are useful tools.
27. Ben Stein and Phil deMuth, *Can America Survive? The Rage of the Left, the Truth, and What to Do About It* (Carlsbad, CA: New Beginnings Press, 2004), 128.
28. Michelle Malkin, "The Truth About Guantanamo Bay," FrontPageMag.com, June 1, 2005, http://www.frontpagemag.com/Articles/ReadArticle.asp?ID=18270 (accessed June 1, 2005).

CHAPTER 10: LOSING THE COMPASS:
EPISODES FROM JOHN KERRY'S CAREER

1. "Daniel Ortega," Wikipedia, http://en.wikipedia.org/wiki/Daniel_Ortega (accessed on May 26, 2005).
2. Ann Coulter, *Treason: Liberal Treachery from the Cold War to the War on Terrorism* (New York: Crown Forum, 2003), 175.
3. S. Steven Powell, *Covert Cadre: Inside the Institute for Policy Studies* (Ottawa, IL: Green Hill Publishers, 1987), 227, 262.
4. Ibid., 243.
5. "Jean-Bertrand Aristide," Wikipedia, http://en.wikipedia.org/wiki/Aristide (accessed May 26, 2005).
6. "Varela Project," Wikipedia, http://en.wikipedia.org/wiki/Proyecto_Varela (accessed on May 26, 2005).
7. Andres Oppenheimer, "Kerry's weapon against Cuba: global pressure,"

Cubanet, posted on June 6, 2004, in the *Miami Herald,* http://www
.cubanet.org/CNews/y04/jun04/07e9.htm (accessed May 26, 2005).

8. "Iyad Allawi," Wikipedia, http://en.wikipedia.org/wiki/Allawi (accessed
   May 26, 2005).

9. "Fire Lockhart and Allawi quote contest," Posse Incitatus, September 24,
   2005, http://posseincitatus.typepad.com/posse_incitatus/2004/09/fire_joe
   _lockha.html (accessed on May 26, 2005).

10. "Kerry: Iraq Election No Big deal," NewsMax.com, January 30, 2005,
    http://newsmax.com/archives/ic/2005/1/30/120434.shtml (accessed May
    26, 2005).

11. Sean Hannity, *Deliver Us from Evil: Defeating Terrorism, Despotism, and Liberalism* (New York: Regan Books/HarperCollins, 2004), 240.

12. "John Kerry's Fellow Travellers," a five-part series. This is derived from
    part 3, posted on October 11, 2004, by an individual known as "Fedora,"
    http://www.freerepublic.com/focus/f-news/1241847/posts (accessed February 18, 2005).

CHAPTER 11: THE ROAD AHEAD

1. The Greens/Green Party USA, http://www.greenparty.org (accessed July
   12, 2004).

2. Ibid.

3. "People for the American Way," http://www.capitalresearch.org/search/
   orgdisplay.asp?Org=PAW100 (accessed March 2, 2005).

4. These ideas may be found in Jesse Ventura, *Do I Stand Alone? Going to the
   Mat Against Political Pawns and Media Jackals* (New York: Simon & Schuster, 2000).

5. Details about the first two itemized events and others pertaining to Congress are found in Kevin Phillips, *Arrogant Capital: Washington, Wall Street
   and the Frustration of American Politics* (New York: Little, Brown and Company, 1994). Details about the last four itemized events and others pertaining to Congress are found in James T. Bennett and Thomas J. DiLorenzo,
   Official Lies: How Washington Misleads Us (Alexandria, VA: Groom Books,
   1992).

6. See Mortimer B. Zuckerman, "Right Down the Middle?" *U.S. News and
   World Report,* June 6, 2005, 63; and Gloria Borger, "Extraordinary Doings," *U.S. News and World Report,* June 6, 2005, 24.

7. "George Galloway," Biogs.com, http://www.biogs.com/famous/galloway
   .html (accessed March 30, 2005). See also Alexis Amory, "The Fall of

George Galloway," FrontPageMagazine.com, May 6, 2003, http://www
.frontpagemag.com/Articles/ReadArticle.asp?ID=7665.

8. Wendell L. Minnick, *Spies and Provocateurs: A Worldwide Encyclopedia of Persons Conducting Espionage and Covert Action, 1946–1991* (Jefferson, NC: McFarland & Company, 1992), 226–27.

9. Ibid., 81–82.

10. "The Soviets' Dirty-Tricks Squad," *Newsweek*, November 23, 1981, 53.

11. "Freedom of Information–Privacy Act," http://foia.fbi.gov/foiaindex/foiaindex_b.htm (accessed June 1, 2005).

12. Central Intelligence Agency, Unclassified Report to Congress on the Acquisition of Technology Relating to Weapons of Mass Destruction and Advanced Conventional Munitions, 1 July Through 31 December 2003. Attachment A.

13. Ibid., 2–3.

14. Ibid., 5–6

15. Ibid., 7–8.

16. U.S. Department of State, Country Reports on Terrorism, April 27, 2005. See also James Hansen, "U.S. Intelligence Confronts the Future," *International Journal of Intelligence and Counterintelligence*, 17, no. 4 (Winter 2004): 692–93.

17. Hansen, "U.S. Intelligence Confronts the Future," 679.

18. Ibid.

19. Mortimer Zuckerman, "Cracking Down on Caracas," *U.S. News and World Report*, February 14, 2005, 72.

20. Ibid.

21. "USA PATRIOT Act," Wikipedia, http://en.wikipedia.org/wiki/USA_PATRIOT_Act (accessed on May 31, 2005).

22. Ibid.

23. Ibid.

24. Ibid.

25. "Bush Supreme Court candidates," Wikipedia, http://en.wikipedia.org/wiki/Potential_Bush_administration_nominees_to_the_Supreme_Court_of_the_United_States (accessed May 31, 2005).

26. John W. Dean, "A Crucial But Largely Ignored 2004 Campaign Issue: The Next President Is Likely to Appoint at Least Three Supreme Court Justices," FindLaw's Legal Commentary, September 24, 2004, http://writ.news.findlaw.com/dean/20040924.html (accessed May 31, 2005).

27. Angie Cannon, "Full Court Press," *U.S. News and World Report*, February 14, 2005, 34.

28. Ibid.

29. Anita Kumar, "Taking the cause of the academic rights of the right," *St. Petersburg Times,* May 29, 2005.

30. Ibid.

31. "Bowling for Fallujah," Cox & Forkum, April 15, 2004, http://www .coxandforkum.com/archives/000320.html (accessed June 1, 2005). There is ample documentation of Moore's activities: David T. Harly and Jason Clarke, *Michael Moore Is a Big Fat Stupid White Man* (New York: Harper-Collins, 2004); and Michael Wilson has produced a film entitled *Michael Moore Hates America.* Moreover, see the Web site entitled Moorewatch: Watching Michael Moore's Every Move, at www.moorewatch.com. Taken together, these paint a very complete portrait.

32. Irene Khan, "Foreword," to 2005 Amnesty International report, http://web.amnesty.org/report2005/message-eng (accessed May 29, 2005).

33. David Remnick, *Lenin's Tomb: The Last Days of the Soviet Empire* (New York: Random House, 1993), 423–24, 442.

BIBLIOGRAPHY

BOOKS

Andrew, Christopher, and Vasili Mitrokhin. *The Sword and the Shield: The Mitrokhin Archive and the Secret History of the KGB.* New York: Basic Books, 1999.

Braudy, Susan. *Family Circle: The Boudins and the Aristocracy of the Left.* New York: Knopf, 2003.

Carville, James, with Jeff Nussbaum. *Had Enough? A Handbook for Fighting Back.* New York: Simon & Schuster, 2003.

Central Intelligence Agency. *Soviet Covert Action and Propaganda.* Provided to the Oversight Committee, House Permanent Subcommittee on Intelligence, February 6, 1980.

Coulter, Ann. *High Crimes and Misdemeanors: The Case Against Bill Clinton.* Washington DC: Regnery Publishing Co., 1998.

———. *Treason: Liberal Treachery from the Cold War to the War on Terrorism.* New York: Crown Forum, 2003.

Courtois, Stephanie, et al. *The Black Book of Communism: Crimes, Terror, Repression.* Cambridge, MA: Harvard University Press, 1999.

DeBenedetti, Charles, and Charles Chatfield. *An American Ordeal: The Antiwar Movement of the Vietnam Era.* Syracuse, NY: Syracuse University Press, 1990.

Dunn, Dennis J. *Caught Between Roosevelt and Stalin: America's Ambassadors to Moscow.* Lexington: University Press of Kentucky, 1998.

Fried, Albert. *FDR and His Enemies.* New York: St. Martin's Press, 1999.

Goldberg, Bernard. *Arrogance: Rescuing America from the Media Elite.* New York: Warner, 2003.

———. *Bias: A CBS Insider Exposes How the Media Distort the News.* Washington DC: Regnery, 2002.

Halberstam, David. *War in a Time of Peace: Bush, Clinton, and the Generals.* New York: Scribner, 2001.

Hannity, Sean. *Deliver Us from Evil: Defeating Terrorism, Despotism, and Liberalism.* New York: Regan Books/HarperCollins, 2004.

Herzstein, Robert Edwin. *Roosevelt and Hitler: Prelude to War.* New York: Paragon House, 1989.

Horowitz, David. *The Politics of Bad Faith: The Radical Assault on America's Future.* New York: Free Press, 1998.

Ingraham, Laura. *Shut Up and Sing: How Elites from Hollywood, Politics, and the UN Are Subverting America.* Washington DC: Regnery, 2003.

Klehr, Harvey, John Earl Haynes, and Kyrill M. Anderson. *The Soviet World of American Communism.* New Haven, CT: Yale University Press, 1998.

Kurtz, Howard. *Spin Cycle: Inside the Clinton Propaganda Machine.* New York: Free Press, 1998.

McQuaid, Kim. *The Anxious Years: America in the Vietnam-Watergate Era.* New York: Basic Books, 1989.

Medved, Michael. *Hollywood vs. America: Popular Culture and the War on Traditional Values.* New York: HarperCollins, 1992.

Moyers, Bill. *The Secret Government: The Constitution in Crisis.* Cabin John, MD: Seven Locks Press, 1988.

O'Neill, John E., and Jerome R. Corsi. *Unfit for Command: Swift Boat Veterans Speak Out Against John Kerry.* Washington DC: Regnery, 2004.

Poe, Richard. *Hillary's Secret War: The Clinton Conspiracy to Muzzle Internet Journalists.* Nashville, TN: WND Books, 2004.

Powell, S. Steven. *Covert Cadre: Inside the Institute for Policy Studies.* Ottawa, IL: Green Hill Publishers, 1987.

Powers, Richard Gid. *Not Without Honor: The History of American Anticommunism.* New York: Free Press, 1995.

Rafalko, Frank J., ed. *A Counterintelligence Reader.* Volume Three: *Post-World War II to Closing the 20th Century.* Washington DC: National Counterintelligence Center, n.d.

Savage, Michael. *The Enemy Within: Saving America from the Liberal Assault on Our Schools, Faith, and Military.* Nashville, TN: WND Books, 2003.

Soros, George. *The Bubble of American Supremacy: Correcting the Misuse of American Power.* New York: Public Affairs, 2004.

Stein, Ben, and Phil DeMuth. *Can America Survive? The Rage of the Left, the Truth, and What to Do About It.* Carlsbad, CA: New Beginnings Press, 2004.

U.S. House of Representatives. *Soviet Active Measures: Hearings Before the Permanent Select Committee on Intelligence, House of Representatives,* 97th Congress, Second Session. July 13–14, 1982. Washington DC: U.S. Government Printing Office, 1982.

U.S. Senate. *Supplementary Detailed Staff Reports on Intelligence Activities and the Rights of Americans. Book III. Final Report of the Select Committee to Study Government Operations with Respect to Intelligence Activities.* Washington DC: U.S. Government Printing Office, 1967.

Viguerie, Richard, and David Franke. *America's Right Turn: How Conservatives Used New and Alternative Media to Take Power.* Chicago: Bonus Books, 2004.

Wells, Tom. *The War Within: America's Battle over Vietnam.* Berkeley and Los Angeles: University of California Press, 1994.

Woods, Thomas E., Jr. *The Politically Incorrect Guide to American History.* Washington DC: Regnery, 2004.

RELATED WEB SITES

Accuracy in Media: www.aim.org

American Enterprise Institute for Public Policy: www.aei.org

Cato Institute: http://cato.org

Center for Media and Public Affairs: www.cmpa (studies of media coverage of campaign)

Center for Public Integrity: www.bop2004.org (about the flow of money)

Center for Responsive Politics: www.crp.org (about the conduct of elections, particularly how money is raised and spent)

CNN political site: www.cnn.com/ALLPOLITICS

Commission on Presidential Debates: www.debates.org (plans the debates and has transcripts of past debates)

Common Cause: www.commoncause.org (about large and unreported contributions and spending)

Congressional Quarterly: www.cq.com (linkages to Congress and its activities, with in-depth information and election analysis)

DemocracyNet: www.dnet.org (sponsored by League of Women Voters, about candidates and their positions)

Democratic National Committee: www.democrats.org

Discoverthenetwork.org. A Guide to the Political Left: www.discoverthenetwork.org

Federal Election Commission: www.fec.gov (data on election turnout, voting, and money; also data on contributions for candidates seeking office as well as for parties and PACs)

First Gov: www.firstgov.gov (U.S. government's official Web portal and comprehensive entry point to link to all facets and levels of government)

Front Page: www.frontpagemagazine.com

Heritage Foundation: www.heritage.org

League of Women Voters www.lwv.org (information about candidates, their positions, and how to register and vote)

National Journal: www.nationaljournal.com (coverage of primaries and caucuses)

National Review Online: www.nationalreview.com

Politics Online: www.politicsonline (source of access to presidential campaigning in the Internet)

Public Citizen: www.citizen.org

Republican National Committee: www.rnc.org

U.S. Congress: http://thomas.loc.org

U.S. Presidency: www.whitehouse.gov

Wikipedia, the free encyclopedia: www.en.wikipedia.org

World Net daily: www.worldnetdaily.com

Yahoo: www.yahoo.com/Government/Politics (many links to political news and information)

INDEX

273

INDEX

277

279

INDEX